39
181

BEST QUOTES OF '54, '55, '56

Best Quotes

OF

'54, '55, '56

Compiled by

JAMES BEASLEY SIMPSON

THOMAS Y. CROWELL COMPANY, NEW YORK

TO

ELLENDER WEAVER SIMPSON

AND IN MEMORY OF

E.O.S.—E.H.B.—E.S.B.

❦

"Lord, thou hast been our dwelling place
in all generations."—Psalms 90:1

Copyright © 1957 by James Beasley Simpson

All rights reserved.

Manufactured in the United States of America
by the Vail-Ballou Press, Inc., Binghamton, New York

Designed by Emil Silvestri

Library of Congress Catalog Card No. 57-6565

All short quotes from Time, Life, and Fortune
are copyrighted by Time, Inc., in their respective years
unless otherwise indicated.

Foreword

BECAUSE the daily rush of news has no more than passing interest there is enduring value in an accurate and more permanent record of the best quotations of our time. To provide such a record is the purpose of this book.

At this very moment, somewhere in the world, someone may be voicing a comment that will be quoted for generations to come. But the flood of unimportant utterance is always likely to obscure those few phrases that have enduring importance. Certainly there is a great deal being said every day that would have been better left unsaid! This collection of quotations attempts to differentiate between the significant and the indifferent, between what is for the moment and what is more likely to have enduring interest. There are bound to be mistakes in evaluation since the author cannot have the perspective provided by the passage of time. Sixty years of reporting and editing justify my personal conclusion that much is said today that is worth keeping for tomorrow. Nuggets of wisdom abound in newspapers and magazines, in biographies and novels, in quotes we hear over the radio and television. They are voiced on the lecture platform and in the pulpit. We hear them on the motion picture screen and in the theater, in interviews and official statements, and in private conversation.

Just as a picture sometimes tells more than a thousand words a single quotation can have more meaning than all the related reporting and interpretation. The words spoken by people in the news often constitute the very heart of the news itself. Indeed reporters and editors have a tremendous responsibility. They must make sure that the quotation marks are never obscured by adjectives, by "color," by sidebars and features. If a person is newsworthy, his exact words at a given moment are the most newsworthy thing about him. The quotation is the key to the man. It sets the pace and mood for the intelligent reporter and analyst.

Quotations from the past have often been helpful to me in analyzing the news at hand. My interview notebooks, covering many years and many countries, are my richest source of raw material for books and articles. The wartime words of Winston Churchill were applicable to his activities when he later became a peacetime Prime Minister. The speeches of General Eisenhower reveal the philosophy he has followed as President Eisenhower.

I frequently use some favorite quotation to start or close a radio broadcast or newspaper column. For the "Words to Live By" feature in *This Week Magazine* I recently cited the Shakespearean quotation, "To thine own self be true. . . ." As a student entering Harvard College I was inspired to read over a gate to Harvard Yard, "Enter here to gain in knowledge." These words have followed me into many new realms of accumulated human wisdom. Another one of my favorite quotations is from Harvard's great late President Charles W. Eliot, "Most profit grows where is most pleasure taken." What a sound educational maxim! And I have always been devoted to the closing lines of Walt Whitman's poem "O, Pioneers!"

These examples suggest that I am well aware of our rich heritage of quotations and how they can be used. We should use more of them more often, but we need not depend on Bartlett and those who compile the best quotations of the past. There is wit and wisdom abroad in the land today. It is reported in all we read and hear. Each day brings a new harvest and we could use these quotations as often as we turn to those of the past.

My interest in this particular project stems from my numerous appearances as a panel member of the radio and television program, "Who Said That?" The compiler of this collection, Jim Simpson, read widely and carefully to gather material for the weekly "Who Said That?" program. He brought in quotations from many sources in many fields. All of them were accurate and provocative and most of those he has retained in this volume have some enduring value. I sincerely hope that a succeeding volume, wrapping up the best quotations of 1957 and 1958, will establish his compilation as a biennial.

We had a lot of fun on the "Who Said That?" program and you will find fun in reading this book for pleasure and in keeping it on hand as a reference volume. It is a delightful departure from the usual book on current affairs and makes a real contribution to the history of this era.

H. V. KALTENBORN

New York
September, 1956

Preface

Best Quotes of '54, '55, '56 is a selection of the best sayings and remarks of people, distinguished and unknown, famous and obscure, who have been inspired by events from all over the world. You will find quotes of many who have been constantly in the news, such as Dwight Eisenhower and Winston Churchill. And there are also memorable remarks made by plain people, who, like most of us, forget they are really the stuff of history.

Best Quotes is arranged in categories, repeated for each of the three years. Among the categories are Armed Forces, Authors, Government, Hollywood, Personalities, Sports, United Nations. Within each category the quotations are placed chronologically (except that all quotes by one person are grouped under the earliest date, and some closely related quotes are arranged together), with their dates, their sources, and circumstances of their delivery included for each one. The term "news reports" usually refers to newspapers and news broadcasts of the day following the event. The term "news summaries" indicates newspapers and magazine round-ups which ordinarily appeared within seven to ten days after the quotation was first reported.

Only the words of President Eisenhower are dated the day on which they were spoken and this is because the President's press conferences and public addresses are such important events in themselves that they warrant particular dating. The President's remarks, like those of Pope Pius XII, are usually quoted in news reports of the next day.

A word of warning in the case of quotes by President Eisenhower and by some of the guests on television programs: they have often been quoted in colloquial statements which make half-completed sentences. The exact meaning of these statements lies in the speaker's way of speaking, in the tone of voice and perhaps the gestures. These quotes deserve the close attention of the reader, for they are not as clear as most other statements.

For much of this material, I am indebted to legions of reliable newspapermen, magazine writers, and reporters of all media who are, really, the keepers of our contemporary diary. Outstanding among this group are the staffs and columnists of *The New York Times, New York Herald Tribune,* the three Manhattan tabloids—the *Daily News,* the *Mirror,* and the *New York Post*—and the two afternoon papers, *The World-Telegram and The Sun* and the *Journal-American,* along with the organizations with which these newspapers exchange news—The Associated Press, United Press Associations, and International News Service.

For many of the more enduring quotes I am indebted to American magazines, which most of us read too quickly and throw away too soon. Among these are *Time, Newsweek, Life,* and *This Week.*

I am grateful to those who urged that this collection be put into book form—Joan Alexander, Jack Bailhe, Morgan Beatty, Ruth Pirkle Berkeley, John Mason Brown, Edward Busyn, Bob Considine, Faye Emerson, Roger Englander, Ray Erwin, Ann Gillis, Eddy Gilmore, William Guthman, Frederic Henry, H. V. Kaltenborn, Janet Kern, Mary Margaret McBride, Don McNeill, William Terence O'Brien, Inez Robb, Eleanor Roosevelt, Senator Margaret Chase Smith, Merriman Smith, James Douglas Stuart, John Cameron Swayze, Raymond Swing, Herbert Bayard Swope, Rhea Talley, Hal Tufty, William Lawrence Wheeler, Earl Wilson, and Thyra Samter Winslow.

I wish to thank the librarians who thought it would make a worthwhile reference book—Clara Clark DeRossett, formerly librarian of Christopher House, Chicago; Mildred Joy, of the NBC Library, New York; Gladys Krone, of the Carnegie Public Library, Fort Smith, Arkansas; Jens Nyholm, Head, Charles Deering Library, Northwestern University; and Rose Williams, librarian for United Press, New York.

In the compilation and editing of this material, my special thanks go to Marie Calderone and Barbara Ketels and to my wife, Shirley Pick Simpson.

JAMES BEASLEY SIMPSON

New York,
November 30, 1956

Contents

1954

THE ARMED FORCES

"At times I just seemed to hang there."
Colonel Willard Millikan, Air National Guardsman, comment on cross-continent flight of four hours, eight minutes, and five seconds which established new speed record between Los Angeles and New York, news summaries of January 4, 1954.

"Nautilus is a symbol of man's dreaming—his bright dreams, certainly, and if man is not wise, his nightmares, too."
Admiral Robert Carney, Chief of Naval Operations, comment on first U. S. atomic-engine submarine, news reports of January 22, 1954.

"Atoms for peace. Man is still the greatest miracle and the greatest problem on this earth."
Brigadier General David Sarnoff, first sentences ever dispatched by electricity produced by atomic energy, news reports of January 27, 1954.

"All of the business of war, and indeed all of the business of life, is to endeavor to find out what you don't know by what you do. That's what I called guessing what was at the other side of the hill."
General Alfred Gruenther, report on problems of a modern-day European commander. First sentence of quotation was attributed to Duke of Wellington, one-time commander of twelve European states, news summaries of February 1, 1954.

1

"Now, at the end of the first half-century of engine-driven flight, we are confronted with the stark fact that the historical significance of aircraft has been primarily military and destructive."

Colonel Charles Lindbergh, comment on accepting medal of Institute of Aeronautical Sciences, news summaries of February 1, 1954.

"Ever since I started flying jets I've been driving cars slower and slower. I can't explain why—just cautious."

Major James Jabara, first U. S. jet ace in Korean War, news summaries of February 10, 1954.

"I climbed in sort of an arc, leveled off at about seventy-thousand feet, and shut it off. That was when I reached maximum speed. When I looked back I could see the wings buffeting and the shock waves on them. It was rather a rough flight."

Major Charles Yeager, after establishing record for flying more than twice the speed of sound, news summaries of February 22, 1954.

"The individual soldier is emerging ever more clearly as the ultimate key to victory."

General Matthew Ridgway, Army Chief of Staff, comment that atomic age has given "new meaning and wider scope to the dimensions of land warfare," news summaries of February 23, 1954.

"We believe man as a weapon is here to stay."

Major General James Gavin, planning and operations officer for Army Chief of Staff, news summaries of April 7, 1954.

"The blackbirds are eating all my marigolds."

General George Marshall, retired, statement on tenth anniversary of the Normandy invasion of World War II, news reports of June 5, 1954.

"History records some unpleasant examples of aggressive wars ending in the ways the aggressors neither planned nor expected."

> *General Matthew Ridgway, opposition to preventive war, news reports of December 5, 1954.*

"I still believe this country can be saved. . . . It's a test of our guts and our resiliency."

> *Lieutenant General John O'Daniel, chief of American Military Advisory Group in Indo-China, call to Americans to resist defeatism, news reports of December 17, 1954.*

"More than three million square miles of territory to protect, ten thousand miles of border to guard, and a fence to build ten, eleven or twelve miles high . . . It is better to have less thunder in the mouth and more lightning in the hand."

> *General Ben Chidlaw, on his job as commander of Continental Air Defense protecting the U.S. from enemy air attack, Time, December 20, 1954.*

"From blackout and sightlessness, I saw bright yellow and then vivid reds. The pain was intense, so intense that I recall very little of the pressure in stopping."

> *Lieutenant Colonel John Stapp, U. S. Air Force, description of his sensations in attaining a record land speed of 632 miles per hour, news reports of December 28, 1954.*

ART

"I've helped some people."

> *"Grandma" Moses' (Anna Mary Moses) reply, at 93, when asked of what she was proudest in her life, news summaries of January 2, 1954.*

"During the Renaissance there was no neurosis because people were surrounded by beauty—which was like spiritual food to them. But today everybody is neurotic because they are surrounded by ugliness."

Salvador Dali, news reports of January 19, 1954.

"It is the same theme I took up again, but this time my soft watch will be explosive so that it is adapted to our present age."

Salvador Dali, comment on sailing for the U.S. with his latest work, "A Soft Explosive Watch," expansion of a theme of two decades earlier when he painted watches dangling from a tree branch under the title "Soft Watches," news summaries of December 14, 1954.

"All the really good ideas I ever had came to me while I was milking a cow."

Grant Wood, comment recalled in critical article on his work, Time, of March 1, 1954.

"I think maybe I have to tip taxi drivers a little more now that I am 'Sir.'"

Sir Jacob Epstein, sculptor, on being knighted, news summaries of March 8, 1954.

"Today everything gets put in cans; why not something romantic, like roses?"

Prince Henry of Hesse, grandson of the late King Victor Emmanuel of Italy, explanation of one of his paintings, news summaries of April 19 and 26, 1954.

"There is no need for alarm; the monster is amenable and responds to kindness."

Augustus John, self-description, news summaries of April 25, 1954.

"A portrait should be what the charwoman sees. That's what I was aiming at."

James Gunn, British portrait painter, on completing a portrait of Queen Elizabeth II, news summaries of May 10, 1954.

"I am the most curious of all to see what will be the next thing that I do."

Jacques Lipchitz, Lithuanian-born artist whose 100 pieces of sculpture formed an exhibit at the New York Museum of Modern Art, news summaries of May 24, 1954.

"To name an object is to do away with the three quarters of the enjoyment . . . which is derived from the satisfaction of guessing little by little: to suggest it, to evoke it—that is what charms the imagination."

Stéphane Mallarmé, poetic creed recalled in essay on French painter Édouard Vuillard, Time, May 24, 1954.

"There is nothing more difficult for a truly creative painter than to paint a rose, because before he can do so he has first to forget all the roses that were ever painted."

Henri Matisse, comment recalled in obituaries reporting his death, news reports of November 5, 1954.

"I offer you, with greatest humility, this chapel which I consider the masterpiece of my life, despite its imperfections, and I hope that those who visit it will be purified and solaced."

Henri Matisse, letter on his design of a chapel for the Dominican Order; the letter was disclosed at a requiem mass held for Matisse at Nice, France; news reports of November 9, 1954.

"Although this commission was interesting, I enormously regret I was asked to paint a national hero. People have their own conception of what a hero is like and too many things other than artistic are involved."

Graham Sutherland, on his eightieth-birthday portrait of Winston Churchill, news summaries of December 3, 1954.

AUTHORS

"I write fast, because I have not the brains to write slow."
> *Georges Simenon, author of an average of six novels per year,*
> *written at a pace of thirty-three hours per novel, quoted in*
> *"The Simenon Phenomenon,"* Look, *December 15, 1953; used*
> *in news summaries of January 2, 1954.*

"A writer should describe reality with a touch of unreality, an element
of distortion. That's the magic of creativeness. A literal transcription—
a photograph—isn't enough. Maybe this is why it's better to write about
places and people you don't know too well. The writer must leave something to his imagination."
> *Jessamyn West, author of best seller* Cress Delahanty, The New
> York Times, *January 3, 1954.*

"The real reason for the universal applause that comforts the declining
years of the author who exceeds the common span of man is that intelligent people, after the age of thirty, read nothing at all. As they
grow older, the books they read in their youth are lit with its glamour,
and with every year that passes they ascribe greater merit to the author
that wrote them."
> *Somerset Maugham, comment recalled in news dispatches re-*
> *porting his eightieth birthday, January 25, 1954.*

"Strange world we lived in—actors do their damnedest to look like gentlemen, and gentlemen do all they can to look like actors."
> *Somerset Maugham. Ibid.*

"The great change in manners today is the relaxation of what is proper.
It makes relations among the young so much easier and more friendly.
You can be companions. When I was a boy, you were expected to protect
young girls. For instance, if you were playing lawn tennis, you would
be considered a cad if you didn't lob her a high ball so she could return it
easily. That made for curious relations and bad tennis."
> *Somerset Maugham. Ibid.*

"The thing I notice in America now is that people have realized that being the most powerful and richest nation puts on their shoulders a great responsibility. They seem rather shy. They feel they ought to take the responsibility; at the same time, they don't see why they should! They seem puzzled, uneasy, rather resentful. That, in the circumstances, is a natural attitude. You're often accused of throwing your weight about over here."
Somerset Maugham. Ibid.

"I remember what the English were like before the First World War; we behaved the same way on the Continent. We had taken responsibility for the world for a hundred years from the Napoleonic Wars. Our people got used to it at last and were very above themselves. We made ourselves very disliked. America will probably do the same thing. No one learns from anyone else's experiences. They just have to go through it."
Somerset Maugham. Ibid.

"The French of course will surprise the rest of us. In the course of history, they've had disaster after disaster. They've always surmounted them and made a comeback. Remember, they are an extremely intelligent people. They will accept help when they can get it. When it stops, they will put their shoulders to the wheel and pull themselves out. They've come back before and they'll come back again this time."
Somerset Maugham. Ibid.

"The real social revolution is the extraordinary change in relations between the sexes. People of course are accepting this change in modern novels, but they aren't admitting it in life, and they won't out and say it in print. The whole relation between the sexes has been completely changed by the invention of modern contraceptives. What used to be called chastity seems to have been a social code based on fear."
Somerset Maugham. Ibid.

"One of the amusements of being old is that I have no illusions about my literary position. I have been taken very seriously, but I have also seen essays by clever young men on contemporary fiction who would never think of considering me. I no longer mind what people think. On the whole, I have done what I set out to do. Now, my age makes

7

everyone take me very seriously. If you are a writer, live a long time. I have found that longevity counts more than talent."
Somerset Maugham. Ibid.

"I didn't write any of them to make money; I wrote each one for a reason of my own. I'm convinced that if I'd written for money, it would never have come."
Mary Chase, comment on her plays, Harvey, Mrs. McThing, *and* Bernardine, Cosmopolitan, *February 1954.*

"My luck, she is running very good."
Ernest Hemingway, comment on reaching Entebbe, Uganda, after surviving two plane crashes in the jungle, news summaries of February 1, 1954.

"We held our breaths about two hours while an elephant twelve paces away was silhouetted in the moonlight, listening to my wife's snores. And when we woke her she said, 'I never snore. You've got a fixation about it.' I replied, 'So has the elephant.'"
Ernest Hemingway. Ibid.

"Literary awards usually come late in life when the recipient is well established. It's like throwing a lifebelt to a shipwrecked man after he has reached safety."
Ernest Hemingway. Ibid.

"If it must be built, let it be built upon one condition—that as soon as it is finished it be burned."
Ernest Hemingway, comment on building designed for Grand Canal of Venice by Frank Lloyd Wright. Ibid.

"If my books didn't sell, I think I'd be a bear trainer. I like to wrestle with bears."
Ernest Hemingway. Ibid.

8

"Worry a little bit every day and in a lifetime you will lose a couple of years. If something is wrong, fix it if you can. But train yourself not to worry. Worry never fixes anything."

Mrs. Ernest Hemingway quoted these as her "Words to Live By" in an essay first published in This Week Magazine, *November 7, 1954; copyright 1954, United Newspapers Magazine Corporation.*

"What a writer must try to do is to write as truly as he can. For a writer of fiction has to invent out of what he knows in order to make something not photographic, or naturalistic, or realistic, which will be something entirely new and invented out of his own knowledge. What a writer should try to do is to make something which will be so written that it will become a part of the experience of those who read him."

Ernest Hemingway, on learning that he had been chosen to receive the Nobel Prize for literature, news reports of November 7, 1954.

"This will notify any friends planning to put the bite on me that the money hasn't arrived from Stockholm yet. . . . I'm not a very solemn man, but I'm serious when I work. I don't expect to live more than five years more and I have to hurry."

Ernest Hemingway, comment on the thirty-six thousand dollars awarded to him as a part of the Nobel Prize, Life, *November 8, 1954.*

"Writing, at its best, is a lonely life. Organizations for writers palliate the writer's loneliness, but I doubt if they improve his writing. He grows in public stature as he sheds his loneliness and after his work deteriorates. For he does his work alone and if he is a good enough writer he must face eternity, or the lack of it, each day."

Ernest Hemingway, statement accepting the Nobel Prize, news reports of December 11, 1954.

"You can only have to do it once to get remembered by some people. But if you can do it year after year after year quite a lot of people remember and they tell their children, and their children and their grandchildren remember, and if it's books they can read them. And if it's good enough it lasts forever."

Ernest Hemingway, comment on gaining fame as a writer, Time, *December 13, 1954.*

"There will be no more real poetry written until people wake up. When you are in a fog you don't want a foggy answer and that's all these poets are giving us."

Lord Dunsany, Irish dramatist and poet, New York Post, *February 28, 1954.*

"Clarity is the first duty of poets and in looking at today's poetry one should realize symbols aren't any good if they aren't clear. This stuff that is called modern verse ought to have a court of appeals to judge what it really is. It's muck, and people ought to be honest. When they don't understand it, they should say they don't. They seem to fear being considered ignorant if they dislike it."

Lord Dunsany, on arriving in New York for a lecture tour. Ibid.

"An archaeologist is the best husband any woman can have: the older she gets, the more interested he is in her."

Agatha Christie, quoted in news reports of March 9, 1954.

"There's absolutely no reason for being rushed along with the rush. Everybody should be free to go very slow. . . . What you want, what you're hanging around in the world waiting for, is for something to occur to you."

Robert Frost, American poet, news reports of March 21, 1954.

"I don't call myself a poet yet. It's for the world to say whether you're a poet or not. I'm one-half teacher, one-half poet and one-half farmer; that's three halves."

Robert Frost, comment on his eightieth birthday, news summaries of March 29, 1954.

"I guess one way of putting it would be that you have freedom when you're easy in your harness."
Robert Frost, news summaries of May 10, 1954.

"I know that my works are a credit to this nation, and I dare say they will endure longer than the McCarran Act. It is even possible that through my plays which have been produced in every theatre in Europe, I have made more friends for American culture than the State Department. Certainly I have made fewer enemies, but that isn't very difficult."
Arthur Miller, playwright, statement on being refused a passport to go abroad, news reports of March 31, 1954.

"Right now, anyone who finds a way to make a lamp out of a Coca-Cola bottle gets more protection than a man who creates a work of art."
Christopher LaFarge, plea for a universal copyright law, news summaries of April 9, 1954.

"Never thank anybody for anything, except a drink of water in the desert—and then make it brief."
Gene Fowler, quoted in Walter Winchell's column, New York Mirror, *April 9, 1954.*

"Sometimes I think it sounds like I walked out of the room and left the typewriter running."
Gene Fowler, author, Newsweek, *November 1, 1954.*

"It is only in the upper-class level that each husband sits next to the other man's wife."
Louis Kronenberger, in Company Manners, *copyright Bobbs-Merrill Company, 1954, quoted in news summaries of April 12, 1954.*

"The trouble with our age is all signposts and no destination."
Louis Kronenberger, Look, *May 17, 1954.*

"Hard-covered books break up friendships. You loan a hard-covered book to a friend and when he doesn't return it you get mad at him. It makes you mean and petty. But twenty-five-cent books are different."
John Steinbeck, news summaries of April 25, 1954.

"Everyone looked like his picture save Winston Churchill, who is blond and quite insignificant-looking."
Mrs. Edith Helm, social secretary at the White House for twenty-five years, letter sent to fiancé while visiting England with President and Mrs. Wilson, recalled in her memoirs, The Captains and the Kings, *G. P. Putnam's Sons, 1954; quoted in news summaries of May 10, 1954.*

"I always knew children were anti-social. But the children of the West Side—they're savage."
Marc Connelly, author and playwright, after being knocked down by a wicker chair thrown from the roof of a New York tenement, news reports of May 28, 1954.

"Practical people would be a lot more practical if they were just a little more dreamy."
J. P. McEvoy, "Charlie Would Love This," Reader's Digest, *June 1954.*

"I work well there. I put on sneakers and shorts and when the perspiration begins to stream down my face, I begin to live."
James Michener, comment on his liking for island retreats in the Pacific, The New York Times, *July 12, 1954.*

"To the alley and the canal and the little houses and the pachinko parlor and to the flutes at night—sayonara. And you, Japan, you crowded islands, you tragic land—sayonara, you enemy, you friend."
James Michener, Sayonara *(meaning "sad goodbye"), novel, copyright by Random House.*

"Dear Mr. Simpson: Your friendly letter concerning Arkansas' interest in that lovable girl Nellie Forbush caused me to go back in my memory some eight years ago to a time when there were, in an Army Base Hospital on the island of Espiritu Santo, a group of two dozen Army nurses completely surrounded by 100,000 unattached American men. I used to have dinner regularly at this hospital in company with four Army doctors from hospitals around Denver, and as we talked after dinner I would see the Army nurses setting out in their jeeps for dates with the various men in our armed services.

"In my own unit there was a young naval officer from somewhere in the South who was much taken by one of the Army nurses. Through me he obtained an introduction to her. I am not sure what state she was from—I think it was Arkansas—but I remember the joy these two southerners found in one another and I was deeply moved by the good sense, simple charm, and heartwarming behavior of this Army nurse. She could have been a very tough customer had she wanted to be for she was courted by at least 500 young men, but miraculously she remained a real paragon of charm and friendliness. I have rarely seen any human being conduct himself so well under such inherently difficult circumstances. I wish I knew her name so that I could at this late date pay my personal respects to a very unusual young woman.

"It is therefore amusing to me to realize that this rare Army nurse has become transposed into the arch type of the rare Navy nurse. Well, that sometimes happens. I was a Navy officer writing about Navy problems and I simply stole this lovely Army nurse and popped her into Navy uniform, where she has done very well for herself.

"You ask if she was a real girl. Indeed she was. You ask if she was from Arkansas. I don't know, but when it came time to write the story I felt that whether this particular girl had actually come from Arkansas or not, she should have done so—and that's how it all happened.

"Warmest regards."

James Michener, letter to James Beasley Simpson on the heroine of South Pacific, *quoted by permission.*

"Here, with whitened hair, desires failing, strength ebbing out of him, with the sun gone down and with only the serenity and the calm warning of the evening star left to him, he drank to Life, to all it had been, to what it was, to what it would be. Hurrah!"

Sean O'Casey, playwright, writing in the third person, told a reporter that this sentence would be the final paragraph of the autobiography he was completing at the age of seventy; Life, *July 26, 1954.*

"It is a nuisance that knowledge can only be acquired by hard work."
Somerset Maugham, Look, *August 24, 1954.*

"A woman can look both moral and exciting—if she also looks as if it was quite a struggle."
Edna Ferber, "Quotable Quotes," Reader's Digest, *December 1954.*

"It is the custom to sneer at the modern apartment-house, television, big-city Christmas with its commercial taint, forced gaiety, office parties, artificial or dyed Christmas trees, the frenetic mechanized Noel of today, but future generations in search of their lost Christmases may well remember its innocence; yes, and its beauty, too."
"The Lost Christmas," by Paul Gallico, Esquire Magazine, *December 1954, copyright 1954 by Esquire, Inc., reprinted by permission of Harold Ober Associates.*

"For the truth seems to be that as long as the miraculous chain of life persists, Christmas will not really have been lost ever, but only strayed during the eternal cycles from youth to maturity, from generation to generation, when at least once on December 25 the eye and the ear is enchanted, the spirit uplifted and Christmas enters the heart never thereafter to be forgotten."
Paul Gallico. Ibid.

"For me, a hearty 'belly-laugh' is one of the beautiful sounds in the world."
Bennett Cerf, foreword to An Encyclopedia of Modern American Humor, *reprinted by permission of Hanover House, Publishers, copyright 1954 by Doubleday & Company, Inc.*

"As far back as I remember, long before I could write, I had played at making stories. . . . But not until I was seven or more, did I begin to pray every night, 'O God, let me write books! Please, God, let me write books!' "

Ellen Glasgow, in her autobiography, The Woman Within, *Harcourt, Brace and Company, 1954. Reprinted by permission of the publisher.*

"Surely one of the peculiar habits of circumstances is the way they follow, in their eternal recurrence, a single course. If an event happens once in a life, it may be depended upon to repeat later its general design. A misadventure in love will be constantly renewed, not in subtle variations, but in a similar pattern. A heart once broken appears to be forever looking for trouble of the same nature."

Ellen Glasgow. Ibid.

"Yes, I have had my life. I have known ecstasy. I have known anguish. I have loved, and I have been loved. With one I loved, I have watched the light breaking over the Alps. If I have passed through 'the dark night of the soul,' I have had a far-off glimpse of the illumination beyond. For an infinitesimal point of time or eternity, I have caught a gleam, or imagined I caught a gleam, of the mystic vision. . . . It was enough, and it is now over. Not for everything that the world could give would I consent to live over my life unchanged, or to bring back, unchanged, my youth. . . . Only on the surface of things have I ever trod the beaten path. So long as I could keep from hurting anyone else, I have lived, as completely as it was possible, the life of my choice. I have been free. Yet I have not ever stolen either the ponderable or the imponderable material of happiness. I have done the work I wished to do for the sake of that work alone. And I have come, at last, from the fleeting rebellion of youth into the steadfast—or is it merely the seasonable—accord without surrender of the unreconciled heart."

Ellen Glasgow, conclusion of autobiography. Ibid.

"I find recorded in my notebook that it was on the afternoon of Wednesday, the sixteenth of November, 1887, when the attention of my friend, Mr. Sherlock Holmes, was first drawn to the singular affair of the man who hated clocks."

Adrian Conan Doyle, youngest son of Sir Arthur Conan Doyle, continuation of character originated by his father, in book published by Random House, 1954.

"There is a famous culinary concoction called 'burgoo' . . . meat, chicken, vegetables and lots of seasonings. These memoirs are going to be somewhat like a 'burgoo.' . . . The recipe is largely in my head, for I have never kept a diary or journal; I have had far too busy a life for that."

Alben Barkley, comment on beginning his memoirs, That Reminds Me, *Doubleday & Company, Inc., 1954.*

"My face, it is far below par,
For I am no beauty by far!
But my face, I don't mind it,
Because I'm behind it;
It's the people out front that I jar!"

Woodrow Wilson, favorite limerick about his personal appearance, recalled by Alben Barkley in his memoirs. Ibid.

"The machine has several virtues. . . . One may lean back in his chair and work it. It piles an awful stack of words on one page. It don't muss things or scatter ink blots around."

Mark Twain's first typewritten letter, addressed to his brother. Quoted by Bruce Bliven in The Wonderful Writing Machine, *Random House, 1954.*

"Breakfast is the one meal at which it is perfectly good manners to read the paper. . . ."

Amy Vanderbilt, etiquette expert, ruling on modern manners, Amy Vanderbilt's Complete Book of Etiquette, *Doubleday & Company, Inc., 1954.*

"Pain makes man think. Thought makes man wise. Wisdom makes life endurable."

John Patrick, playwright, widely quoted line from his Broadway hit, Tea House of the August Moon.

"For sixteen years I existed in a nightmare world, one which many enter but not many leave. That one can come back, that there is a way out from shame and despair and utter hopelessness—that is the sum and substance of my book."

Lillian Roth, introduction to I'll Cry Tomorrow, *Frederick Fell Inc., 1954.*

"From defending the common man we pass on to exalting him and we find ourselves beginning to imply not merely that he is as good as anybody else but that he is actually better. Instead of demanding only that the common man be given an opportunity to become as uncommon as possible, we make his commonness a virtue and, even in the case of candidates for high office, we sometimes praise them for being nearly indistinguishable from the average man in the street. Secretly, no doubt, we hope that they are somehow superior, but we feel at the same time that a kind of decency requires them to conceal the fact as completely as possible."

Reprinted from "Is the Common Man Too Common? A Survey of Our Cultural Resources and What We Are Doing About Them," by Joseph Wood Krutch and others. Copyright 1954, by University of Oklahoma Press. Used by permission.

BUSINESS

"We are not the gloom and doom boys [but] it is easier to stop a snowball than an avalanche."

Walter Reuther, president of the Congress of Industrial Organizations (CIO), statement urging the Administration to take action against an economic recession, New York Post, *January 1, 1954.*

"Anybody who has any doubt about the ingenuity or the resourcefulness of a plumber never got a bill from one."

George Meany, President, American Federation of Labor, himself a former plumber, to Edward R. Murrow, "Person to Person," CBS-TV, January 8, 1954.

"Just put me on the lazy, no-account list."

John Nance Garner, former Vice-President of the U.S., announcement of retirement from business as a bank director, news reports of January 30, 1954.

"All elephants traveling by air are accompanied by a live hen which makes its home on the elephant's head during the trip. Elephants do not like to travel alone and the feathered companion has a calming effect on the truculent beast."

KLM, Royal Dutch Airlines, transporters of many animals from jungles to zoos, news summaries of January 31, 1954.

"I don't sell just this coffee. That's nothing. I sell gentility. I sell companionship."

Proprietor of New York coffee house, quoted by Rhea Talley in Louisville, Ky., Courier-Journal of January 31, 1954.

"All the problems of the world could be settled easily if men were only willing to think. The trouble is that men very often resort to all sorts of devices in order not to think, because thinking is such hard work."

Thomas J. Watson, head of International Business Machines, statement on his eightieth birthday, news summaries of February 22, 1954.

"Millionaires are marrying very often their secretaries because they're so busy making money they haven't time to see other girls."

Doris Lilly, author of How to Marry a Millionaire, *G. P. Putnam's Sons, new summaries of March 8, 1954.*

". . . This demand is not enough to enable us to maintain profitable schedules. . . . After all they don't need them."
A Troy, New York, woolen mill announcement that it was closing its doors after manufacturing long woolen underwear for sixty-eight years, news summaries of March 8, 1954.

"I never want *Who's Who* to fall into irresponsible hands . . . you cannot buy, bribe or flatter your way into *Who's Who*."
Wheeler Sammons, owner and editor of Who's Who, *announcement of plans for board of trustees to put book's profits into fund for biographical research, news summaries of March 8, 1954.*

"A man's worth is counted in the things he creates for the betterment of his fellow men."
Harry Morrison, president, Morrison-Kundsen Co., world's largest heavy-construction firm, Time, May 3, 1954.

"Every day I have a matutinal indisposition that emanates from the nauseous effluvia of that oppressive slave statute."
John L. Lewis, comment on Taft-Hartley Act, news reports of May 10, 1954.

"The woman who climbs to a high post and then wants everybody to know how important she is is the worst enemy of her own sex."
Mrs. Claire Giannini Hoffman, only woman director of the Bank of America, news reports of July 7, 1954.

"Every woman can learn something from Senator McCarthy—how important it is to confuse everybody. You get noticed that way."
Lilly Daché, Look, July 13, 1954.

"When I was six I made my mother a little hat—out of her new blouse."
Lilly Daché, hat designer, comment on the start of her career, news summaries of December 3, 1954.

"Maybe you heard the complaint which was voiced, not long ago, by a leading lady of the New York stage. She said that with taxes as they are today, a girl might as well marry for love!"

Benjamin F. Fairless, chairman of the board, United States Steel Corporation, address to Charleston, South Carolina, Chamber of Commerce in October 1954, text printed and distributed by U. S. Steel.

"I hope that a world of peace will permit the building to live out its life expectancy of two hundred years."

Colonel Henry Crown, son of a Lithuanian immigrant, on completing payments of $49,500,000 to become owner of the Empire State Building, news reports of October 15, 1954.

"In advertising there is a saying that if you can keep your head while all those around you are losing theirs—then you just don't understand the problem."

Hugh M. Beville, Jr., director of Research and Planning, National Broadcasting Company, NBC brochure, November 18, 1954.

"The business has busted its britches. I doubt if more than three houses are operating in the black this year."

Freeman Lewis, executive vice president of Pocket Books, Inc., report on excessive production of paper-backed books, Wall Street Journal, December 12, 1954.

"Men are just starting to use cosmetics. And this part of the business should expand into untold millions in the next fifty years. Men are just as vain as women, and sometimes even more so."

Helena Rubenstein, founder and director of one of the world's largest lotion and cosmetics empires, quoted in interview with Art Buchwald, New York Herald-Tribune Syndicate, 1954.

"When he came out after the war with his New Look he saved Paris like the Battle of the Marne."

> *Carmel Snow, fashion editor, comment on Christian Dior's contribution to the fashion economy, interview with Art Buchwald. Ibid.*

"Fath was sexy, Dior was simple, Balmain was accented, Givenchy was youthful, Balenciaga was classic, Schiaparelli was eccentric, Lanvin was wearable, Desses was himself and Patou was breathless."

> *Carmel Snow, comment on 1954 fashion showings in Paris. Ibid.*

"Every man wants to live like a king, but you can't anymore unless you are in the innkeeping business. . . . Besides it's the ideal life because you never are alone."

> *Ludwig Bemelmans, writer and artist, on opening a bar in an old house in Paris. Ibid.*

"Public Relations is the management function which evaluates public attitudes, identifies the policies and procedures of an individual or an organization with the public interest, and executes a program of action to earn public understanding and acceptance."

> *Definition of public relations composed by the editors of* Public Relations News, *New York City, printed on cards distributed to the public relations profession, 1954.*

WINSTON CHURCHILL

"One does not leave a convivial party before closing time."

> *Sir Winston Churchill, reply to queries on when he might retire as Prime Minister, news summaries of March 22, 1954.*

"I am in almost hourly correspondence with the United States Government."

> *Churchill, reply to Laborites' complaints at lack of Anglo-American consultations on hydrogen bomb experiments, news summaries of April 5, 1954.*

"We are all naturally concerned with the prodigious experiments which are being carried out in the Pacific, but I do not think that there will be any difference between us that we would rather have them carried out there than in Siberia."

Churchill, comment to House of Commons on hydrogen bomb detonations, April 5, 1954, news reports of April 6, 1954.

"I am not a lawyer but I have had to obey a lot of laws and helped to make a few."

Churchill, acceptance of an honorary degree, Doctor of Laws, from New York State Board of Regents, news reports of April 10, 1954.

"The honorable member must not, in his innocence, take the bread from the mouths of the Soviet secret service."

Churchill, reply to question asked in Parliament on Britain's protection against atom bomb attack, news summaries of April 26, 1954.

"I have a feeling that people who go in for involved, unexpected super-original—if I may coin that word—forms of art ought to have credentials."

Churchill, The New York Times, May 1, 1954.

"All over the globe there has been a sense of kindly feeling and generous admiration. Even envy wore a friendly smile."

Churchill, address asking Commons to adopt a resolution welcoming home Queen Elizabeth from her first tour of the Commonwealth, news reports of May 18, 1954.

"It will be the same, I trust, as it has been since the days of Adam and Eve."

Churchill, reply when asked by an ardent American feminist about the role of women in the future, news summaries of May 31, 1954.

"The people of Russia have had a very rough time in the twentieth century, the century of the common man. The common man in no country has had a worse time than they have had in the twentieth century, with all the bloody struggles in which they have had to engage, in the revolution and the disciplinary measures, internal stresses which have fallen upon them."

Churchill, remark at news conference held in New York City, during visit to U.S., news reports of June 29, 1954.

". . . I don't know whether you have them here but football pools, and all that, constitutes the sustaining background of the life of a man upon whose faithful daily toil and exertion all the progress of society depends."

Churchill, evaluation of the football pool, a game of chance highly popular in Britain. Ibid.

"I am an optimist. It does not seem too much use being anything else."

Churchill, address to the Lord Mayor's banquet, London, news reports of November 10, 1954.

"I am proud but also, I must admit, awe-struck at your decision to include me. I do hope you are right. I feel we are both running a considerable risk and that I do not deserve it. But I shall have no misgivings if you have none."

Churchill, message read by Lady Churchill as acceptance speech for Nobel Prize for literature, recalled in news reports on his eightieth birthday, November 30, 1954.

"This Man, in darkness saw, in doubtings led;
In danger did; in uttermost despair,
Shone with a Hope that made the midnight fair.
The world he saved calls blessings on his head."

John Masefield, poet laureate of England, tribute "On the Birthday of a Great Man," Winston Churchill's eightieth birthday, news summaries of November 30, 1954.

"It was the nation and the race dwelling all 'round the globe that had the lion's heart. I had the luck to be called upon to give the lion's roar. I also hope that I sometimes suggested to the lion the right place to use his claws."

Churchill, address at London ceremonies marking his eightieth birthday, news reports of December 1, 1954.

"In modern times, war should not be decided on questions of nationality or on the past conduct of any nation but only on the new guilt of aggression."

Churchill, recommendation for rearming of German forces, news reports of December 2, 1954.

CRIME

"There is scarcely a deed more commonplace than the lie. Children lie; hysterics lie, and likewise do persons deemed most honorable."

Guillaume Duprat, statement recalled at time of the Army-McCarthy hearing, New York Post, March 24, 1954.

". . . I defended about one hundred forty people for murder in this country and I think in all of the cases I received just one Christmas card, from all of these defendants. . . ."

Samuel Leibowitz, judge, King's County Court, Brooklyn, New York, in an interview with Edward R. Murrow, "Person to Person," CBS-TV, May 28, 1954.

"There are only about twenty murders a year in London and not all are serious—some are just husbands killing their wives."

Commander G. H. Hatherill, Scotland Yard, news reports of July 1, 1954.

"Before this hot August Sunday is over one of us in this city will have been murdered. Another of us will have died as the result of criminal negligence. Twenty-seven of our people will have been feloniously assaulted. Three women will have been raped. One hundred and forty of our homes and businesses will have been burglarized. Forty of us will have had our cars stolen. Thirty-one of us will have been held up and robbed on the streets of this city. Sixty-nine grand larcenies will have taken place before this day is over. And there will have been fifteen other miscellaneous felonies—such as frauds, possession of dangerous weapons and sex offenses other than rape and the like. The property which will be stolen from New Yorkers on this one day will amount to more than one hundred forty thousand dollars—enough to pay the salaries of twenty-eight policemen for a year. Even in the brief half hour in which I will talk to you, seventeen crimes will be committed in the city of New York—more than one every two minutes. This then is an average day in this city—far from quiet, far from peaceful."

Police Commissioner Francis Adams, statement warning that New York "is on the verge of becoming a community of violence and crime" because of an undermanned and underpaid police force; news reports of August 2, 1954.

"Astounding is the word for the verdict. . . . I heard the same evidence the jury heard. . . . I could not have convicted him of anything except possibly negligence in not locking his front door. . . . I have covered a score and more of murder trials. . . . It is the first time I have ever been scared by the jury system, and I mean scared."

Dorothy Kilgallen, of the Hearst newspapers, report on the conviction December 21, 1954, of Dr. Sam Sheppard of the murder of his wife, news summaries of January 3, 1955.

DEFINITIONS

"Back in Detroit we had a saying that an expert is a mechanic away from home."

Charles E. Wilson, Secretary of Defense, news summaries of January 11, 1954.

"Modern poets are bells of lead. They should tinkle melodiously but usually they just klunk."

Lord Dunsany, Irish poet, news summaries of January 11, 1954.

"Humanity, let us say, is like people packed in an automobile which is travelling down hill without lights on a dark night at terrific speed and driven by a four-year-old child. The signposts along the way are all marked 'Progress.' "

Lord Dunsany. Ibid.

"The guitar is a little island—and music is the ocean around it."
Andres Segovia, famed guitarist, news summaries of January 25,
1954.

"Middle age is when your age starts to show around your middle."
Bob Hope, quoted by Nick Kenny's column in New York Daily
Mirror, *and in news summaries of February 15, 1954.*

"Life is something like this trumpet. If you don't put anything in it you
don't get anything out. And that's the truth."
W. C. Handy, comment during Negro History Week, news sum-
maries of February 15, 1954.

"I didn't get sophisticated—I just got tired. But maybe that's what
sophisticated is—being tired."
Rita Gam, actress, quoted in Earl Wilson's column in New York
Post *and in news summaries of February 15, 1954.*

"The future begins when you cut every tie with the lost past."
Heinz Nordhoff, German General Motors executive, comment on
his postwar success as an automotive executive, Time, *February*
15, 1954.

"I define a recession as when your neighbor loses his job, but a depression
is when you lose your own."
Dave Beck, Teamsters' Union president, Time, *February 22,*
1954, and other news summaries of that date.

"Obscenity is whatever happens to shock some elderly and ignorant
magistrate."
Bertrand Russell, Look, *February 23, 1954.*

"The public is like a piano. You just have to know what keys to poke."
Al Capp, cartoonist, news summaries of March 1, 1954.

"A bohemian is a man who plays all night and sleeps all day. I have always worked too hard to be considered a bohemian."

Sir Jacob Epstein, the sculptor, news summaries of March 8, 1954.

"A gossip is one who talks to you about others; a bore is one who talks to you about himself; and a brilliant conversationalist is one who talks to you about yourself."

Lisa Kirk, singer, bon mot, concluding Cholly Knickerbocker's column, New York Journal American, *March 9, 1954.*

"Baloney is the unvarnished lie laid on so thick you hate it. Blarney is flattery laid on so thin you love it."

Bishop Fulton Sheen, news reports of March 22, 1954.

"A true sonnet goes eight lines and then takes a turn for better or worse and goes six or eight lines more."

Robert Frost, news summaries of March 29, 1954.

"Humor is falling downstairs if you do it while in the act of warning your wife not to."

Kenneth Bird, editor of Punch, *news summaries of May 3, 1954.*

"Eleanor Roosevelt is the jet plane with a fringe on top."

Anna Rosenberg, news summaries of May 17, 1954.

"An egghead is one who stands firmly on both feet in mid-air on both sides of an issue."

Senator Homer Ferguson, news summaries of May 28, 1954.

"It is a belief in the universal obligation to work . . . and certain miscellaneous traits such as overheated houses and a passion for rocking chairs and ice water."

Arthur Schlesinger, Harvard professor and historian, comment on traits that stamp Americans, news summaries of June 6, 1954.

"Any attempt at definition would put the sausage manufacturers up in arms. The sausage has been the subject of pantomime jokes. Humorous articles have been written about it. But, as yet, nobody has been bold enough to lay down rules as to its composition."

Gwilym Lloyd George, food minister for Great Britain, reply to a demand that he define the composition of sausage, news summaries of June 14, 1954.

"Memory is when you look back and the answers float in to who, what, when, where. . . ."

Carl Sandburg, news summaries of June 30, 1954.

"A committee is a group that keeps minutes and loses hours."

Milton Berle, news summaries, July 1, 1954.

"A fanatic is one who can't change his mind and won't change the subject."

Sir Winston Churchill, news summaries of July 5, 1954.

"An appeaser is one who feeds a crocodile—hoping it will eat him last."

Sir Winston Churchill, Reader's Digest, December 1954.

"Security is when I'm very much in love with somebody extraordinary who loves me back."

Shelley Winters, news summaries, July 9, 1954.

"Politics is the diversion of trivial men who, when they succeed at it, become important in the eyes of more trivial men."

George Jean Nathan, news summaries, July 9, 1954.

"Religion is a candle inside a multicolored lantern. Everyone looks through a particular color, but the candle is always there."

Mohammed Naguib, former President of Egypt, news summaries of July 10, 1954.

"America is a large, friendly dog in a very small room. Every time it wags its tail, it knocks over a chair."
Arnold Toynbee, news summaries, July 14, 1954.

"A sports writer is a guy who could get himself slugged regularly each Tuesday and Thursday if fist fighters, ball players, and such didn't have a commendable and wholly unreasonable awe for something called 'the power of the press.'"
Red Smith, sports editor of the New York Herald-Tribune, *news summaries of July 29, 1954.*

"Playing 'bop' is like playing Scrabble with all the vowels missing."
Duke Ellington, band leader, Look, *August 10, 1954.*

"An elder statesman is somebody old enough to know his own mind and keep quiet about it."
Bernard Baruch, news reports of August 20, 1954.

"The library is not a shrine for the worship of books. It is not a temple where literary incense must be burned or where one's devotion to the bound book is expressed in ritual. A library, to modify the famous metaphor of Socrates, should be the delivery room for the birth of ideas —a place where history comes to life."
Norman Cousins, editor of the Saturday Review, *writing in the American Library Association* Bulletin, *October 1954.*

"An atheist is a guy who watches a Notre Dame–SMU football game and doesn't care who wins."
President Eisenhower, remark to newsmen during the 1954 football season, news summaries of November 6, 1954.

"Bravery is the capacity to perform properly even when scared half to death."
General of the Army Omar Bradley, The American Weekly, *November 7, 1954.*

"Our democracy is like a reluctant knight going out to engage the dragon. His armor is on awry and he drives out his horse with no flash of enthusiasm, but somehow in the end the dragon poops out and our knight wins."

Norman Thomas, comment on American democracy on eve of his seventieth birthday, news reports of November 20, 1954.

"An after-dinner speech is like a love letter. Ideally, you should begin by not knowing what you are going to say, and end by not knowing what you've said."

Lord Jowitt, Look, *December 14, 1954.*

"The art of acceptance is the art of making someone who has just done you a small favor wish that he might have done you a greater one."

Russell Lynes, Reader's Digest, *December 1954.*

"A bad little boy is a canoe—behaves better if paddled from the rear."

Don McNeill, frequently used on his radio program, "The Breakfast Club," in 1954.

"A bore is a fellow who opens his mouth and puts his feats in it."

Henry Ford, humorous jottings made public on fiftieth anniversary of founding of Ford Motor Company, printed privately by the Company.

"The twenties are better than the teens, the thirties are better than the twenties, and the forties are just dandy."

Emily Kimbrough, Forty Plus and Fancy Free, *Harper & Brothers, 1954, news summaries of March 8, 1954.*

"Happiness is not having what you want, but wanting what you have."

Dr. Hyman Judah Schachtel, rabbi, favorite sentence in his book, The Real Enjoyment of Living, *E. P. Dutton & Company, 1954.*

"Protocol may be defined as the code of etiquette which protects royalty from the competition of intellectual and social superiors."
Elsa Maxwell in her autobiography, RSVP, *copyright 1954 by Elsa Maxwell; Little, Brown and Company, Boston, reprinted by permission.*

". . . The Four Hundred is an archaic figure of speech in New York and any other social center. It is a fairly accurate census of the combined elite on the face of the earth."
Elsa Maxwell. Ibid.

"A vice-president in an advertising agency is a 'molehill man.' A molehill man is a pseudo-busy executive who comes to work at 9 A.M. and finds a molehill on his desk. He has until 5 P.M. to make this molehill into a mountain. An accomplished molehill man will often have his mountain finished even before lunch."
Fred Allen, Treadmill to Oblivion, *copyright 1954 by Fred Allen; Little, Brown and Company, reprinted by permission.*

"A celebrity is a person who works hard all his life to become well known, then wears dark glasses to avoid being recognized."
Fred Allen. Ibid.

EDUCATION

"Work 'em hard, play 'em hard, feed 'em up to the nines, and send 'em to bed so tired that they are asleep before their heads are on the pillow."
Dr. Frank Boyden of Deerfield Academy, advice on how to run a successful prep school, news summaries of January 2, 1954.

"More free time means more time to waste. The worker who used to have only a little time in which to get drunk and beat his wife now has time to get drunk, beat his wife—and watch TV."
Robert Hutchins, news summaries of January 2, 1954.

"It is just as important, perhaps more important, for the teacher to have the benefit of personal counseling when he needs it as it is for the student."

Dr. William Menninger, noted psychiatrist, address to Milwaukee convention, National Association of Secondary School Principals, news reports of February 24, 1954.

"The true business of liberal education is greatness."

Dr. Nathan Pusey, president, Harvard University, Time "profile" story, March 1, 1954.

"Our task is to keep American life reasonable. This is more than any two institutions alone—or sometimes, I think, all of us together, can do."

Dr. Nathan Pusey, address on receiving honorary Doctor of Laws degree from Yale University, news reports of June 14, 1954.

"When you leave here, don't forget why you came."

Adlai Stevenson, comment to Princeton University Class of 1954, news reports of March 22, 1954.

"If we are to compete with Russia and China, then each American child actually must be three or four times as well trained and as effective as each Asiatic if our balance of progress is to be maintained."

Dr. Samuel M. Brownell, United States Commissioner of Education, news reports of April 8, 1954.

"It is perhaps treason for me to say it but cast aside the richest book to listen to the right person."

Dr. Herbert Putnam, for forty years librarian of Congress until retirement in 1939, news summaries of April 19, 1955.

"To our public school teachers we turn over the most precious thing in America. But all too frequently we ask these teachers to carry on their vital work in cramped, outmoded physical plants which we would never tolerate in our businesses—and at salaries less than we pay our secretaries."

Richard Bowditch, president, U. S. Chamber of Commerce, news summaries of May 3, 1954.

"We come then to the question presented: Does segregation of children in public schools solely on the basis of race, even though the physical facilities and other 'tangible' factors may be equal, deprive the children of the minority group of equal education opportunities? We believe that it does. . . . We conclude that in the field of public education the doctrine of 'separate but equal' has no place."

Text of Supreme Court decision outlawing Negro segregation in the public schools, as read by Chief Justice Earl Warren, May 17, 1954, news reports of May 18, 1954.

"They screen the country for talented kids more than we do. We're enamored of the idea of mass education."

Dr. Vannevar Bush, comment on belief that Russia trains more scientists because U.S. "still lets too many gifted youths slip through our hands," news reports of June 13, 1954.

"My final warning to you is always pay for your own drinks. . . . All the scandals in the world of politics today have their cause in the despicable habit of swallowing free drinks."

Y. Yakigawa, president of Kyoto (Japan) University, in advising the graduating class, news summaries of June 13, 1954.

"What the Lunts have joined together Dartmouth will not set asunder. . . ."

Dartmouth College citation in awarding a joint L.H.D. honorary degree to Alfred Lunt and Lynn Fontanne. The citation continued, "It can be said of your performing art that words are never put to better use or needed less . . . ," news reports of June 14, 1954.

"The Italian navigator arrived at the shores of the new world."

Dr. Arthur Compton, coded telephone message to Dr. James Conant, head of the National Defense Research Committee, when Dr. Enrico Fermi, in 1942, set an atomic furnace into successful operation for the first time. The quotation was recalled in obituaries reporting death of Dr. Fermi, news reports of November 29, 1954.

"If the schools cannot or do not send the colleges properly qualified students, the whole fabric of higher education becomes a bridge built on rotten pilings."

Dr. Whitney Griswold, president, Yale University, annual report to alumni, news reports of December 1, 1954.

"This is a world in which each of us, knowing his limitations, knowing the evils of superficiality and the terrors of fatigue, will have to cling to what is close to him, to what he knows, to what he can do, to his friends and his tradition and his love, lest he be dissolved in a universal confusion and know nothing and love nothing."

Dr. J. Robert Oppenheimer, director, Institute for Advanced Study, address marking the close of Columbia University bicentennial celebration, news reports of December 27, 1954.

"Philanthropy is an American habit and the modern foundation is an American invention. To make human beings healthier, happier, wiser, more conscious of the rich possibilities of human existence and more capable of realizing them. . . ."

Charles Dollard, president, Carnegie Corporation of New York, reply to a congressional committee investigating alleged subversive activities on the part of tax-free foundations, news summaries of December 28, 1954.

". . . And when in turn my time came to share the vitality of this experience with others, I was resolved to sustain and preserve in my college the bite of the mind, the chance to stand face to face with truth, the good life lived in a small, various, highly articulate and democratic society."

Virginia Gildersleeve, dean emeritus of Barnard College, in her autobiography, Many a Good Crusade, The Macmillan Company, 1954, reprinted by permission of the publisher.

". . . For me the most moving moment of the celebration came when a short telegram from an absent alumna was opened. 'Don't ever dare,' read the message of Alice Duer Miller, 'to take your college as a matter

of course—because like freedom and democracy, many people you'll never know anything about have broken their hearts to get it for you.'"
Virginia Gildersleeve, recollection of 1939 celebration of fiftieth anniversary of Barnard College. Ibid.

"Perhaps the pleasantest part of the San Francisco Conference for me was the photograph which was taken just as I was rising from the table after signing and was shaking hands with President Truman. The expressions on the faces of my colleagues of the delegation as they look at me and applaud, warm my heart. They seem to approve of me and to like me. Senator Vandenberg especially looks like a proud uncle who has had a lot to do with bringing me up."
Virginia Gildersleeve. Ibid. (Miss Gildersleeve was the only woman member of the U. S. delegation which signed the United Nations charter.)

"The ability to think straight, some knowledge of the past, some vision of the future, some skill to do useful service, some urge to fit that service into the well-being of the community—these are the most vital things education must try to produce. If we can achieve them in the citizens of our land, then, given the right to knowledge and the free use thereof, we shall have brought to America the wisdom and the courage to match her destiny."
Virginia Gildersleeve. Ibid. (closing paragraph)

AMERICAN GOVERNMENT

"Liberty, not communism, is the most contagious force in the world."
Earl Warren, speech before Association of Alumni of Columbia College, first major address after becoming Chief Justice, news reports of January 15, 1954.

"My regards to the brothers of the federation. Their kindness to me has always been more than a one-time poor clarinet player deserved."
Earl Warren, Supreme Court Chief Justice, letter thanking International Brotherhood of Musicians for their congratulations

on his appointment to the high court; Warren had been a charter member of union's local in Bakersfield, California, in 1906, news reports of January 20, 1954.

"People listen, to a large extent, because of vacuity of mind."
Felix Frankfurter, U. S. Supreme Court Justice, news reports of January 20, 1954.

"This problem of definition involves the related questions of wardship or trusteeship, tribal membership, and maintenance of tribal rolls. The question is complex, but until it is settled by law, the problem remains open-ended and not even a gradual narrowing of the federal responsibility will be possible."
Department of Interior report on "Who is an Indian?" to determine school tuition, and other aids for persons with at least one-quarter Indian blood, news summaries of January 20, 1954.

"It is one thing to recognize evil as a fact. It is another thing to take evil to one's breast and call it good."
John Foster Dulles, Secretary of State, comment on Russian propaganda during address to Big Four Foreign Ministers' conference, Berlin, news report of January 26, 1954.

"There is only one defense—a defense compounded of eternal vigilance, sound policies, and high courage."
John Foster Dulles, address to Overseas Press Club, New York, news reports of March 30, 1954.

"The United States is a member of a goodly company who in the past have stood together in the face of great peril, and who have shown those qualities and who have overcome the peril."
John Foster Dulles. Ibid.

"Only incredible blindness, or the most wishful of thinking, could lead us to believe that the danger is over and that each free nation could now safely go its separate way. We must stay united."
John Foster Dulles, statement before the House Foreign Affairs Committee, news reports of April 6, 1954.

"We will play our part in collective defense of the area but we are not going to play gladiator for the world."

> *John Foster Dulles, comment in advance of the Geneva Conference, news reports of May 4, 1954.*

"Neighborly love, in political action, means loving others, based on the brotherhood that was created with God as the Father of all. It means that the political power of any government must be considered an opportunity, not to favor individuals but to do well for all."

> *John Foster Dulles, reply to a Danish student who asked if the secretary believed "Love thy neighbor" still applied to the world today, news summaries of May 7, 1954.*

"Foreign policy will be dynamic or inert, steadfast or aimless, in proportion to the character and unity of those who serve it."

> *John Foster Dulles, on scholarships to interest students in the Foreign Service, news summaries of June 28, 1954.*

"The President's main complaint is that we don't give him enough time to think. Finally we had to set aside a half hour in the morning and the same time in the afternoon in order to give the President the time he requires."

> *Bernard Shanley, special counsel to President Eisenhower, address to college students at South Orange, N.J., news reports of January 19, 1954.*

"We're not advocating the plowing under of every fourth farmer."

> *Ezra Taft Benson, Secretary of Agriculture, defense of presidential recommendation that so-called marginal farmers should turn to other work, news reports of February 2, 1954.*

"Abundance must be a reservoir serving the people's needs, not a stagnant pool, a breeding place of depressed markets."

> *Ezra Taft Benson, comment on goals of Administration's farm program, news summaries of March 1, 1954.*

"Even after one and a half years in Washington one's skin doesn't become so thick as to resist sunshine."

Ezra Taft Benson, commenting on his suntan, New York Post, *July 24, 1954.*

"I personally wish we would quit rattling the atom bomb."

Charles E. Wilson, Secretary of Defense, comment to news conference, news reports of February 3, 1954.

"In some cases, all you can do is ask the Lord."

Charles E. Wilson, comment on policy of retaliation to enemy attack, news summaries of March 15, 1954.

"I think that we oughtn't to scare everybody so that they don't sleep nights."

Charles E. Wilson, comment to reporter when queried about the advisability of acquainting the people with the realities of the Hydrogen Age, news reports of March 31, 1954.

"In the volunteer class, we can reject a man if we think he's flat-headed as well as if he's got flat feet."

Charles E. Wilson, at hearing of Senate Armed Forces Committee on security risks in the Armed Forces, news reports of April 9, 1954.

"As I stated previously, one single Communist or disloyal member in the Armed Forces is one too many."

Charles E. Wilson. Ibid.

"If you can't stand the heat, get out of the kitchen."

Charles E. Wilson, words he said comforted him in enduring his first weeks as a member of the President's cabinet, The Saturday Evening Post, *May 1, 1954.*

"You never give anyone orders to such a degree. . . . I mean it's like trying to tell someone how to suck eggs. You give him a job and let him go and suck it his way."

Charles E. Wilson, during the McCarthy-Army hearings, news summaries of May 5, 1954.

"It was never intended by the Founding Fathers that the President of the United States should be a ventriloquist's dummy sitting on the lap of Congress."

Senator J. William Fulbright, of Arkansas, speech against amendment to limit President's treaty-making power, news reports of February 7, 1954.

"That 'rolling readjustment' is a lovely phrase. It seems to suggest springtime and laughing children on jogging ponies. But to the man out of work, it's just a ten-ton tank rolling over him."

Senator J. William Fulbright, on use of term "rolling readjustment" by Republican leaders, news summaries of March 8, 1954.

"Production is the goose that lays the golden egg. Payrolls make consumers."

George Humphrey, Secretary of the Treasury, news summaries of February 8, 1954.

"It's a terribly hard job to spend a billion dollars and get your money's worth."

George Humphrey, Look, February 23, 1954.

". . . I think what I am trying to do is do the same thing for all of America that each good American tries to do in his own home. We are trying to live within our income; we are trying to cut out waste; we are trying to have an efficient management; we are trying to improve our position as we go along. . . ."

George Humphrey, on his objectives, in an interview with Edward R. Murrow, "Person to Person," CBS-TV.

"I've always considered writing important. I went through all the stages that economists go through, from jargon to lucidity, and on the way I passed through the sesquipedalian stage."

Arthur Burns, chairman, President's Council of Economic Advisers, comment on goal of making government reports readable and nontechnical; he defined "sesquipedalian" as weakness for using big words; news summaries of February 8, 1954.

"When you yield to international blackmail, it is surrender on the installment plan."

Senator William F. Knowland of California, on fear that the British and French were prepared to negotiate a "far-eastern Munich" by yielding to Communist pressure, news reports of February 23, 1954.

"According to the rules of the House nothing can interfere with the taking of a vote. But something did today."

Joseph W. Martin, Jr., of Massachusetts, Speaker of the House, comment on assassination attempt in the House by shooting from visitors' gallery, news reports of March 1, 1954.

"I love this House. . . . In this forum is worked the will of the people, a forum that we must ever strengthen, never weaken. Here lies the true citadel of the Republic."

Representative Joseph W. Martin, Jr., Forty-fifth Speaker of the House of Representatives and veteran congressman from Massachusetts, news reports of November 4, 1954.

"If we exonerate the last of the Salem witches, what will happen to our tourist trade?"

George Evans, Massachusetts state senator, comment against resolution to exonerate Ann Pudeator, Salem woman convicted of witchcraft 287 years ago, news reports of March 6, 1954.

"We would no longer be the United States of America. We would be the United States of America and the Pacific and the Arctic and the Caribbean and only the good Lord knows where it would end."

Senator George Smathers of Florida, speech against statehood for Alaska and Hawaii, news reports of April 2, 1954.

"In sixteen years we have seen the first of radar, jet planes, guided missiles, atomic bombs, and all the misery and slavery and tragedy the world's great war has wrought, but we still retain our faith in the partnership of God and liberty that has preserved our country."

Arthur Summerfield, Postmaster General, announcement of first U. S. stamp to carry inscription, "In God We Trust," news summaries of April 5, 1954.

"And above all not too much zeal."

Talleyrand, motto hanging on office wall of Clare Boothe Luce, U. S. ambassador to Italy, news reports of April 5, 1954.

"We are not only a treadmill, but we can't keep up with the tread."

Senator Charles Potter of Michigan, discouraged comment on the Army-McCarthy hearings, news reports of April 6, 1954.

"The modern ideal of feminine perfection seems to be a punk actress with platinum hair and an overstuffed bosom. The ideal of manhood is a character who toots a horn and smokes marijuana."

Governor Robert B. Meyner of New Jersey, news reports of April 8, 1954.

"Attorney generals come and go. Most of them are great. Some are not. They're subject to the human frailties—prejudice, lack of knowledge and downright unfairness."

Representative Sam Rayburn of Texas, speech in House defending decision to put authority to tap telephone wires into hands of federal courts instead of Attorney General's office, news reports of April 9, 1954.

"I would rather be alive with an empty pocketbook than dead with a full one."

Representative Sam Rayburn, expression of hope that defense budget had not been drastically cut. Ibid.

"You mean I have to think right now?"

Army Secretary Robert Stevens, reply to a question from Senator Karl Mundt during the Army-McCarthy hearings, news reports of April 26, 1954.

"I want to make it clear that I'm not covering up for anybody at any time."

Army Secretary Robert Stevens. Ibid.

"When an Italian talks with an American he's inclined to feel a twinge of inferiority. America is rich and strong. Italy is poor. But when he talks to me, he's more at ease. I still represent a big, strong nation but I am a woman—and he's a man."

Clare Boothe Luce, U. S. ambassador to Italy, news reports of May 4, 1954.

"If we're headed on the train for economic perdition, it's the first time I've ever seen the trip being made with all the parlor-car seats sold."

Senator Mike Monroney of Oklahoma, disagreeing with predictions of depression, news reports of May 4, 1954.

"I pledge allegiance to the flag of the United States of America and to the republic for which it stands, one nation, under God, indivisible, with liberty and justice for all."

Representative Louis Rabaut of Michigan, bill to insert the words "under God" in the pledge of allegiance to the American flag, news reports of May 6, 1954.

"My sympathy often goes out for the humble decimal point. He has a pathetic and hectic life wandering around among regimented ciphers, trying to find some of the old places he used to know when budgets were balanced."

Herbert Hoover, at a farm conference on government economy, news summaries of May 31, 1954.

"Thirty years ago we used to believe there were only two occasions in which the American people would respect the privacy of the President —in prayer and fishing. I now detect you have lost the second part of this. . . . That is one of the degenerations of the last thirty years."

Herbert Hoover, comment that the decrease in privacy is the worst change in the presidency since he left the White House, while vacationing with President Eisenhower in Fraser, Colorado, news reports of September 2, 1954.

"When you differ with a man, show him, by your looks, by your bearing and by everything that you do or say, that you love him."

Senator Paul Douglas of Illinois, comment on "the best advice I ever had," heard at a Quaker meeting as a boy, Reader's Digest, *June 1954.*

"Most people say that as you get old, you have to give up things. . . . I think you get old because you give up things."

Senator Theodore Francis Green of Rhode Island, comment as he sought re-election on eve of his eighty-seventh birthday, news summaries of June 23, 1954.

"Out visiting these people, they put on the table Kentucky ham, fried chicken, turnip greens, boiled potatoes, three-story cake, and the other good eats. It's hard for a healthy man to resist."

Senator John Sherman Cooper of Kentucky, comment on perils of campaigning in his home state, news summaries of July 5, 1954.

"Always remember your first obligation is to your conscience. If you have to make a difficult decision, ask yourself how your conscience will react to it tomorrow, the next day and the next year."

> *Senator Irving Ives of New York, recalling advice of his grandfather, first published in* This Week Magazine, *July 11, 1954, copyright 1954, United Newspapers Magazine Corporation; later reprinted in "The Best Advice I Ever Had,"* Reader's Digest.

"I hope he doesn't send me one and if he does, I hope it gets lost in the mail."

> *Senator Joseph McCarthy of Wisconsin, on being told that Roy Cohn had written out copies of his resignation from the senator's staff, news reports of July 20, 1954.*

"My colleagues in the Senate can now go to bed, because I am going to talk to the country for a few hours."

> *Senator Wayne Morse of Oregon, opening of a Congressional filibuster that ran from midnight to noon, news summaries of August 9, 1954.*

"We women don't care too much about getting our pictures on money as long as we can get our hands on it."

> *Ivy Baker Priest, United States Treasurer,* Look, *August 10, 1954.*

FOREIGN GOVERNMENTS

"The recovery of the lost territory must be paid with our own blood and flesh."

> *Generalissimo Chiang Kai-shek, New Year's message broadcast from Taipei to Nationalist Chinese troops, news reports of January 1, 1954.*

"I expected the worst. But all they wanted was a ride to Tokyo. I took them in and they offered me chocolate bars and cigarettes."

Prime Minister Shigeru Yoshida of Japan, comment on his first meeting with American occupation troops in Japan, news summaries of January 10, 1954.

"For heaven's sake, don't stop smoking. I'm getting six hundred million pounds a year out of the tobacco tax."

R. A. Butler, British Chancellor of the Exchequer, report to House of Commons on Britain's finances, Look, January 12, 1954.

"It takes two to make love and two partners to make trade agreements work. Unrequited trade or unrequited exports pay no better than unrequited love."

R. A. Butler, comparison of the affairs of state to affairs of the heart, news summaries of January 29, 1954.

"I left him there, telling the pretty nursemaid about the mysteries of unrequited exports."

R. A. Butler, comment on walk in St. James Park, London, with Anthony Eden, both of whom were unrecognized, news reports of April 4, 1954.

"The essence of all successful international negotiation is compromise."

Anthony Eden, British Foreign Secretary, broadcast from London prior to Foreign Ministers' conference in Berlin, news reports of January 25, 1954.

"Don't ask for the moon or you will get something else."

Anthony Eden, warning to Communist Chinese Foreign Minister Chou En-lai during the Far Eastern conference at Geneva, news summaries of June 12, 1954.

"It was all I could do to catch my breath. It was now late September 1941, and, if the international situation continued to intensify, the attack plan called for execution in December. There was no time to lose in training for this all-important mission."

Captain Mitsuo Fuchida, Imperial Japanese Navy, recollection of receiving assignment to lead attack on Pearl Harbor; report was published by the U. S. Naval Institute and in the Reader's Digest, *February 1954.*

"My plane was about the last to get back to the fleet. . . . I urged another attack. Admiral Nagumo, however—in a decision which has since been the target of much criticism by naval experts—chose to retire. Immediately flag signals were hoisted, and our ships headed northward at high speed."

Captain Fuchida, conclusion of report on Pearl Harbor raid. Ibid.

"The work was killing me; they called me out of bed at all hours of the night to receive the resignations of prime ministers."

Vincent Auriol, comment on retirement as President of France, news summaries of February 1, 1954.

"Photographers are the only dictators in America."

Celal Bayar, President of Turkey, comment during visit to U.S., news summaries of February 1, 1954.

"This, Madam, is where your husband gives me so much trouble. After all, I am alone against three of them."

V. M. Molotov, Soviet Foreign Minister, comment to Mrs. John Foster Dulles, wife of U. S. Secretary of State, on showing her Big Four conference room in Russian Embassy in East Berlin, The New York Times, *February 5, 1954.*

"I believe it is proposed to have a bigger show in the middle of April. This only reminds me of the genie that came out of the bottle, ultimately swallowing man."

Jawaharlal Nehru, Prime Minister of India, on American hydrogen bomb tests, news summaries of April 3, 1954.

"These experiments show man is unleashing power which can ultimately get out of control."

Jawaharlal Nehru. Ibid.

"Apart from my dislike of their cutting off other people's heads, the tribesmen are fine men."

Jawaharlal Nehru, report to Parliament on a tribal clash in which fifty-seven persons were slain, news summaries of December 3, 1954.

"More than once British courage and British initiative have saved Europe. British initiative may well save world civilization."

Clement Attlee, opposition leader in Parliament, speech asking that Britain take question of hydrogen bomb control to UN, news reports of April 16, 1954.

"I have been exposed to lots of eyewash in my time. I know it when I see it."

Clement Attlee, British Labour party leader on his proposed tour of Communist China, news reports of August 1, 1954.

"I was France. I was the state, the government. I spoke in the name of France. I was the independence and sovereignty of France. . . ."

General Charles de Gaulle, wartime head of French provisional government, remarks against a current government of France, news summaries of April 19, 1954.

"We have imported the British parliamentary machine but we have blown off its brakes."

Paul Reynaud of France, news summaries of April 23, 1954.

"When it comes to laying cards on the table, the Russians never play anything but clubs."

Georges Bidault, French Foreign Minister, on Soviet diplomacy, news summaries of April 26, 1954.

"He never spares himself in conversation. He gives himself so generously that hardly anybody else is permitted to give anything in his presence."
Aneurin Bevan, leader of British left-wing Socialists, comment on Sir Winston Churchill, news summaries of April 26, 1954.

"We want the internationalization of peace and not the internationalization of the war."
Christian Pineau, French Socialist, protest against calling for U.S. participation in the Indo-China war, news reports of May 7, 1954.

"It is dangerous to confuse children with angels."
Sir David Maxwell Fyfe, British Home Secretary, on the problem of juvenile delinquency, Look, May 18, 1954.

"When the world seems large and complex, we need to remember that great world ideals all begin in some home neighborhood. . . . So history shows us that our moments of discouragement can become the moments for our new starts. . . . We are each more important than we think."
Konrad Adenauer, Chancellor of West Germany; "Words to Live By," This Week Magazine, May 23, 1954, copyright 1954, United Newspapers Magazine Corporation.

"I hate politics, I do not indulge in politics. I am not a politician."
Pierre Mendes-France, Time, July 2, 1954.

"This is now behind us. For us, the clock is already turning."
Pierre Mendes-France, comment on being informed that he had been named twentieth Premier of France since World War II, news summaries of July 12, 1954.

"It is the day we have all been looking forward to for over fourteen years. It is the last day of food rationing. I regard it as a great privilege to be the Minister of Food on this day."

Major Gwilym Lloyd George, British Minister of Food, the day Britons threw away their ration books as controls were finally lifted on the last rationed item—meat, news reports of July 4, 1954.

"There is no doubt that Your Excellency is a political genius, but the trouble with Your Excellency is that your love of yourself is greater than your love for the country."

K. C. Wu, former governor of Formosa, in a letter to Generalissimo Chiang Kai-shek, news summaries of August 4, 1954.

"To the wrath of my enemies I leave the legacy of my death. I take the sorrow of not being able to give to the humble all that I wished."

Getulio Vargas, Brazil's "old man," suicide note when he shot himself to death after fifty-eight generals forced him to quit as President, news reports of August 24 and August 25, 1954.

". . . You don't have a democracy. It's a photocracy."

Prime Minister Robert Menzies of Australia, on being followed by news photographers during a visit to Washington, D.C., news reports of November 6, 1954.

"Sir, the venerable age of this great man, his merited rank, his superior eloquence, his splendid qualities, his eminent services, the vast space he fills in the eyes of mankind . . . will not suffer me to censure any part of his conduct. I am afraid to flatter him. I am sure I am not disposed to blame him. Let those who have betrayed him by their adulation insult him with their malevolence."

Herbert Morrison, quoting Edmund Burke on the Earl of Bhatham in 1774, in asking for resignation of Sir Winston Churchill as Prime Minister, news reports of December 4, 1954.

HOLLYWOOD

"It is my hope that the day may not be far off when the court will go further and eliminate all political censorship of motion pictures so the screen will enjoy the same freedom of expression as the press under our constitution."

Eric Johnston, president, Motion Picture Association of America, on U. S. Supreme Court ruling that states may not censor films as "immoral" or "inciting to crime," news summaries of January 19, 1954.

"Before your fortieth birthday keep circulating the story that you're thirty-nine. If people hear it often enough they'll believe it for years."

Jack Benny, Collier's, February 19, 1954.

"God makes the star. God gives them the talent. It is up to the producers to recognize that talent and develop it."

Samuel Goldwyn, comment, "Person to Person," CBS-TV, February 19, 1954.

"The average Hollywood film star's ambition is to be admired by an American, courted by an Italian, married to an Englishman and have a French boy friend."

Katharine Hepburn, quoted in E. V. Durling's column, New York Journal-American, news summaries of February 22, 1954.

"Treat kids like adults and adults like kids."

William Boyd, the Hopalong Cassidy of western films, comment on how to win friends and fans; quoted by Bob Considine, New York Journal-American, March 3, 1954.

"Oscar, as far as I'm concerned, is a monster. How can anybody decide who's best actor unless every actor is playing the same part?"

Celeste Holm, herself an Oscar winner, news summaries of April 9, 1954.

"I was a loathsome bearded lady in *The Big Top,* a resurrected corpse in *The Bride of Frankenstein,* and I'll play the wicked stepmother in *Cinderella.* I've played so many repulsive characters that I sometimes have to stop and check to make sure that I have arms and legs and am quite normally human."

Elsa Lanchester, recollection of some of her roles in motion pictures, Time, *May 3, 1954.*

"I deliberately do routines with no dialogue. No dialogue is a great relief to audiences."

Buster Keaton, dead-pan star of silent films, news summaries of May 13, 1954.

"The American motion picture has had much to do with the fact that through a large part of the world when somebody has an inclination to bang his neighbor on the head, he stops and thinks twice before doing it. I have learned that generally the movies oppose intolerance. Without them the peoples of the world would know much less about each other. . . ."

Dag Hammarskjold, Secretary-General of the United Nations, address to a Hollywood dinner of the Association of Motion Picture Producers, news reports of May 15, 1954.

"The movie-makers are able to put more reality into a picture about the terrors of life at the ocean bottom than into a tale of two Milwaukeeans in love."

Ben Hecht, news reports of June 13, 1954.

"Heaven knows, women harbor some strange notions, but one of the strangest is the conviction that their brains are like icebergs—only one-eighth should show above the surface."

Nina Foch, "Should Women Let Their Brains Show," reprinted from This Week Magazine, *June 13, 1954.*

"I never was allowed to speak while my husband was alive and since he's gone no one ever has been able to shut me up."
Hedda Hopper, Hollywood columnist, news summaries of June 15, 1954.

"A Frenchwoman, when double-crossed, will kill her rival; the Italian woman would rather kill her deceitful lover; the Englishwoman simply breaks off relations—but they all will console themselves with another man."
Charles Boyer, news summaries of July 20, 1954.

"There's one way to find out if a man is honest—ask him. If he says 'yes,' you know he is crooked."
Groucho Marx, news summaries of July 28, 1954.

"I keep myself in puffect shape. I get lots of exercise—in my own way —and I walk every day. . . . Knolls, you know, small knolls, they're very good for walking. Build up your muscles, going up and down the knolls."
Mae West, at sixty-one, pronounces herself in "puffect" health. At the time, she was breaking attendance records at a Times Square night club in an act that featured nine muscle-men in loincloths, news summaries of November 1, 1954.

"There's nothing funnier than the human animal."
Walt Disney, announcement on changing from shows about animals to shows about people, news reports of December 5, 1954.

"After my screen test, the director clapped his hands gleefully and yelled: 'She can't talk! She can't act! She's sensational!' "
Ava Gardner, recollection of how she crashed Hollywood, news summaries of December 11, 1954.

MUSIC

"To play great music, you must keep your eyes on a distant star."
*Yehudi Menuhin, citing words of his old music teacher, "The
Best Advice I Ever Had," Reader's Digest, December, 1953; news
summaries of January 1, 1954.*

"Contemporary American jazz, without harmony or melody, is the very
quintessence of crazy formalism."
*Leonid Utyosov, "Soviet king of jazz," writing in the magazine
Soviet Music, news reports of January 8 and 9, 1954.*

"The past twenty years has been an age of discovery in America. There
have been ages of scientific discovery but in the past twenty years Americans have discovered music. It is like people had just discovered color
—that they were seeing red and blue and green for the first time, where
all had been but black and white before."
André Kostelanetz, news reports of January 13, 1954.

"A good education is usually harmful to a dancer. A good calf is better
than a good head."
Agnes de Mille, news summaries of February 1, 1954.

"I'd hate this to get out but I really like opera."
*Ford Frick, baseball commissioner, acknowledgment of a "sec-
ond love," news summaries of February 8, 1954.*

"Its members are quite hopeless—drooling, driveling, doleful, depress·
ing, dropsical drips."
*Sir Thomas Beecham, comment on some music critics, news sum-
maries of February 13, 1954.*

"Too often we mistake talent for genius. But talent fades while genius never dies."

Mary Garden, Town Hall lecture during visit to U.S., news summaries of February 15, 1954.

"If you have a great career, why should you want a man trailing around after you?"

Mary Garden, comment on marriage. Ibid.

"Only life suffered can transform a symphony from a collection of notes into a message for humanity."

Dimitri Mitropoulos, conductor of the New York Philharmonic Symphony, news summaries of February 19, 1954.

"I didn't know if I could make it. My ears kept popping. When this is over, there's one thing I know I can do—sleep."

Risë Stevens, comment between acts of singing Carmen at the Metropolitan Opera, New York, only thirty-six hours after she had sung the leading role at La Scala in Milan, Italy, and then flown to the U.S., news reports of April 3, 1954.

"And now the sad time has come when I must reluctantly lay aside my baton and say goodbye to my orchestra. . . ."

Arturo Toscanini, letter of resignation as conductor of the NBC Symphony, news summaries of April 5, 1954.

"I love, you love, we all love, why do we love, who do we love, how much do we love, where do we love, why did you stop loving me?"

Mitch Miller, comment that prevailing moods in American songs of 1954 were frustration, nostalgia, and love, news summaries of May 24, 1954.

"Beethoven had real prospects as a composer. If he had lived longer, he might have fulfilled his promise."

Pierre Monteux, comment while conducting a concert in Chicago, Time, August 2, 1954.

"Music itself is the purest expression of emotion. To me, emotion is the guts of theatre. With music you can say in one moment what an author would take a whole scene to tell you in a drama."

Joshua Logan, theatrical producer, Theatre Arts, *October 1954.*

"It takes perhaps a thousand poor musicians to produce one virtuoso."

Ralph Vaughan Williams, dean of British composers, The New York Times Magazine, *December 5, 1954.*

"I wrote it as a so-called 'throw away' to cover a stage wait. No one visualized what the song would eventually become, especially myself."

Irving Berlin, comment on his song, "There's No Business Like Show Business," news reports of December 17, 1954.

"If a guy's got it, let him give it. I'm selling music, not prejudice."

Benny Goodman, first conductor to integrate Negroes into a big-time band, The Saturday Evening Post, *December 18, 1954.*

". . . I want to tell their mothers and fathers of our great country never to permit their children to become professional musicians, because if they do they are going into a starvation business."

James Caesar Petrillo, comment in interview with Edward R. Murrow, "Person to Person," CBS-TV, October 16, 1953, recalled in news summaries of January 1, 1954.

"There are two kinds of relaxation . . . compulsory relaxation and voluntary relaxation. Right now I am on the compulsory one . . . waiting for the phone to ring for me to get some employment. . . ."

Ethel Waters, comment in interview with Edward R. Murrow, "Person to Person," CBS-TV, January 8, 1954.

". . . I think we as a whole—speaking for my race—I think we are all gifted. That is our inheritance, fun, pleasure, laughter, and song."

Ethel Waters. Ibid.

PERSONALITIES

"I feel as though someone hit me on the head."
Barbara Hutton, Woolworth fortune heiress, comment on arrival at the home of the Dominican Consul in New York to marry Porfirio Rubirosa, a marriage lasting less than three months, news summaries of January 4, 1954.

"He who slings mud generally loses ground."
Adlai Stevenson, on politics, news summaries of January 11, 1954.

"What is needed is a little lock-jaw."
Adlai Stevenson, comment on the Oppenheimer case, news reports of January 11, 1954.

"Peace is not the work of a single day, nor will it be the consequence of a single act. Yet every constructive act contributes to its growth; every omission impedes it. Peace will come, in the end, imperceptibly, until we realize one day in incredulous surprise that the child is almost grown."
Adlai Stevenson, address to Democratic Committee meeting in New Orleans, news reports of December 5, 1954.

"Age is no matter. . . . You can be ravishing at twenty, charming at forty, and irresistible the rest of your life. . . ."
Madame Gabrielle Chanel, French designer, news summaries of January 15, 1954.

"I always play a party by ear."
Perle Mesta, famed as a hostess, comment that she tries to start some new action at a party when she senses that the guests are losing interest, news summaries of January 16, 1954.

"The only place I've ever been homesick for is Missouri."

Harry Truman, comment one year after leaving the White House, news summaries of January 30, 1954.

". . . If I had carried out the recommendations of many, there would have been the most terrible slaughter in the history of the world. I'm taking credit for preventing it."

Harry Truman, refutation of frequent charges "of murder and everything else in the book because it was necessary to stop aggression in Korea," address to Kansas City reunion with World War I buddies of Battery D, 129th Field Artillery, news summaries of April 5, 1954.

"We weren't sharing our secrets with the British. They were sharing theirs with us."

Harry Truman, comment to reporter regarding the British-American atomic agreement of 1943, news summaries of April 7, 1954.

"It was a good agreement. There was no secret about it to the people who were entitled to know about it."

Harry Truman. Ibid.

"When you become forty, you should take it a little slower, work a little harder, take a little more time to think, and you will be all right. . . . I guess the best assurance of a long life is to get yourself a set of long-living parents like I did."

Harry Truman, on his seventieth birthday, news summaries of May 7, 1954.

"People come by here to see me. . . . They expect to see some big, imposing man. And it's me. I'm just a little old Democrat."

John Nance Garner, former Vice-President of the United States, news summaries of January 30, 1954.

"You have to do a little bragging on yourself even to your relatives—man doesn't get anywhere without advertising."
John Nance Garner, news summaries of February 15, 1954.

"First she stood stiffly at attention. However, being naturally histrionic, she relaxed as we chatted and the beauty that unfolded was of the quality of a flower."
Cecil Beaton, on photographing Greta Garbo, news summaries of February 15, 1954.

"She has a face that belongs to the sea and the wind, with large rocking horse nostrils and teeth that you know just bite an apple every day."
Cecil Beaton, comment on aspects of photographing Katharine Hepburn, news summaries of March 29, 1954.

"I have a hankering to go back to the Orient and discard my necktie. Neckties strangle clear thinking."
Lin Yutang, Chinese-American philosopher and writer, news summaries of February 22, 1954.

"The story of my boyhood and that of my brothers is important only because it could happen in any American family. It did, and will again."
Earl Eisenhower, a brother of the President, conclusion to his article, "I Grew Up With Eisenhower," The American Weekly, *April 4, 1954.*

"I was determined to be an old-maid school teacher after my college graduation."
Mrs. Wheeler Howard Tolbert, Columbus, Georgia, selected by the Golden Rule Foundation as the 1954 American Mother-of-the-Year, news reports of May 1, 1954.

"The boys have invited me to stay for the siege."
Nurse Genevieve de Gallard-Terraube, "the angel of the battle of Dien Bien Phu," news reports of May 4, 1954.

"We are not trying to obtain a list of prominent names for our letter-head, since in this age of suspicion such a letterhead may make people less willing to give."

Corliss Lamont, philanthropist and liberal, announcement of his gift of fifty thousand dollars to establish a fund to defend the Bill of Rights, news reports of May 5, 1954.

"I thought I would prefer to be technically wrong and alive than technically right and dead."

Aneurin Bevan, British left-wing leader, testimony to an English court that he swerved from his side of the road and ran into a bus to avoid a head-on collision with another car, news reports of May 8, 1954.

"A smell of incense mingled with the scent of wood. It was faint and mystic, like the odor of a cathedral."

Kamal El-Malakh, Egyptologist and architect, description of discovery of burial ship built by a Pharaoh in 2900 B. C. to carry his soul to heaven, news summaries of May 31, 1954.

"The past is over and I'm looking forward to the future."

Mrs. Barbara Rockefeller, comment on receiving a divorce and a five million five hundred thousand dollar settlement from her husband, Winthrop Rockefeller, news reports of August 4, 1954.

"I doubt if there is anything in the world uglier than a midwestern city."

Frank Lloyd Wright, address in Evanston, Illinois, news reports of August 8, 1954.

"I'm one of the few people in the world without worries. Many might be glad to change places with me."

Fred Snite, Jr., Chicagoan who lived for more than eighteen years in an iron lung, married, fathered three children, and became world famous for his courage; remark recalled in obituaries reporting his death, news reports of November 22, 1954.

"We had a little excitement around here. A meteor fell through the roof."

Mrs. Ann Elizabeth Hodges of Sylacauga, Alabama, first human ever struck by a meteorite, remark to her husband when he arrived home, Time, December 13, 1954.

"Homo Americanus, 1954," compilation by the Gallup poll, Time, December 13, 1954, reprinted by permission of the American Institute of Public Opinion:

"Out of 102 million U. S. adults, approximately half have visited Chicago and New York City. About 5.5 million men have been to London, 6.5 million to Paris—a large percentage of them by courtesy of the U. S. armed forces.

"Ten million women and 7.5 million men have read the Bible all the way through.

"Eleven million men and 10 million women have written their Congressmen.

"Slightly more than half the adult population have eaten lobsters.

"Some 62% of all men and 27% of the women have played poker for money; 17 million men and 11 million women have bet money at a race track.

"Half of all U. S. men have had a fist fight since they were 15, but only one woman in ten has engaged in a hair-pulling match. Seventeen percent of men admit they have hit their wives, and 18% of women say they have struck their husbands.

"A total of 32 million men and 10 million women have gone swimming in the nude.

"Eighteen million Americans have seen Harry Truman in person.

"Nineteen million have gone hungry for lack of money.

"Half of American adult males and a third of females have stayed out all night on a party.

"Ten million men and 4,000,000 women have pawned something in their lifetime.

"Some 28.5 million men and 11.5 million women claim they have caught a fish weighing more than two pounds.

"Twenty percent of all women and 8% of the men have been telephoned on a radio-TV quiz."

"I let Earl go with me to a delicatessen just once. We never could afford it again."

Mrs. Earl Warren, wife of the Supreme Court Chief Justice, explaining that she does her marketing by telephone, news summaries of December 14, 1954.

"I want to hug my wife, kiss my children, roll up my sleeves, and dig those crazy books."

Reinhold Pabel, Chicago bookshop owner who was permitted re-entry into U.S. after being deported as an escaped German prisoner of war. While "at large" he had married and bought a book store in Chicago. News summaries of December 16, 1954.

"You're so strategic!"

Gwen Cafritz, Washington hostess, favorite saying, news summaries of December 17, 1954.

"I can see, and that is why I can be so happy, in what you call the dark, but which to me is golden. I can see a God-made world, not a man-made world."

Helen Keller, reply to question, "Can you see a world?" in The Unconquered, *filmed documentary of her life.*

"It is a moment I shall never forget. I was alone and unable to communicate with anyone. I did not know the names of anything. I did not even know things had names. Then one day, after she had tried a number of approaches, my teacher held my hand under the water pump on our farm. As the cool water ran over my hand, and arm, she spelled the word water into my other hand. She spelled it over and over, and suddenly, I knew there was a name for things and that I would never be completely alone again."

Helen Keller, recollection of her most memorable discovery, quoted in Cosmopolitan Magazine, *December 1954.*

"So often we rob tomorrow's memories by today's economies."

John Mason Brown, essay in The Arts of Living, *Simon & Schuster, Inc., 1954.*

"The French approach to food is characteristic; they bring to their consideration of the table the same appreciation, respect, intelligence, and lively interest that they have for the other fine arts, for painting, for literature, and for the theatre."

Alice B. Toklas, The Alice B. Toklas Cook Book, copyright 1954 by Alice B. Toklas; reprinted by permission of Harper & Brothers.

". . . What is sauce for the goose may be sauce for the gander but is not necessarily sauce for the chicken, the duck, the turkey or the guinea hen."

Alice B. Toklas. Ibid.

"Gigot de la Clinique—A surgeon living in the provinces, as fond of good cheer as he was learned, invented this recipe which we acquired by bribing his cook. No leg of venison can compare with a simple leg of mutton prepared in the following manner. Eight days in advance you will cover the leg of mutton with the marinade called Baume Samaritain, composed of wine—old Burgundy, Beaune or Chambertin —and virgin olive oil. Into this balm to which you have already added the usual condiments of salt, pepper, bay leaf, thyme, beside an atom of ginger root, put a pinch of cayenne, a nutmeg cut into small pieces, a handful of crushed juniper berries and lastly a dessertspoon of powdered sugar (effective as musk in perfumery) which serves to fix the different aromas. Twice a day you will turn the gigot. Now we come to the main point of the preparation. After you have placed the gigot in the marinade you will arm yourself with a surgical syringe of a size to hold ½ pint which you will fill with ½ cup cognac and ½ cup of fresh orange juice. Inject the contents of the syringe into the fleshy part of the gigot in three different spots. Refill the syringe with the same contents and inject into the gigot twice more. Each day you will fill the syringe with the marinade and inject the contents into the gigot. At the end of the week the leg of mutton is ready to be roasted; perfumed with the condiments and the spices, completely permeated by the various flavours, it has been transfused into a strange and exquisite venison. Roast and serve with the usual venison sauce to which has been added just before serving 2 tablespoons of the blood of a hare."

Alice B. Toklas. Ibid.

"I enjoy photographing creative men. I can provoke them and they can provoke me. . . . I love temperamental subjects. I hate to photograph 'yes-men.' "
> *Yousuf Karsh, Canadian photographer, quoted in interview with Art Buchwald for* New York Herald-Tribune *syndicate.*

"One couldn't get homesick for the White House. One might miss the beauty of the White House because, of course, it has wonderful proportions and is a lovely house. But one couldn't be homesick for the White House."
> *Eleanor Roosevelt, in interview with Edward R. Murrow, "Person to Person," CBS-TV.*

"There are certain compensations for overweight women. Men do not suspect them and other women do not fear them as competition."
> *Elsa Maxwell in her autobiography,* RSVP, *copyright 1954 by Elsa Maxwell, reprinted by permission of the publisher, Little, Brown and Company.*

"There was no one around to make me go to school, least of all my family, so I just ran wild. I hunted, fished and crabbed, and cooked what I caught. On special occasions I would stoop to conquer a chicken. To catch chickens I used a piece of corn attached to a long string, with myself at the other end. The chicken swallowed the corn and was then gently drawn toward me and sure death. The chicken didn't belong to me, but I figured the corn didn't belong to the chicken either."
> *Jacqueline Cochran, recollection of her childhood in her autobiography,* The Stars at Noon, *Little, Brown & Company, 1954, reprinted by permission.*

"It was along about this same time that I conquered fear. . . . I had to pass a small cemetery on the way home and they said a ghost that was there would go after me and that I would get scared and come back. Past the cemetery there was a raised wooden walk over a low spot of ground. As I started along this raised section the 'ghost' rose up from the walk in front of me. I retreated and studied the problem. I had to choose between turning back to hear the jeers of my friends and fighting

the ghost. I chose the latter. Yelling at the top of my lungs, I charged. As the ghost rose to grab me I plunged in to grapple with it. It proved to be a calf with its hind legs stuck down through a broken board. I had won. Since then all ghosts in my life have turned out to be just scared calves caught by the hind legs."
Jacqueline Cochran. Ibid.

"The pay was good: about six cents an hour for the twelve-hour night shift, and I was supremely happy. I had no shoes but I had dreams."
Jacqueline Cochran, recollection of one of her first jobs in a cotton mill. Ibid.

"I wanted to go higher than Rockefeller Center, which was being erected across the street from Saks Fifth Avenue and was going to cut off my view of the sky. I decided that if I could fly I could really start a new career. One fine day in the later summer of 1932 I took the three weeks' holiday I had coming to me and learned to fly. Flying got into my soul instantly but the answer as to why must be found somewhere back in the mystic maze of my birth and childhood and the circumstances of my earlier life. Whatever I am is elemental and the beginnings of it all have their roots in Sawdust Road. I might have been born in a hovel, but I determined to travel with the wind and stars."
Jacqueline Cochran, on how she became an internationally famous aviatrix in addition to heading her own 3½ million-dollar cosmetic company. Ibid.

THE PRESIDENCY

"This Administration believes that we must not and need not tolerate a boom-and-bust America. We believe that America's prosperity does not and need not depend upon war or the preparation for war."
President Eisenhower, address to the nation, January 4, 1954, less than forty-eight hours before presentation of his State of the Union message to Congress.

"Slowly but surely the free world gathers strength. Meanwhile, from behind the Iron Curtain, there are signs that tyranny is in trouble and reminders that its structure is as brittle as its surface is hard."

President Eisenhower, State of the Union Message, January 7, 1954.

". . . That precious intangible, the initiative, is becoming ours."

President Eisenhower. Ibid.

"A professional corps is the heart of any security organization. It is necessarily the teacher and leader of those who serve temporarily in the discharge of the obligation to help defend the Republic."

President Eisenhower, statement recommending standing army of career militarymen. Ibid.

"For the first time, mobilization officials know what are the requirements for one thousand major items needed for military uses. . . . We shall speed their attainment. This nation is to at last have an up-to-date mobilization base that is the foundation of a sound defense program."

President Eisenhower, report on national defense. Ibid.

"We should recognize by law a fact that is plain to all thoughtful citizens—that we are dealing here with actions akin to treason—that when a citizen knowingly participates in a Communist conspiracy he no longer holds allegiance to the United States."

President Eisenhower, recommendation that convicted Communists be made to forfeit American citizenship. Ibid.

"The American economy is one of the wonders of the world."

President Eisenhower. Ibid.

"I am flatly opposed to the socialization of medicine. The great need for hospital and medical services can best be met by the initiative of private plans . . . [however] federal government can do so many helpful things and still avoid the socialization of medicine."

President Eisenhower. Ibid.

"For years our citizens between the ages of eighteen and twenty-one have, in time of peril, been summoned to fight for America. They should participate in the political process that produces the fateful summons."
President Eisenhower, recommendation that Congress lower voting age to eighteen. Ibid.

"No government can inoculate its people against the fatal materialism that plagues our age. Happily, our people, though blessed with more material goods than any people in history, have always reserved their first allegiance to the kingdom of spirit, which is the true source of that freedom we value above all material things."
President Eisenhower. Ibid.

"It will be continually a challenge to government to sense the aspirations of the working people of our country, that all may have the opportunity to fairly share in the results of the productive genius of our time, from which comes the material blessings of the present and a greater promise for the future."
President Eisenhower, conclusion of Labor Message to Congress, January 11, 1954.

"When it comes down to dealing with the relationships between the humans in this country and his government, the people in this Administration believe in being what I think we would normally call liberal, and when we deal with the economic affairs of this country, we believe in being conservative."
President Eisenhower, news conference of January 27, 1954.

"Just one word of warning, however, by popular choice you are now an elected official. That means that your former colleagues will expect you to reduce their club dues, balance the club's deficit, and serve bigger and better meals and refreshments at drastically lower prices. If you find out how to do it, please let me know."
President Eisenhower, message to Tony Vaccaro of the Associated Press, new president of the Washington National Press Club, news summaries of February 1, 1954.

"Let us be courageous. Let us lift our chins, our heads, and square our shoulders, and walk right square into it like Lincoln would have walked into it."

President Eisenhower, address at Lincoln Day box supper, comment on challenging times ahead, Washington, February 6, 1954.

". . . To work in a manner consistent with the traditions of liberty, with all those who with us struggle for the cause of liberty, is to gain their trust and in the end, to win the struggle."

President Eisenhower, letter to the American Association for the United Nations, February 28, 1954.

"I am doing nothing in the security departments that I don't believe is for the welfare and the security and the continued safety of the United States of America and I am not going to demagogue about it."

President Eisenhower, news conference of March 10, 1954.

"Seventy cents out of each dollar spent by your government still go for defense purposes. The remaining thirty cents go for many things: to meet our obligations to veterans; to carry on important obligations overseas; to pay the interest on the gigantic public debt; and to do within our country what Abraham Lincoln described as 'those things which the individual cannot at all do or so well do for himself.'"

President Eisenhower, address to the nation on tax program, March 15, 1954.

"I simply do not believe for one second that anyone privileged to live in this country wants someone else to pay his own fair and just share of his government."

President Eisenhower. Ibid.

". . . I mustn't overlook those among us who are professionally fainthearted . . . viewing with gloom is only to be expected in the spring of an election year."

President Eisenhower. Ibid.

"Every single day things change in this world. . . . You cannot possibly say that the kind of a unit and organization that I took to war or took across the channel in 1944 would have any usefulness today whatsoever."

President Eisenhower, news conference of March 17, 1954, comment on "new look" of the military.

". . . Our most valued, our most costly asset, is our young men. Let's don't use them any more than we have to."

President Eisenhower. Ibid.

"The most terrible job in warfare is to be a second lieutenant leading a platoon when you are on the battlefield."

President Eisenhower. Ibid.

"The world is suffering from a multiplicity of fears. . . . There is a little element of truth in each, a little element of danger in each, and that means that finally there is left a little residue that you can meet only by faith, a faith in the destiny of America."

President Eisenhower. Ibid.

". . . In America, if a man is a party to a dispute, directly or indirectly, he does not sit in judgment on his own case, and I don't believe that any leadership can escape responsibility for carrying on that tradition and that practice."

President Eisenhower, news conference of March 24, 1954, comment on Senator Joseph McCarthy's statement that McCarthy would not participate in an investigation in which he was involved.

"The destiny of the nation is as great in promise as its young people are great in character. In that light, we need constant and profound appreciation of the mother as a builder of a brighter and better future."

President Eisenhower, message to annual convention of the National Catholic Family Life Conference, New Orleans, March 25, 1954.

"NATO symbolizes the unity of free men in an age of peril."
*President Eisenhower, comment on the fifth anniversary of the
North Atlantic Treaty Organization, April 4, 1954.*

"None of the questions that bother us today have an easy answer and
many of them have no answer at all. . . ."
*President Eisenhower, address entitled, "Multiplicity of Fears,"
delivered to the nation, April 6, 1954.*

". . . The problems of America are the family problems multiplied a
million-fold."
President Eisenhower. Ibid.

"From personal experience in war and peace I have come to recognize
your dedication to truth and to the welfare of your country. You deserve
the applause of free men everywhere."
*President Eisenhower, address to dinner of the American
Newspaper Publishers Association, New York, April 22, 1954.*

". . . I am quite aware, after sitting between the St. Louis Post-Dispatch
and the Minneapolis Star and Tribune that you are not members of a
one-party press."
President Eisenhower. Ibid.

"The words 'Dien Bien Phu' are no longer just a funny-sounding name to
be dismissed from the breakfast table conversation because we don't
know what it is or what it means. We begin to understand that in a far-
off corner of the world is an agony of conflict which, no matter how it
started, has become again a testing ground between dictatorship and
freedom."
*President Eisenhower, address at Transylvania College, Lexing-
ton, Kentucky, April 23, 1954.*

"We cannot forever be an Atlas . . . supporting the rest of the world."
*President Eisenhower, address to U. S. Chamber of Commerce,
Washington, April 26, 1954.*

71

". . . A long face never solved any difficult problem."
President Eisenhower. Ibid.

"If at times we are torn by doubts, by unworthy scenes in our national capital, we know that we are Americans. The heart of America is sound."
President Eisenhower, address to Armed Forces Day dinner, Washington, May 13, 1954, at height of Army-McCarthy hearings.

"Any American who had any modicum of modesty would at times be overcome by the intensity and the importance of the problems that he would meet if he were called upon to serve in the chief official position of the country."
President Eisenhower, address at Charlotte, North Carolina, May 18, 1954.

"The Supreme Court has spoken and I am sworn to uphold . . . the constitutional processes in this country, and I am trying—I will obey."
President Eisenhower, backing Supreme Court ruling that segregation in U. S. public schools is unconstitutional, comment made during news conference of May 19, 1954.

"The American people are honored to have you here on their shores, so that they may salute one who has established a reputation as a defender of freedom and a supporter of progress."
President Eisenhower, welcome to Emperor Haile Selassie of Ethiopia on visit to the White House, May 26, 1954.

". . . All that service is limited to what must be and what need be and doesn't overstep and get into something where they are being merely busybodies and taking over those functions of individuals' lives that must be sustained if we are to remain the great country we have become."
President Eisenhower, on government and its citizens, address at Washington College, Chestertown, Maryland, June 7, 1954.

"From this day forward, the millions of our school children will daily proclaim in every city and town, every village and rural school house, the dedication of our nation and our people to the Almighty."

President Eisenhower, on signing message for inclusion of the words "under God" in the pledge of allegiance to the flag, June 14, 1954.

"The first professional concern of the men and women who attend this conference is the increase of sound information and wide knowledge throughout the country. Through generations, observance to that principle has been characteristic of our way of life. The rewards are manifest on every page of our history."

President Eisenhower, letter to the American Library Association convention at Minneapolis, June 21, 1954.

". . . For any American who had the great and priceless privilege of being raised in a small town there always remains with him nostalgic memories of those days. And the older he grows the more he senses what he owed to the simple honesty and neighborliness, the integrity that he saw all around him in those days. . . ."

President Eisenhower, address to the National Editorial Association, Washington, June 22, 1954.

"I will not be a party to any agreement that makes anybody a slave; now that's all there is to it."

President Eisenhower, statement of belief in peaceful coexistence with the Communists but not appeasement or recognition of their enslavement of peoples, news conference of June 29, 1954.

". . . I never give up a battle until I am licked completely, utterly, and destroyed, and I don't believe in giving up any battle as long as I have got a chance to win."

President Eisenhower, comment on admittance of Red China to the United Nations, news conference of July 7, 1954.

"I would be guilty of misrepresentation if I just said all the world is rosy, and all the roses are gilded."
President Eisenhower, comment on the degree of his approval of Republican legislative program. Ibid.

"It is only governments that are stupid, not the masses of people."
President Eisenhower, address to the World Christian Endeavor Community, Washington, July 25, 1954.

"I think it is a sorry reward, at the end of at least fifty years of service to this country, to say that he is not a loyal, fine American, and that he served only in order to advance his own personal ambitions."
President Eisenhower, statement defending General George Marshall from criticism in press, news conference of August 3, 1954.

"A platoon leader doesn't get his platoon to go by getting up and shouting and saying, 'I am smarter. I am bigger. I am stronger. I am the leader.' He gets men to go along with him because they want to do it for him and they believe in him."
President Eisenhower, comment on American leadership in the world. Ibid.

"When I get back to familiar sights of the farmlands, the corn and the wheat, the vast horizons, the friendly people with whom I was raised, I feel more at home than I do any other place in this world that I have been roaming for long over forty years."
President Eisenhower, address at Illinois State Fair, Springfield, August 19, 1954.

"This is money you spend for yourselves now instead of the government spending it for you. Moreover, it's money that you were using for all the things that you need to do, you are using your own decisions instead of using a bureaucrat's decision."
President Eisenhower, comment on tax reduction and revision, address to the nation from Denver, Colorado, August 23, 1954.

"The American people are determined to protect themselves and their institutions against any organization in their midst which, purporting to be a political party within normally accepted meaning, is actually a conspiracy dedicated to overthrow of our entire form of government. The American people, likewise, are determined to accomplish this in strict conformity with the requirements of justice, fair play, and the Constitution of the United States."

President Eisenhower, comment on signing legislation to outlaw the Communist party and penalize Red-infiltrated labor unions, Denver, August 24, 1954.

"I know of nothing, particularly for one who has to spend a great deal of his time in Washington in an official position, that can take the place of going out and trying again to meet Americans that are making a living and paying taxes, rather than just taking it unto themselves to spend the taxes."

President Eisenhower, speech at McCook, Nebraska, during vacation tour of western states, September 3, 1954.

"Among these treasures of our land is water—fast becoming our most valuable, most prized, most critical resource. A blessing where properly used—but it can bring devastation and ruin when left uncontrolled."

President Eisenhower, speech dedicating McNary Dam in Oregon, September 23, 1954.

"I can't tell you what a relief it is to me to address an audience where there is nothing political expected of me one way or the other."

President Eisenhower, address to the annual convention of the American Federation of Labor, Los Angeles, September 24, 1954.

"Just the welfare, the local welfare of one hundred sixty million people is certainly enough to tax the ingenuity of the greatest Administration that could be put together."

President Eisenhower, comment on tasks of the presidency. Ibid.

"Just give me a little time and I will be back in the crowd, cheering for some other poor sucker who is up here."
President Eisenhower, at a luncheon of the West Point Society, October 21, 1954.

"Drawing on the richly varied abilities of our entire citizenry, we can foresee that in less than a decade the national output will increase from today's 356 billion dollars to 500 billion. This would equal an average increase of more than three thousand dollars for every American family of today. And these can be real dollars—dollars of staple buying power, not simply more dollars of cheapened value."
President Eisenhower, address to the National Security Industrial Association, New York, October 25, 1954.

". . . The external characteristics of home are not the same for each of us. On the coast of Maine, families labor to bring in their livelihood from the gray seas. In the vast reaches of the West many families live isolated from their neighbors. For each American, the meaning of home is unique and personal."
President Eisenhower, address to the National Council of Catholic Women, Boston, November 8, 1954.

"I say with all the earnestness that I can command that if American mothers will teach our children that there is no end to the fight for better relationships among the people of the world, we shall have peace. . . . Gradually the age-old longing of the human kind for peace will be reflected in better governmental structures, governmental structures that will be forced to comply with the demands of a great and enlightened citizenry throughout the world."
President Eisenhower. Ibid.

". . . I am bold enough to speak for every Eisenhower I know, or have known, for those representatives of six generations of the Eisenhowers who lie buried in this county or in the neighboring county of Geary, for all of them, for each generation to which they belong, and for those who bear our name or shall be related to us in the future, to express our humble pride that today we may be here to dedicate this shrine to the future citizens of a great and glorious America."

President Eisenhower, address at opening of the Eisenhower Museum, Abilene, Kansas, November 11, 1954.

"Now, as you reach fourscore, we Americans salute you as world statesman, as unconquerable warrior in the cause of freedom, as our proven friend of many valiant years."

President Eisenhower, "Dear Winston" letter to Prime Minister Winston Churchill on the British Prime Minister's eightieth birthday, November 30, 1954.

". . . If we are going to take such a fateful decision as leads us one step toward war, let us, by no means, do it in response to our human emotions of anger and resentment, but let's do it after we have prayerfully considered it and found as [President] Wilson expressed it, 'no other means of protecting our rights.'"

President Eisenhower, news conference of December 2, 1954.

". . . Too often politicians look into a looking glass instead of through a window."

President Eisenhower, reply to charge by National Democratic Committee Chairman Paul Butler that the President had shown a lack of capacity to govern and unite the American people, news conference of December 8, 1954.

"Through many years I have had good reason to count the press corps as a vital arm of the force of freedom. In war, I saw its members strive tirelessly, endure hardship, dare battlefield peril, that our people might be fully and quickly informed. On every front they were worthy of our fighting men. Now, as President, I find that each day emphasizes anew for me the fairness, the discernment, the dignity of the American reporter; in peace he is still a valuable soldier for the truth that makes men free. . . . In the unending struggle to maintain our freedom, the American reporter is ever in the front line."

President Eisenhower, address at the dedication of the Overseas Press Club Building, New York, December 13, 1954.

"This year, even as two thousand years ago when the Prince of Peace was born into the world, the drums of war are still. . . . Mankind's unquenchable hope for peace burns brighter than for many years."
President Eisenhower, on lighting the 1954 national Christmas tree at the White House.

THE PRESS

"It's the problem of the cartoonist to try to relate these characters to people rather than to the animals they represent and in the case of Pogo he looks a little bit more like a little boy than he looks like a possum, and the reason for that is that more of us have little boys in our families than have possums. He has that round head and needs a haircut like his father. . . . He is the first character in the strip and after him comes one called Albert the alligator."
Walt Kelly; comment in interview with Edward R. Murrow, "Person to Person," CBS-TV, January 1, 1954.

"The Yellows see such stories only as opportunities for sensationalism. When *The Times* gives a great amount of space to such stories it turns out authentic sociological documents."
Adolph Ochs, publisher of The New York Times, *definitive statement made during the Hall-Mills murder case of the 1920s, recalled during the Sheppard murder trial at Cleveland, Ohio, in 1954;* Newsweek, *January 3, 1955.*

"It takes a long time to educate a community and it can't be done by spellbinders, moneybags, hypnotizers or magicians . . . or Aladdin's lamp. Character is what matters on a paper."
Harry Grant, publisher, Milwaukee Journal, Time, *February 1, 1954.*

"We're not a loved paper. But we're a respected one."
Harry Grant. Ibid.

"I think it would be in bad taste if the head were held a little higher so the neck would show with the blood dripped out."

William Gaines, comic-book publisher, definition of the difference between good taste and poor taste, in testimony before a Senate investigating committee. Gaines said that "poor taste" was not implied in a "horror comic" cover showing an ax-wielding man holding aloft the severed head of a blonde, news summaries of May 13, 1954.

"Nobody knows anything and nobody tells you anything, and that means a good reporter can go out and get a beat every day."

Robert Capa, reporter-photographer, on covering war in Indo-China; comment recalled in obituaries of May 26, 1954, reporting his death when he stepped on a land-mine near Hanoi.

"I suppose I will go on selling newspapers until at last will come the late night final."

Lord Beaverbrook, British newspaper publisher, address to six hundred staffers who feted him on his seventy-fifth birthday, new summaries of June 7, 1954.

"I am always in favor of the free press but sometimes they say quite nasty things."

Sir Winston Churchill, comment during visit to Ottawa, Canada, on remarks in the U. S. press that British policy in Asia was comparable to British appeasement at Munich, news reports of July 1, 1954.

"The reason I got that information is that I don't break confidences, and I'm not going to break them now."

James A. Hagerty, announcement on retirement, after thirty-four years on The New York Times, that he would not be tempted to break confidences by writing a book on his career of news and political reporting, news reports of July 1, 1954.

"The trouble with me is that I am a vindictive old shanty-Irish bitch."
Cissy Patterson, late American heiress and newspaper publisher,
quoted in an article on her niece, Alicia Patterson, New York
publisher, Time, *September 13, 1954.*

"I have never discovered a genius who spoke of talent. Or even of inspiration. Only brutal work. So, if you or I or my children don't succeed, might it not be more fitting to blame it, perhaps, on a measure of laziness rather than lack of talent?"
Wilfred Funk, American publisher, reprinted from This Week
Magazine, *October 3, 1954; copyright 1954, United Newspapers*
Magazine Corporation.

"From winding and tortuous paths where the known faded into fogs of the unknown they did their best at sending home to press and radio the story of what has happened from day to day."
Carl Sandburg, address at dedication of Overseas Press Club
Building, New York, news reports of December 14, 1954.

"Valor is a gift. Those having it never know for sure whether they have it till the test comes. And those having it in one test never know for sure if they will have it when the next test comes. No one knows better than the tested overseas correspondent how a brave man can be rash, can take such risks that he goes down and never lives to file what might have been his greatest story."
Carl Sandburg. Ibid.

"Habits form our pattern of living, and when we have become accustomed, through the years, to traverse the whole world every morning through the imposing size of your newspapers and the abundance of your news reports, it is going to be hard to give up this intellectual morning feast. It is to me the little glass of white wine that the workman in my country still prefers to milk before setting out on his hard day's work."
Henri Bonnet, French ambassador to U.S., farewell address to
the National Press Club, Washington, news reports of December
16, 1954.

"The composing room has an unlimited supply of periods available to terminate short, simple sentences."

Turner Catledge, managing editor of The New York Times, *memo calling for shorter and sharper writing in news stories,* Time, *December 20, 1954.*

"Once *Vogue* showed two or three dresses for stout women, but we were so shaken by the experience we haven't repeated it in fifty-seven years."

Edna Woolman Chase, for nearly sixty years editor of Vogue, *writing in her autobiography,* Always in Vogue, *by herself and Ilka Chase. Copyright by Edna Woolman Chase and Ilka Chase, reprinted by permission of Doubleday & Company, Inc.*

"Fashion can be bought. Style one must possess. I have seen a Texas cowboy swing himself into his saddle with more real elegance, more style, than many gentlemen on the hunting field."

Edna Woolman Chase. Ibid.

"There are gatherers and scatterers of work. You, Edna, are a gatherer."

Edna Woolman Chase, quotation of a comment from Vogue *publisher Condé Nast. Ibid.*

RADIO AND TELEVISION

"You meet people and, well, it is like your own child when you look at his face. You say he has father's eyes and mother's nose and when you create a character it is a little bit of everybody you have ever known I think."

Gertrude Berg, comment on twenty-five years of writing the life and times of Mollie Goldberg, interview with Edward R. Murrow, "Person to Person," CBS-TV, June 4, 1954.

". . . Talking about Molly I just want to say I always remember the first script that I wrote. Jake came home for supper with a little ambitious bug in his brain. He wanted to go into business and he told this to Molly and Molly had some money she had put away anticipating just such a time and she gave it to him, and as they sat down to the dinner table he said to her, 'Molly, darling, some day we will be eating out of golden plates,' and Molly turned to him and said, 'Jake, darling, will it taste any better?' I always remember that."

Gertrude Berg. Ibid.

"I wish I could get some way of getting word to my dentist—not a Communist—that part of one of my teeth fell off in the auto today. . . ."

Joseph Welch, special Army counsel at the Army-McCarthy hearings, first man in history to make a dental appointment by television, news reports of May 1, 1954.

"Me Gotta Have You," lyrics by Roy Alfred, music by Marvin Fisher.

> "Shave need Burma. . . .
> Adler got to have shoe. . . .
> Hair need Toni. . . .
> Swift bologna
> Me, I gotta have you. . . .
> Smith need brother. . . .
> Halo need a shampoo. . . ."

Song, "Me Gotta Have You," considered one of the most loaded with commercials of many commercially slanted songs. Many were banned by radio and television stations as free advertising. Quoted in Time, *June 14, 1954, reprinted by permission of the publisher, Marvin Music Company.*

"All this boogie-woogie and jazz—I often curse radio for being a medium for that. But I like good music. When radio is used for that, I'm well satisfied."

Lee DeForest, "the father of the radio," comment shortly before his eighty-first birthday, New York Times Magazine, *August 22, 1954.*

"The American arrives in Paris with a few French phrases he has culled from a conversational guide or picked up from a friend who owns a beret. He speaks the sort of French that is really understood by another American who also has just arrived in Paris."

Fred Allen, introduction to Paris After Dark, *by Art Buchwald, Little, Brown and Company, 1954.*

"Whether he knows it or not, the comedian is on a treadmill to oblivion. When a radio comedian's program is finally finished it slinks down Memory Lane into the limbo of yesteryear's happy hours. All that the comedian has to show for his years of work and aggravation is the echo of forgotten laughter."

Fred Allen, Treadmill to Oblivion, *copyright 1954 by Fred Allen, reprinted by permission of the publisher, Little, Brown and Company.*

RELIGION

"American soldiers have taught me better than I could have learned in any other way what America means to me."

Francis Cardinal Spellman, archbishop of New York, on third consecutive Christmas visit to troops in Korea, news summaries of January 4, 1954.

"Even the Milwaukee Braves have no pitcher who can pitch a double-header."

Francis Cardinal Spellman, declining to make two speeches on successive days in Milwaukee, news summaries of August 31, 1954.

"May the Lord bless you real good."

Billy Graham, considered at thirty-five to be "the world's No. One revival preacher," favorite benediction, Newsweek, *February 1, 1954.*

"I felt as if I were shaking hands with Mr. History."
Billy Graham, comment after meeting Sir Winston Churchill, news summaries of May 31, 1954.

"Just pray for a thick skin and a tender heart."
Ruth Graham, wife of Evangelist Billy Graham, comment on being the wife of a famous preacher, news reports of April 22, 1954.

"It was not the outer grandeur of the Roman but the inner simplicity of the Christian that lived on through the ages."
Colonel Charles Lindbergh, comment in address at Institute of Aeronautical Sciences dinner in New York, news summaries of February 1, 1954.

"You've shown your gesture. Now I order you to use it for a better cause."
The Aga Khan, comment after the ancient Moslem ceremony of matching his weight in a like amount of platinum. The precious load was turned over to charity for aid to Pakistan, news summaries of February 3, 1954.

"Before these perplexing, troublesome days pass it may be necessary to move mountains. It is good that we keep the faith together."
Earl Warren, U. S. Supreme Court Chief Justice, comment in address to breakfast meeting of International Council for Christian Leadership, news summaries of February 5, 1954.

"In cities, no one is quiet but many are lonely; in the country, people are quiet but few are lonely."
The archbishop of Canterbury, Dr. Geoffrey Fisher, news summaries of February 22, 1954.

"Dare I say that when he is at home, I wish he were overseas? And still more profoundly, when he is overseas, I wish he were at home."
The archbishop of Canterbury, Dr. Geoffrey Fisher, comment on the "Red Dean" of Canterbury, Hewlett Johnson. Ibid.

"There are only two kinds of people in the modern world who know what they are after. One, quite frankly, is the Communist. The other, equally frankly, is the convinced Christian. . . . The rest of the world are amiable nonentities."

The archbishop of Canterbury, Dr. Geoffrey Fisher, comment at Evanston, Illinois, conference of the World Council of Churches, news summaries of August 26, 1954.

"The world is covered with places I'm going to retire to—New Zealand, America, and every county of England."

The archbishop of Canterbury, Dr. Geoffrey Fisher, speaking as Britain's most-traveled archbishop, news summaries of August 27, 1954.

". . . I call these children exceptional children because they give us an exceptional opportunity to manifest our love for God by loving the least of his children and these tots certainly are the least of the children of the Lord."

Archbishop Richard Cushing of Boston, comment on new home for children mentally handicapped, in interview with Edward R. Murrow, "Person to Person," CBS-TV, April 16, 1954.

". . . We will tirelessly endeavor to bring about by means of international agreements—always in subordination to the principle of legitimate self-defense—the effective proscription and banishment of atomic, biological, and chemical warfare."

Pope Pius XII, Easter message, 1954, news reports of April 19, 1954.

"He is the Saint that Providence presents to our era."

Pope Pius XII, on canonization of Pius X, news reports of May 30, 1954.

"I am grateful for those many prayers. From now on my prayers will be offered up for others."

Marie Dionne, at birth the smallest and weakest of the Dionne quintuplets, comment while a novice in a community of clois-

tered nuns at Quebec City, Canada, news summaries of May 31, 1954.

"I consider myself a living example of what prayer can do if it is sincere enough."

Representative Alvin Bentley of Michigan, on receiving a standing ovation when he returned to the House of Representatives for the first time since he and four other congressman were shot down by Puerto Rican fanatics on March 1, 1954. Bentley had been given only a fifty-fifty chance to live, news reports of September 13, 1954.

"When we had means we worked, when we had none we waited on God in prayer."

The Right Rev. Henry Benjamin Whipple, first Episcopal bishop of Minnesota in the 1860s, quotation recalled when the worldwide Anglican Congress was held in his diocese in the summer of 1954, news reports of September 13, 1954.

"I feel it is time that I also pay tribute to my four writers, Matthew, Mark, Luke, and John."

Bishop Fulton Sheen on receiving a Look *award for his television addresses, quoted in Faye Emerson's column,* New York World-Telegram & Sun, *December 24, 1954.*

ROYALTY

"To that new conception of an equal partnership of nations and races I shall give myself heart and soul, every day of my life."

Queen Elizabeth II, outline of a new ideal of the British Commonwealth, address from Auckland, New Zealand, during a world tour, news reports of December 26, 1953; used in news summaries of January 1, 1954.

"I must be careful. Once in Canada, the train started off without me."
Queen Elizabeth II, remark while making a brief stop in Palmerston, New Zealand, news reports of January 7, 1954.

"It is . . . a joy for me today to address you, not as a Queen from far away, but as your Queen and part of your Commonwealth. In a real sense you are here as my colleagues, friends, and advisers. When I add to this consideration the fact that I am the first ruling sovereign to visit Australia, it is clear that the events of today make a piece of history which fills me with deep pride and most heartfelt pleasure, and which I am confident will serve to strengthen in your own hearts and minds the feeling of comradeship with the Crown and that sense of duty shared which we must all have as we confront our common tasks."
Queen Elizabeth II, speech from the throne opening a session of the Australian Parliament at Melbourne, news reports of February 16, 1954.

"They have done so, I am proud to say, because of the great qualities of my peoples, qualities which have shown themselves through labours manfully performed, duties courageously done by men and women, sorrows sustained and happiness earned."
Queen Elizabeth II, comment on survival of governments of parliamentary sovereignty in the Commonwealth. Ibid.

". . . It is my resolve that under God I shall not only rule but serve. That is not only the tradition of my family. It describes, I believe, the modern character of the British Crown."
Queen Elizabeth II. Ibid.

"I couldn't resist the impulse, so I leaned over and said, 'No, it's me!'"
Queen Elizabeth II, recollection of riding through a park of Auckland, New Zealand, and overhearing a young girl insisting that the royal personage was Princess Margaret. (Said The New York Times, "Not spoken in the Queen's English!") News summaries of February 23, 1954.

"It is a wonderful moment."

> *Queen Elizabeth II, signaled message to the Home Fleet which welcomed her return to England after her fifty-thousand-mile around-the-world trip—the longest journey ever made by a reigning monarch—news reports of May 15, 1954.*

"In the turbulence of this anxious and active world many people are leading uneventful, lonely lives. To them dreariness, not disaster, is the enemy. They seldom realize that on their steadfastness, on their ability to withstand the fatigue of dull repetitive work and on their courage in meeting constant small adversities depend in great measure the happiness and prosperity of the community as a whole. . . . The upward course of a nation's history is due in the long run to the soundness of heart of its average men and women."

> *Queen Elizabeth II, Christmas message broadcast to the Commonwealth from Sandringham, news reports of December 26, 1954.*

"Home from abroad
I rest at Karizawa
And the coloring woods
Are full of my country's scent."

> *Crown Prince Akihito, poem written for the annual Japanese Imperial Poetry Party Contest of the royal household. Akihito had recently become the first crown prince to make a world tour. News reports of January 13, 1954.*

"There is only one Franz Josef. That's me. I want to become plain Mr. Josef."

> *Archduke Franz Josef of Hapsburg-Lothrigen, comment on his role as a New Yorker, news reports of February 28, 1954.*

"The whole world knows that I became a Queen in spite of myself."

> *Ex-Queen Narriman, comment that it was against her wishes to marry King Farouk of Egypt, news reports of April 30, 1954.*

"We have a radiant rose, our royal head
Now coming from the summers of our kin
After such welcome few have ever seen. . . ."
John Masefield, sonnet to mark return to England of Elizabeth II after a world tour, news summaries of May 17, 1954.

"Yes, but I'd rather go by bus. There is nothing nicer in the world than a bus."
Prince Charles of England, reply when asked if he was excited about sailing on the royal yacht to meet his mother, Queen Elizabeth II, in Tobruk, news summaries of May 21, 1954.

"This is the one, the very one."
Prince Charles, pointing out his favorite bicycle to a London department store Santa Claus, news summaries of December 21, 1954.

"To succeed as both husband and subject, I believe you need a tightrope walker's sense of balance—and an understanding wife."
Prince Bernhard of the Netherlands, comment on five years as consort to a reigning sovereign, Collier's, June 6, 1954.

"After he got up and banged his fist, out he walked and slammed the door so hard the plaster wall shattered. I was told later that as he was walking to get into the car, he and his interpreter were both laughing their heads off."
Ex-King Michael of Rumania, recollection of a palace call paid by Andrei Vishinsky, Russian ambassador to Bucharest when Rumania first fell under Soviet domination; Michael told the story for a committee of U. S. congressmen meeting in London, Time, June 28, 1954.

"Dalai Lama first. Dalai Lama top man."
The Dalai Lama, statement to a British newsman who attempted to secure the autograph of a Lama backed by the Chinese Communists, Time, September 27, 1954.

"The Atlantic, once a wide gulf between us, is surely now a lake that links us."

Queen Mother Elizabeth of England, in New York, expression of thanks for a scholarship fund of more than four hundred thirty-three thousand dollars honoring her late husband, King George VI, news summaries of November 4, 1954.

SPORTS

"Americans are very kind and very energetic about celebrating. It's a bit tiring of course."

Sir Edmund Hillary, New Zealand mountaineer who successfully scaled Mount Everest, comment on finding New York exhausting when compared with the Everest expedition, news reports of January 28, 1954.

"I'd like to see how the lifts work."

Sir Edmund Hillary, continuing an interest in heights during a visit to Empire State Building, New York. Ibid.

"Coaching is a life of heartaches, but it's the life for you and me."

Knute Rockne, advice recalled by Frank Leahy, quoted in reports of Leahy's resignation from the post in which he had succeeded Rockne, news reports of January 31, 1954.

"I believe in security—if the seeking for security is based on personal contribution and sound method. I do not believe in killing today's goose for sake of a possible omelet tomorrow."

Ford Frick, baseball commissioner, address at thirty-first annual dinner of Baseball Writers' Association, comment on player pension funds, news summaries of February 1, 1954.

"Nobody with gumption is what you would call a good loser. But I try to be gracious."

Terry Brennan, Notre Dame football coach, news summaries of February 8, 1954.

"It's a tremendous weight off my mind to get out of the game, as much as I love it."

Frank Leahy, comment on resigning as head coach at Notre Dame, news summaries of February 8, 1954. (Since 1941, his teams had played eighty-seven games, lost eleven, tied nine.)

"Rodeoing is about the only sport you can't fix. You'd have to talk to the bulls and horses, and they wouldn't understand you."

Bill Linderman, holder of the title "All-Around Cowboy of the U.S.," news summaries of March 8, 1954.

"If I know I make this much trouble, I never climb Everest."

Tensing Norkay, Sherpa guide who was member of expedition to Mount Everest, comment on becoming involved in international politics in an attempt to secure a passport to U.S., news summaries of March 29, 1954.

"The horse ran well and at the eighth pole, when I looked around, I knew I had the race."

Ray York, jockey who guided the winner of the 1954 Kentucky Derby, "Determine," news reports of May 2, 1954.

"Naturally, we wanted to achieve the honor of doing it first, but the main essence of sport is a race against opponents rather than against clocks."

Roger Bannister, British athlete who ran a mile in three minutes, fifty-nine and four-tenths seconds to break a twenty-year record, news reports of May 7, 1954.

"Hey, Charlie, does that mean I won't have to think any more?"
Rocky Marciano, reply to his trainer's praise for fighting by instinct, The New York Times Magazine, *May 13, 1954.*

"This bum picked me up when I didn't have a quarter to my name. Now I owe twenty thousand dollars."
Ex-boxer Maxie Rosenbloom, recollection of the kindness of a benefactor, Look, *May 18, 1954.*

"Anything I got, I got through the fights."
Jack Dempsey, comment on thirty-fifth anniversary of becoming heavyweight boxing champion of the world, news reports of July 4, 1954.

"It is well known that the older a man grows, the faster he could run as a boy."
Red Smith, sports editor of the New York Herald-Tribune, Reader's Digest, *August 1954.*

"If you break 100, watch your golf. If you break eighty, watch your business."
Walter Winchell, columnist, Reader's Digest, *August 1954.*

"Steel is a man's weapon. It has always been the great equalizer. Little men have brought big men crashing like storm-stricken oaks by sliding six inches of it gently into their bodies. Speed and guile offset brawn and size; trickery can take the measure of knowledge."
Paul Gallico, "Gentle Art of Swordplay," Sports Illustrated, *September 20, 1954, copyright 1954, Time, Inc.; reprinted by permission.*

"The fundamental difference between intercollegiate and professional athletics is that in college the players are supposed to be students first and foremost. This does not mean that they should all be Phi Beta Kappas or physics majors, but neither should they be subnormal students majoring in ping-pong."
The Rev. Theodore Hesburgh, C.S.C., president, University of Notre Dame, "Spirit of Notre Dame," Sports Illustrated, *September 27, 1954, reprinted by permission.*

"Here is no sentiment, no contest, no grandeur, no economics. From the sanctity of this occupation, a man may emerge refreshed and in control of his own soul. He is not idle. He is fishing, alone with himself in dignity and peace. It seems a very precious thing to me."

John Steinbeck, "Of Fish and Fishermen," Sports Illustrated, October 4, 1954; copyright 1954 by John Steinbeck; reprinted by permission of McIntosh & Otis, Inc.

"You just walk up there and hit it."

Hugh Duffy, the heaviest hitter of any season in baseball history, remark recalled in obituaries reporting his death at the age of eighty-seven. The remark had often been compared to the Ballet Russe's late Vaslav Nijinsky who, when asked how he made his incredible floating leaps, once explained, "You have just to go up and pause there a little."—Time, November 1, 1954.

"They surprised me by agreeing so quick. Maybe I made a mistake. I should-a asked for more."

Yogi Berra, recollection of the moment he signed for a reported forty-one thousand dollars for 1954 to become highest-salaried catcher in history of the Yankees, news reports of December 10, 1954.

"O'er the stadiums snowfalls hover,
Losing coaches run for cover.
Never got around to winning,
Open season just beginning."

Poem for coaches with nonwinning teams, quoted by Herman Hickman in Sports Illustrated, December 13, 1954.

THEATER

"When you're a star in France, you are just a French star. When you're a star in Italy, you are just an Italian star. But when you're a star in New York, you're a star of the whole world."

Lilo, French star of the Broadway musical, Can Can, *news summaries of March 1, 1954.*

"One's strong. One's weak. And in between one is always in a growing up process that never ends."

Joan Greenwood, English actress, news summaries of March 8, 1954.

"The most difficult secret for a man to keep is his own opinion of himself."

Marcel Pagnol, French playwright and author, news summaries of March 15, 1954.

"I could play Lady Macbeth when I was nine years old. No one told me it was difficult."

Constance Collier recalls her early interest in Shakespeare. She spoke at a New York luncheon marking the 391st anniversary of Shakespeare's birth, news reports of April 30, 1954.

"Women never use their intelligence—except when they need to prop up their intuition."

Jacques Deval, French playwright, news summaries of May 10, 1954.

"The only thing that happens overnight is recognition. Not talent."

Carol Haney, on her sudden success as the star of Pajama Game, *news summaries of May 24, 1954.*

"Bad notices will cook you. It's impossible to grin and bear it."
Margaret Webster, director, news reports of June 27, 1954.

"So long as there is one pretty girl left on the stage, the professional undertakers may hold up their burial of the theatre."
George Jean Nathan, critic, news summaries of June 28, 1954.

"Whenever I get hungry, whenever I start getting nasty notes from the collector of internal revenue, I become fascinated with the summer theatre. I pine for a season amid the sumac."
Tallulah Bankhead, comment on the straw-hat circuit, news summaries of July 12, 1954.

"Behind the footlights you can look like William Bendix and be a glamorous actress—but in front of the camera they expect you to be beautiful."
Geraldine Page, remark on the difference between Hollywood and Broadway, news summaries of August 13, 1954.

"I'm an old girl now; I'm the grandmother of the world, but stardom is so new to me that I'm not sure I like it."
Josephine Hull, news summaries of October 11, 1954.

"Playing Shakespeare is very tiring. You never get to sit down unless you're a King."
Josephine Hull. Ibid.

"If I hadn't been blessed with a little talent I would have worn green hair on the stage. The first function of an artist is to be noticed."
Sir Cedric Hardwicke, news summaries of October 27, 1954.

"We read the lines so that people can hear and understand them; we move about the stage without bumping into the furniture or each other. . . ."
Lynn Fontanne, definition of the art of acting, news reports of October 31, 1954.

"The cinema tried to ruin the theatre, then radio came along and had its way with the cinema, then TV came along and had its way with radio. But there'll always be a theatre."

Lionel Barrymore, comment recalled in obituaries of November 16, 1954, reporting his death.

"No Barrymore ever amounted to anything until after the age of twenty-eight."

Lionel Barrymore. Ibid.

". . . I felt I was being gently appraised, and when I heard, 'Zorina! You're looking wonderful and fit,' I felt as if I had again officially become public property. This is the challenge that everyone in the theatre feels after a period of absence, and it happens over and over, not only in interviews but in photographic sessions, in rehearsals, and on innumerable other occasions. It will culminate at the moment when I shall take a deep breath and face the opening-night audience."

Vera Zorina, description of her return to Broadway in the musical, On Your Toes, Theatre Arts, *November 1954.*

". . . At the end of a successful evening, one really does feel that one is at last a part of a world united by that bond which has been consummated in the theatre between the audience and the actors."

Gloria Vanderbilt, comment on her theatrical debut at the Pocono Playhouse in Pennsylvania, Theatre Arts, *November 1954.*

"A setting is a presence, a mood, a great warm wind fanning the drama to flame."

Robert Edmond Jones, dean of American stage designers, rejection of the traditional idea of a stage design as simply a decoration, quoted in obituaries reporting his death, news reports of December 4, 1954.

"It will cover my life and loves from Chaplin to Valentino—and those who came before and after!"

Pola Negri, actress, comment on a forthcoming autobiography, news summaries of December 12, 1954.

"Actors should be overheard, not listened to, and the audience is fifty percent of the performance."

Shirley Booth, citing her two guiding rules for a successful stage career, news summaries of December 13, 1954.

"A low trick I hate to stoop to is tying and untying my shoelaces. It seems to fascinate audiences . . . probably because so many women in the audience have their shoes off, or wish they did."

Edward Everett Horton, on scene-stealing, news summaries of December 14, 1954.

"When you're a blonde, people sort of lean forward when you ask them a question. They take your arm to keep you from falling into an open manhole. But when you're a brunette . . . you're just one of the bunch."

Carol Channing, comment on changing her hair color on completion of her role in Gentlemen Prefer Blondes, *news reports of December 30, 1954.*

"Manliness is not all swagger and swearing and mountain climbing. Manliness is also tenderness, gentleness, consideration. You men think you can decide on who is a man, when only a woman can really know."

Robert Anderson, Tea and Sympathy, *copyright 1953 by Robert Anderson, reprinted by permission of the author and Random House, Inc., speech for the housemother in the play, Laura Reynolds; award play of 1954.*

"Did it ever occur to you that you persecute in Tom, that boy up there, you persecute in him the thing you fear in yourself?"

Robert Anderson. Ibid.

"I'll tell you the real secret of how to stay married. Keep the cave clean. They want the cave clean and spotless. Air-conditioned, if possible. Sharpen his spear, and stick it in his hand when he goes out in the morning to spear that bear, and when the bear chases him, console him when he comes home at night, and tell him what a big man he is, and then hide the spear so he doesn't fall over it and stab himself. . . ."

Anniversary Waltz, wife's speech, by Jerome Chodorov and Joseph Fields, copyright 1954 by Jerome Chodorov and Joseph Fields, reprinted by permission of the publisher, Random House, Inc.

"Before you're married, everything seems so simple. You're in love and that's it. You take your girl dancing on the Starlight Roof, you don't know it, but looking over that lovely girl's shoulder is the Sunshine Diaper Service. And right through the strains of Guy Lombardo, though you don't hear it, Millie, comes the roar of the vacuum cleaner. And instead of I love you, pretty soon you're looking into your loved one's eyes and saying, 'The baby didn't throw up again, darling?' I tell you, Millie, by the time you get that wonderful girl you took to the Starlight Roof away from the children, your father-in-law, your mother-in-law, the PTA, the A&P, Dr. Spock and Dr. Gesell, and should they go to the same camp this summer; by the time you close the door to the bedroom at night, you're just too exhausted to give a damn. No, Millie, love is one thing and marriage and children another. And never the twain shall meet. They're ships that pass in the night, Millie, one ship is you and your loved one, sending out an SOS, and the other ship is full of children—firing on the lifeboats."

Anniversary Waltz, husband's speech. Ibid.

" 'Do you hear that? Do you know what it means? It means that never, never, never again will we have to eat in a Third Avenue restaurant.' "

David Belasco, whispered comment to Mrs. Leslie Carter as they received on-stage ovations after the first performance of The Heart of Maryland; *Craig Timberlake,* The Bishop of Broadway, David Belasco, His Life and Work, *Library Publishers, 1954, reprinted by permission.*

"Praise is never more grudgingly rendered than by a subordinate critic, who inevitably feels constrained to write a suave, knowing, completely superior critique. The result is that he is usually completely insulated and fireproofed before the first note of the overture has been played, and he spends the rest of the evening busily resisting the enthusiasm of those about him. His concentration suffers; he misses a good deal of the play and finally is unable to write a cogent review of what he has seen and heard."
Craig Timberlake. Ibid.

"In New York people don't go to the theatre—they go to see hits."
Louis Jourdan, on his belief that high cost of tickets makes American audiences seek plays which have received good reviews, quoted by Art Buchwald, New York Herald Tribune *Syndicate.*

UNITED NATIONS

"I do not think Rome is burning at such a pace we should sacrifice our lunch."
Andrei Vishinsky, comment during a UN session that threatened to last through his lunch hour, news summaries of January 4, 1954.

"I would rather see the United States respected than loved by other nations."
Henry Cabot Lodge, Jr., U. S. ambassador to the United Nations, news summaries of January 28, 1954.

". . . My own belief is that the Soviets have done themselves more harm than good on many occasions, because they do not understand that in the United Nations they are not talking to the terrified and isolated people of Communist-controlled countries but to people in the United Nations who know what's what and what's going on in the world."
Henry Cabot Lodge, Jr. Ibid.

"This organization is created to prevent you from going to hell. It isn't created to take you to heaven."

Henry Cabot Lodge, Jr., comment on purpose of UN. Ibid.

"If it succeeds, it will be because of the work of hard-headed men who knew what they wanted and who made sacrifices for it. This operation should be run on a business basis."

Byron Price, comment on retirement as one of the American staff members of the UN Secretariat, news reports of February 2, 1954.

"Many times have I consulted them as one consults an oracle. If we are to believe the ancients, the voice of the people must be taken very seriously indeed."

Sir Gladwyn Jebb, British ambassador to the UN, comment on his numerous conversations with New York cab drivers, news reports of February 24, 1954.

"TV is all right for recording scenes of historic interest, but delicate negotiations become impossible when millions of people watch every time you scratch your head."

Sir Gladwyn Jebb, comment on the televising of UN sessions, news summaries of April 24, 1954.

"My TV rating was reckoned equal to the top comics."

Sir Gladwyn Jebb. Ibid.

". . . It would seem that those eminent gentlemen must know that there is nothing to spy on in the United Nations and therefore, there could be no spies. That is the obvious reason why the Soviets never fill their quota."

Eleanor Roosevelt, former member of U. S. delegation to the UN, comment on charges that UN is a nest of Communist spies, "My Day," New York World-Telegram & Sun, March 9, 1954.

"We intend to travel on this road with the assistance, and in the company, of our friends, if possible; without them, if necessary."

> Ramj Ram Saksena, speaking in the Economic and Social Council of the UN, regarding the U.S. Point Four program, news reports of April 8, 1954.

"Don't move without knowing where to put your foot next, and don't move without having sufficient stability to enable you to achieve exactly what should be the next step."

> Dag Hammarskjold, UN Secretary-General, remark that rules of mountaineering also apply to international negotiations, news summaries of April 12, 1954.

"Whenever a real challenge to freedom has arisen the British quality of reliability has always stood us and our friends in good stead."

> Sir Pierson Dixon, British ambassador to the UN, news summaries of April 30, 1954.

"I am not a gentleman, I am representative of the Soviet Union here."

> Semyon Tsarapkin, Soviet delegate to the UN, reply to Ambassador Lodge's inquiry on why "the gentleman" was asking for the floor. Lodge replied, "The two are not necessarily mutually exclusive," news reports of June 26, 1954.

". . . The United Nations was not set up to be a reformatory. It was assumed that you would be good before you got in and not that being in would make you good."

> John Foster Dulles, Secretary of State, comment on UN Charter, news reports of July 9, 1954.

"I have now come to believe that the United Nations will best serve the cause of peace if its Assembly is representative of what the world actually is, and not merely representative of the parts which we like."

> John Foster Dulles. Ibid.

"You are no longer dealing with a king here, a pasha there, a feudal lord elsewhere!"

Dr. Charles Malik of Lebanon, Arab spokesman on the UN Security Council, report on a new spirit of nationalism in the Middle East, news summaries of August 3, 1954.

"I believe that jaw is better than war, that it is good to have a place where we can talk and let off steam."

Anthony Nutting, British Minister of State for Foreign Affairs, on arriving in New York to head his country's delegation to the UN, news summaries of November 8, 1954.

"I don't think this mixture of chopped carrots and bamboo cane will go over well with the lovers of French cuisine."

Anthony Nutting, British UN delegate, comment on belligerent tone of Russian and Chinese efforts to prevent ratification of Paris agreements to arm West Germany, news reports of December 12, 1954.

1955

THE ARMED FORCES

"Underway on nuclear power at 11:01."

The Nautilus, *world's first atomic submarine, flashed this historic message on January 17, 1955, as it headed into the Atlantic, at Groton, Connecticut, on its initial sea tests, reportedly the first time the atom had propelled man, news reports of January 18, 1955.*

"Battles are not won by arms alone. There must exist above all else a spiritual impulse—a will to victory. In war there can be no substitute for victory."

General Douglas MacArthur, a quotation inscribed on a monument dedicated to him in Los Angeles on his seventy-fifth birthday, news reports of January 18, 1955.

"Youth . . . is not wholly a matter of ripe cheeks, red lips, or supple knees. It is a temper of the will, a quality of the imagination, a vigor of the emotions, a freshness of the deep springs of life. It means a temperamental predominance of courage over timidity, of an appetite for adventure over love of ease. Nobody grows old by merely living a number of years. People grow old only by deserting their ideas. Years may wrinkle the skin, but to give up interest wrinkles the soul. Worry, doubt, self-distrust, fear, and despair—these are the long, long years that bow the head and turn the growing spirit back to dust. Whatever your years, there is in every being's heart the love of wonder, the undaunted challenge of events, the unfailing child-like appetite for what next, and the joy and the game of life. You are as young as your faith, as old as your doubt; as young as your self-confidence, as old as your fear; as young as your hope, as old as your despair. In the central place of every heart there is a recording chamber; so long as it receives messages of beauty, hope, cheer, and courage, so long are we young. When the wires are down and your heart is covered with the snows of pessimism and the ice of cynicism, then, and then only are you grown old—and then, indeed, as the ballad says, you just fade away."

General MacArthur, speaking at dedication (quotation in part from Samuel Ullman, From the Summit of Years Four Score). Ibid.

"Much to my surprise, the emperor himself first brought up the question of war responsibilities. To my utter astonishment the emperor declared, 'I wish to assume full responsibility for every event connected with the prosecution of the war. I assume responsibility for the actions of every military commander and every statesman of Japan. Whatever your judgment is as to what my fate may be, go ahead. I assume all responsibility.' I could have kissed him. His part has never been adequately or fairly publicized. . . . But when the history of the era is written, it may very well be that Emperor Hirohito will be recognized and acclaimed as the father of the New Japan."

General Douglas MacArthur, comment to Japanese Foreign Minister Mamoru Shigemitsu recalling the Japanese occupation; when Shigemitsu called on MacArthur during a visit to the U.S., news reports of September 3, 1955.

"I realize that advice is worth what it costs—that is nothing."

General Douglas MacArthur. Ibid.

"You don't sit down with murderers and discuss business. The longer we wait, the more awful the war will be."

Brigadier General Frank Howley, U. S. Army, retired, former U. S. commandant in Berlin, appearing before the Senate Internal Security Subcommittee to testify against negotiations with Communist China, news summaries of May 9, 1955.

"As the bomb fell over Hiroshima and exploded, we saw an entire city disappear. I wrote in my log the words: 'My God, what have we done?'"

Captain Robert Lewis, copilot of the B-29, Enola Gay, from which the atom bomb was dropped on Hiroshima, appearing on the television program, "This Is Your Life," with a minister injured in the bombing, news reports of May 19, 1955.

"It was easier than driving through the traffic in downtown Los Angeles."

Lieutenant John Conroy, thirty-four, on completing a record dawn-to-dusk flight from Los Angeles to New York, and back, in eleven hours, 26 minutes and 33 seconds, May 21, 1955, news reports of May 22, 1955.

"The Academy's long-range mission will be to train generals, not second lieutenants."

General Hubert Harmon, first commander of the newly established U. S. Army Air Force Academy, Newsweek, June 6, 1955.

"It must be a flexible, all-purpose weapon ready for all emergencies, large and small."

General Maxwell Taylor's goal for the U. S. Army, a statement made on being sworn in as chief of staff, news reports of July 1, 1955.

"A child decided not to go home—a man decided to go home."

William Cowart, Dalton, Georgia, serviceman who spent two years with the Chinese Communists before requesting repatriation to the U.S., news reports of July 11, 1955.

"War is like a giant pack rat. It takes something from you, and it leaves something behind in its stead. It burned me out in some ways, so that now I feel like an old man but still sometimes act like a dumb kid. It made me grow up too fast."

Audie Murphy, most decorated soldier of World War II, comment to columnist Hal Boyle, New York Journal-American, August 30, 1955.

"The human body comes in only two shapes and three colors. I don't expect there will be any changes, so what we learn about it now will serve us for a long time to come."

Lieutenant Colonel Paul Stapp, comment on human endurance for space travel, Time, September 12, 1955.

"No woman has ever stepped on Little America—and we have found it to be the most silent and peaceful place in the world."

Rear Admiral Richard Byrd, comment in Washington on eve of his fifth expedition to the Antarctic, news reports of November 27, 1955.

"When we are wrong, make us easy to change.
When we are right, make us easy to live with."

General Alfred Gruenther, supreme commander, North Atlantic Treaty Organization, prayer for Americans to be patient when dealing with their allies, Time, December 12, 1955.

ART

"My house, I trust, does express my needs, my tastes and aspirations. It is a library with living rooms attached."

Critic Bernard Berenson at eighty-nine describes the Italian villa in which he had lived for two decades, Time, April 25, 1955.

"I have always disclaimed being a collector. Such a one loves to compete, to get the better of the seller, to gloat over the object as a scalp or trophy. . . ."

Critic Bernard Berenson, speaking of his art collection, considered one of the finest privately owned collections in the world. Ibid.

"I wonder whether art has a higher function than to make me feel, appreciate, and enjoy natural objects for their art value? So, as I walk in the garden, I look at the flowers and shrubs and trees and discover in them an exquisiteness of contour, a vitality of edge or a vigor of spring as well as an infinite variety of color that no artifact I have seen in the last sixty years can rival. . . . Each day, as I look, I wonder where my eyes were yesterday."

Critic Bernard Berenson. Ibid.

"An artist cannot speak about his art any more than a plant can discuss horticulture."

Jean Cocteau, refusing to discuss an exhibit of his work in Rome, Newsweek, May 16, 1955.

"I am so sorry I must go. It is too bad that when you know the most and can do the most, you must go."

Carl Milles, noted American sculptor, on the eve of his eightieth birthday regrets that he will not live long enough to execute "2000 more dreams" in sculpturing, news summaries of June 27, 1955.

"If my husband would ever meet a woman on the street who looked like the women in his paintings, he would fall over in a dead faint."

Mrs. Pablo Picasso, Quote, July 3, 1955.

"I'd like to live to be two thousand years old and just sculp all the time."

Daniel Chester French, a remark recalled by his daughter, Margaret French Cresson, in a report on the opening of his studio to the public, The New York Times Magazine, July 10, 1955.

"I'm modest enough to say that they're all great."

Sir Jacob Epstein, comment when asked if he thought that his "Social Consciousness" group of sculptured figures, in Philadelphia, was his greatest work, Newsweek, July 25, 1955.

"It is naturally difficult to assess one's place in the period one lives in, perhaps impossible. It is a process similar to painting one's own portrait, or rather to working on a portrait in the round, a really difficult undertaking. The artist usually dramatises himself, and that is why few self-portraits bear the imprint of truth. My outstanding merit in my own eyes is that I believe myself to be a return in sculpture to the human outlook, without in any way sinking back into the flabby sentimentalising, or the merely decorative, that went before."

Sir Jacob Epstein, comment in his autobiography, Epstein, *E. P. Dutton & Company, 1955, reprinted by permission.*

"I shot without plan. I was not out for subject matter. All I wanted was to connect my moods with those of Paris. Beauty pains, and when it pained most, I shot."

Ernst Haas, comment on his photographic essay, "The Glow of Paris," published in Life, *August 1, 1955.*

"I found it was a lot easier than embroidering."

Grandma Moses (Anna Mary Moses), comment on her success as an artist, news reports of September 6, 1955.

"I think a true form ought to suggest infinity. The surfaces ought to look as though they went on forever, as though they proceeded out from the mass into some perfect and complete existence."

Constantin Brancusi, sculptor, Time, *November 3, 1955.*

"I picked him up in a gutter, and saved him for France."

Madame Lucie Utrillo, comment about her artist-husband, Maurice Utrillo, recalled in obituaries reporting his death, news reports of November 6, 1955.

"All emotion comes to me through the elbow."

Salvador Dali, comment during lecture at the Sorbonne on the subject "Phenomenological Aspects of the Critical Paranoiac Method," Time, *December 26, 1955.*

AUTHORS

"It is music to my ears. I have always said that if I were a rich man, I would employ a professional praiser."

Sir Osbert Sitwell, comment about a program when one of his books was read aloud, interviewed in "The Elder Wise Men" series, NBC-TV, January 2, 1955; printed by permission.

"The critics will say as always that the literature is decaying. From the time of the first critic up to now they have said nothing else."

Sir Osbert Sitwell. Ibid.

> "Vermont's a place where barns
>   come painted
> Red as a strong man's heart,
> Where stout carts and stout boys
>   in freckles
> Are highest forms of art."

"Vermont Looks Like a Man," by Robert Tristram Coffin, last poem contributed to the New York Herald Tribune *editorial page before his death, January 20, 1955, reprinted by permission of his estate.*

"The last half century has been a retrogression of humanity, a frightening atrophy of culture of the most sinister kind, a loss in education, in decorum, in feeling for law, in truth and faith, in the most simple dependability."

Thomas Mann, part of an identical lecture delivered in West Germany and in East Germany a few weeks before his eightieth birthday, news reports of January 28, 1955.

"Deep down I believe that creation of the universe out of nothingness and that of life out of inorganic state ultimately aimed at the creation of man. I believe that man is meant as a great experiment whose possible failure by man's own guilt would be paramount to the failure of creation itself. Whether this belief be true or not, man would be well advised if he behaved as though it were."

Thomas Mann, statement prepared in 1952, at the age of seventy-eight, on the theme, "This I Believe," recalled in obituaries reporting his death, news reports of August 13, 1955.

"There simply is no more Hornblower. I've used him up. I've filled his life from childhood to old age through the end of the Napoleonic wars—in 1815."

C. S. Forester, creator of Horatio Hornblower series, since 1935 author of ten short stories and seven novels about that indomitable British naval officer, news reports of January 29, 1955.

"The writer in America isn't part of the culture of this country. He's like a fine dog. People like him around, but he's of no use. . . . The artist is still a little like the old court jester. He's supposed to speak his vicious paradoxes with some sense in them, but he isn't part of whatever the fabric is that makes a nation. It is assumed that anyone who makes a million dollars has a unique gift, though he might have made it off some useless gadget."

William Faulkner, interviewed during a visit to New York to receive the National Book Award for A Fable, The New York Times, *January 30, 1955.*

"I save writing for the four months of bad weather from December through April, when there's nothing else to do. I never take up serious writing in good weather. I'm outdoors too much."

William Faulkner, New York Mirror, May 15, 1955.

"Maybe it will be enough so that I can even bet the horses here."

William Faulkner, on being notified at Louisville, Kentucky, that he had been awarded the Pulitzer Prize (for A Fable), *Tempo, May 16, 1955.*

"In the end I thought: 'Here I am, making a living, enjoying my friends here, I don't like being a squatter, I might as well take the full responsibility.'"

T. S. Eliot, comment on his decision to become a British subject,
Life, *February 1, 1955.*

"You have to look at so much inferior stuff all the time that, like a tea-taster, or a chocolate-maker, you may lose your appetite for literature altogether."

T. S. Eliot, comment on his work as an editor and publisher.
Ibid.

"When I started to write I thought I would spend five years on this one project and keep track of the time so that if, when I was finished, no one would want to publish it, my father, at least, couldn't say I hadn't worked hard enough, so I kept track of all the time and I spent one thousand three hundred and three hours reading and three hundred and eighty hours indexing and three thousand two hundred and eighty-four hours writing, and the total hours was four thousand nine hundred and sixty-nine. . . . The total pages was nine thousand two hundred and forty-two."

Kathleen Winsor, comment in interview with Edward R. Murrow, "Person to Person," CBS-TV, February 4, 1955, on Forever Amber.

". . . I was certainly surprised. I was so surprised that I woke one morning and started to get up and fainted dead away on the floor, tried to get up again, fainted again, and fainted five times in two hours."

Kathleen Winsor, description of reaction to success of Forever Amber. *Ibid.*

"To divide one's life by years is of course to tumble into a trap set by our own arithmetic. The calendar consents to carry on its dull wall-existence by the arbitrary timetables we have drawn up in consultation with those permanent commuters, Earth and Sun. But we, unlike trees, need grow no annual rings."

Clifton Fadiman, "On Being Fifty," Holiday, February 1955, reprinted by permission.

"What makes a good writer of history is a guy who is suspicious. Suspicion marks the real difference between the man who wants to write honest history and the one who'd just rather write a good story."

Jim Bishop, newspaperman and author of The Day Lincoln Was Shot *and other books,* The New York Times, *February 5, 1955.*

"I write what I would like to read—what I think other women would like to read. If what I write makes a woman in the Canadian mountains cry and she writes and tells me about it, especially if she says, 'I read it to Tom when he came in from work and he cried, too,' I feel I have succeeded. People have said I write according to formula. Long ago an editor of one of the women's magazines told me, 'Get a girl in all kinds of trouble and then get her out.' . . . Their one warning was, 'Keep it clean.' I didn't need to be told that because it never occurred to me to write otherwise, with my Irish Catholic upbringing."

Kathleen Norris, at seventy-four commenting on the publication of her seventy-eighth book, The New York Times, *February 5, 1955.*

"He writes and rewrites and rewrites. He is the scourge of publishers with his proof changes. I've known him to keep a poem in his desk for twenty years."

Mrs. Carl Sandburg, commenting on the work habits of her poet-husband, Newsweek, *February 14, 1955.*

"The time a man is difficult is before he's found himself."

Mrs. Carl Sandburg. Ibid.

"I've always believed in writing without a collaborator, because where two people are writing the same book, each believes he gets all the worries and only half the royalties."

Agatha Christie, British mystery writer, news summaries of March 15, 1955.

"The best time for planning a book is while you're doing the dishes."

Agatha Christie. Ibid.

"All my major works have been written in prison. . . . I would recommend prison not only to aspiring writers but to aspiring politicians, too."
Prime Minister Nehru of India, speaking of the years he spent as a political prisoner, Look, April 5, 1955.

"When I had got my notes all written out, I thought that I'd polish it off in two summers, and it took me twenty-seven years."
Arnold Toynbee, on completing the ten volumes known as A Study of History, *comment made during television interview with Christopher Wright, teaching fellow at Harvard University, "Elder Wise Men" series, NBC-TV, April 17, 1955; printed by permission.*

"I think the explanation is really my mother. Not that she suggested it, but she just was an historian herself and I grew up assuming that I was going to be one, too, because of her. . . . When I was small and she used to put me to bed at night, she used to tell me the history of England in bits, till after about a year we finally had gone all through it."
Arnold Toynbee, comment on how he became interested in history. Ibid.

"I don't believe a committee can write a book. There are all kinds of things a committee can do. It can, oh, govern a country, perhaps, but I don't believe it can write a book. I think a book has to be written by some single mind. But, of course, that's a very large and formidable undertaking, and I think if a writer is wise, he gets all the help he can from other people. The responsibility is on him, it must pass through his mind, but he takes help where he can get it."
Arnold Toynbee, comment when asked if A Study of History *could have been written by a group of people working together. Ibid.*

"History not used is nothing, for all intellectual life is action, like practical life, and if you don't use the stuff—well, it might as well be dead."
Arnold Toynbee. Ibid.

"I believe that it [history] partly does repeat itself. I believe you can discover a certain number of uniformities in past history. At the same time, I am not a determinist and I don't believe we have no free will, and I don't believe past patterns just foretell and foredoom the future. I think there's an element of freedom and an element of patterns."

Arnold Toynbee. Ibid.

"Literature is like any other trade; you will never sell anything unless you go to the right shop."

George Bernard Shaw, message on a postcard sent to a young author; card exhibited in a New York department store, New York Herald Tribune, May 4, 1955.

"I was a code clerk in Washington at the time, when we received an urgent message that twelve code clerks were needed by President Wilson at the Versailles Peace Conference. What they really wanted were twelve code books, but somebody got the message mixed up."

James Thurber, interviewed on how he got his first trip to Paris, New York Herald Tribune Syndicate, May 15, 1955.

"With sixty staring me in the face, I have developed inflammation of the sentence structure and a definite hardening of the paragraphs."

James Thurber, comment on the trials of a writer at age fifty-nine, New York Post, June 30, 1955.

"All of my poems spill from life, from feelings . . . tender and thunderous, serene and raging and unique and true. . . . Nothing is anything unless it is done from feeling, which is the same thing as nothing is anything unless it is done from and with love."

Gloria Vanderbilt, comment a few months before publication of her first volume of poetry, Time, June 6, 1955.

"It's what I meant it to be. It's a tender Valentine that's going out into the world."

Gloria Vanderbilt, comment on the publication of her first book, Love Poems, news reports of August 14, 1955.

"One of the very few advantages of writing in my middle twenties is that it is still possible to remember adolescence as a time of both turmoil and frustration. Perhaps only the young should be allowed to reminisce, because only they can remember turmoil and frustration as well as happiness. They are not old enough to see everything in the distorted mirror of time or dimmed by the haze of forgetfulness."

Roger Bannister, English champion runner, on writing his autobiography, Sports Illustrated, *June 20, 1955.*

"The books are full of familiar and affectionate talk about the little lands: the countries made out of islands in the sea, or river valleys, or a circle of mountains. 'Map of Ireland!' they say of a young Gael, meaning you'd know him for Irish anywhere by the light in his eyes and the set of his jaw. Nobody says, 'Map of America!' of any of us—not even of the slender girls with the long legs and the fine ankles who walk the streets of the world as other women never walked them. People know us well enough. They know us everywhere. They know what we are and where we come from. But nobody thinks 'The map of America!' when we go by. You don't talk about continents that way."

Archibald MacLeish, "Sweet Land of Liberty," Collier's, *July 8, 1955; reprinted by permission.*

"The map of America is a map of endlessness, of opening out, of forever and ever. No man's face would make you think of it but his hope might, his courage might."

Archibald MacLeish. Ibid.

"Spring has many American faces. There are cities where it will come and go in a day and counties where it hangs around and never quite gets there. . . . Summer is drawn blinds in Louisiana, long winds in Wyoming, shade of elms and maples in New England. . . . Autumn is the American season. In Europe the leaves turn yellow or brown, and fall. Here they take fire on the trees and hang there flaming. We think this frost-fire is a portent somehow: a promise that the continent has given us. Life, too, we think, is capable of taking fire in this country; of creating beauty never seen."

Archibald MacLeish. Ibid.

"To our neighbors, East and West, the symbols of the Republic are enormous chimneys leaking their pink smoke into the clean, blue sky, or huge derricks wading into the sea itself for oil, or deserted mining towns where gold and silver were once dug. But we ourselves—what do we think of the world's talk? . . . Do steel and oil alone explain it? Is it only metal that speaks here and an ooze pumped out of muck? Or have the minds of men imagined these tall towers?"

Archibald MacLeish. Ibid.

"Poetry ennobles the heart and the eyes, and unveils the meaning of all things upon which the heart and the eyes dwell. It discovers the secret rays of the universe, and restores to us forgotten paradises."

Dame Edith Sitwell, "Of What Use Is Poetry," Reader's Digest, August 1955.

"Poetry is the light of the Great Morning wherein the beings whom we see passing in the street are transformed for us into the epitome of all beauty, or of all joy, or of all sorrow."

Dame Edith Sitwell. Ibid.

"It gives a man character as a poet to have a daily contact with a job. I doubt whether I've lost a thing by leading an exceedingly regular and disciplined life."

Wallace Stevens, American poet, comment on his daytime position as a specialist in surety-bond work and vice-president of the Hartford Accident and Indemnity Company, Hartford, Connecticut; recalled in news summaries of August 15, 1955 reporting his death.

"You will find that at the times when life becomes most real, in the great times of life, almost every man or woman becomes a poet at heart, as when in love or in the moments of great loss or bereavement, or coming very close to reality."

John Hall Wheelock, American poet and editor, news summaries of September 13, 1955.

"I am convinced that all writers are optimists whether they concede the point or not. . . . How otherwise could any human being sit down to a pile of blank sheets and decide to write, say two hundred thousand words on a given theme?"

Thomas Costain, author of The Silver Chalice *and other best-selling books,* Guideposts, *October 1955.*

"You can't make the Duchess into Rebecca of Sunnybrook Farm. The facts of life are very stubborn things."

Cleveland Amory, comment on why he stopped helping the Duchess of Windsor with the writing of her memoirs, news reports of October 6, 1955.

"A poet can write about a man slaying the dragon, but not about a man pushing a button that releases a bomb."

W. H. Auden, Pulitzer Prize winning poet, observation that twentieth-century verse often puzzles the writer as well as the reader, Newsweek, *October 31, 1955.*

"It has always been much like writing a check. . . . It is easy to write a check if you have enough money in the bank, and writing comes more easily if you have something to say."

Sholem Asch, comment on seventy-fifth birthday on publication of The Prophet, *fifth in his cycle of Biblical narratives,* New York Herald-Tribune *book review, November 6, 1955.*

"That's the way I write a poem—getting a small piece of it in my hands and pulling it out and not knowing whether it is a man or a woman. I have never started a poem yet whose end I knew. Writing a poem is discovering."

Robert Frost, The New York Times *book review, November 7, 1955.*

"I would love to be the poet laureate of Coney Island. I would feel enormous satisfaction in being regarded as the voice of the average American."

Thornton Wilder, New York Journal-American, *November 11, 1955.*

"The most salient fact about Africa is that 190,800,000 people are suddenly making the transition with unbelievable velocity from wearing a string of beads to driving a Ford."
John Gunther, comment on the publication of his book, Inside Africa, *quoted in interview with Sidney Fields,* New York Daily Mirror, *November 13, 1955.*

"Africa is safer than Central Park at night."
John Gunther. Ibid.

"The duty of dramatists is to express their times and guide the public through the perplexities of those times."
Robert Sherwood, comment recalled in obituaries reporting his death, news reports of November 15, 1955.

"The critics will be waiting for you with meat cleavers the next time around."
John P. Marquand, warning to Herman Wouk, author of The Caine Mutiny, *news reports of November 18, 1955.*

"This is the great folly of grownups—wanting what lasts, wanting to last. Only two things last: shoes too small and foolishness."
Minou Drouet, eight-year-old Parisian girl who in late 1955 caused a lively controversy among French critics over whether she was a literary genius or a fraud, news summaries of November 19, 1955.

"i use capitals ONLY for emphasis, after all, that's what they were invented for, weren't they?"
e. e. cummings, explanation of his aversion to use of capital letters, Time, *December 5, 1955.*

"When people are free to do as they please, they usually imitate each other."
Eric Hoffer, The Passionate State of Mind, *copyright 1954, 1955, by Eric Hoffer, reprinted by permission of Harper & Brothers.*

"Intolerance is the 'Do Not Touch' sign on something that cannot bear touching. We do not mind having our hair ruffled, but we will not tolerate any familiarity with the toupee which covers our baldness."
Eric Hoffer. Ibid.

"Our credulity is greatest concerning the things we know least about. And since we know least about ourselves, we are ready to believe all that is said about us. Hence the mysterious power of both flattery and calumny."
Eric Hoffer. Ibid.

"Louis says that I have the soul of a peasant, not so much that I love working in the earth and with the earth, but because I like to know that it is my own earth that I am delving in. Had I the soul of an artist, the stupidity of possessions would have no power over me. He may be right. I would as soon think of renting a child to love as a piece of land. When I plant a seed, or a root, I plant a bit of my heart with it and do not feel that I have finished when I have had my exercise and amusement. But I do not feel so far removed from God when the tender leaves put forth and I know that in a manner I am a creator."
Fanny Van de Grift Osbourne Stevenson, wife of Robert Louis Stevenson, in a diary she kept during the Stevensons' memorable residence in Samoa in the 1890s. (This portion was among some crossed-out sections of the diary brought to light by radiation photography early in 1955.) Reprinted by permission from Our Samoan Adventure, *Harper & Brothers, 1955.*

"If you set to work to believe everything you will tire out the muscles of your mind and then you'll be so weak you won't be able to believe the simplest true things. Only last week a friend of mine set to work to believe Jack-the-Giant-Killer. He managed to do it, but he was so exhausted by it that when I told him it was raining (which was true) he couldn't believe it, but rushed out into the street without his hat or umbrella."
Lewis Carroll, author of Alice in Wonderland, *quoted in the biography,* Lewis Carroll, *by Derek Hudson, The Macmillan Company, copyright 1955; reprinted by permission of the publisher.*

"The most exhausting thing in life, I have discovered, is being insincere. That is why so much social life is exhausting; one is wearing a mask." *Anne Morrow Lindbergh,* Gift from the Sea, *Pantheon Books, Inc., 1955; reprinted by permission of the publisher.*

"I believe that what woman resents is not so much giving herself in pieces as giving herself purposelessly." *Anne Morrow Lindbergh. Ibid.*

"If one sets aside time for a business appointment, a trip to the hairdresser, a social engagement, or a shopping expedition, that time is accepted as inviolable. But if one says: I cannot come because that is my hour to be alone, one is considered rude, egotistical or strange. What a commentary on our civilization, when being alone is considered suspect; when one has to apologize for it, make excuses, hide the fact that one practices it—like a secret vice!" *Anne Morrow Lindbergh. Ibid.*

"Nothing feeds the center [of being] so much as creative work. . . . The curtain of mechanization has come down between the mind and the hand." *Anne Morrow Lindbergh. Ibid.*

"One resents any change, even though one knows that transformation is natural and part of the process of life and its evolution. Like its parallel in physical passion, the early ecstatic stage of a relationship cannot continue always at the same pitch of intensity. It moves to another phase of growth which one should not dread, but welcome as one welcomes summer after spring." *Anne Morrow Lindbergh. Ibid.*

"Perhaps both men and women in America may hunger, in our material, outward, active, masculine culture, for the supposedly feminine qualities of heart, mind and spirit—qualities which are actually neither masculine nor feminine, but simply human qualities that have been neglected.

It is growth along these lines that will make us whole, and will enable the individual to become world to himself."
Anne Morrow Lindbergh. Ibid.

"The Upsons lived the way every family in America wants to live—not rich, but well-to-do. They had two of everything: two addresses, the flat on Park and a house in Connecticut; two cars, a Buick sedan, and a Ford station wagon; two children, a boy and a girl; two servants, man and maid; two clubs, town and country; and two interests, money and position. Mrs. Upson had two fur coats and two chins. Mr. Upson also had two chins, two passions—golf and business—and two aversions, Roosevelt and Jews."
Patrick Dennis in his novel, Auntie Mame, *the best-selling novel of 1955, copyright 1955 by Patrick Dennis, published by the Vanguard Press, reprinted by permission.*

"Gladys, at thirteen, was a wanton little nymphomaniac. Edmund, at fifteen, was a complete thug with halitosis and an advanced case of satyriasis. . . . Eleven-year-old Enid was a kleptomaniac, and whenever anything was missing one only had to look in Enid's room to find it. Ginger was an illegitimate child who exploded the old theory that love children are always the loveliest. . . . Albert, at ten, was just despicable, and his little sister, Margaret Rose, although the best of the lot, was a chronic bed wetter and no bargain."
Patrick Dennis, describing adoption of six English war refugees.
Ibid.

BUSINESS

"If I had to state the formula for a young lawyer's success, and you would permit such an oversimplification, I would use the following symbols: W.Q. stands for work quotient; S.Q. for stamina quotient; I.Q. for intelligence quotient; S. for success. The formula is, I.Q. plus S.Q. plus W.Q., equals Success."
Louis Nizer, trial attorney, Esquire, January 1955.

" 'A giant business that's growing all the time' is the way a spokesman for Union News Company describes its coffee-break catering; it now serves ten thousand to twelve thousand people a day. Far bigger, however, is Schrafft's, which started five years ago with a single coffee-break client. Today it serves 'close to five hundred' companies. Each day Schrafft's waitresses dole out three thousand gallons of coffee, plus uncounted oceans of tea, milk and soft drinks, not to mention food. About one thousand Schrafft employes are involved in the operation."
Wall Street Journal, January 25, 1955, reports on a new development in American business—"The Coffee Break: Workers' Pause to Sip Attains New Magnitude, Brews Many Problems. . . . Some Employers Note Higher Productivity; Others Cite Losses Up to Forty-five Minutes."

"Men get their pictures on money but women get their hands on it."
Mrs. Ruth Sherrill, vice-president of the First National Bank of Memphis, Tennessee, commenting on a report that women spend eighty-five cents of every consumer dollar; news summaries of January 26, 1955.

"What happens at our house to that other fifteen cents?"
Wall Street Journal, commenting editorially two days later on Mrs. Sherrill's statement (see above).

"I never speculate unless the elements of speculation have been removed, and I turn the wheels, or the man who turns them is on my payroll."
Serge Rubinstein's statement to a government investigator studying Rubinstein's international financial holdings; news reports, January 28, 1955, recalling his career after his murder.

"We are pooling our resources so we can take on the task of organizing the great mass of unorganized workers in America and build a greater industrial democracy. It is our belief that a united labor movement will be able to devote the talent and strength of our trade unions to greater service to the people of the United States."
Walter Reuther, head of the Congress of Industrial Organizations (CIO), and George Meany, president of the American

Federation of Labor, announce the merger of their fifteen million members. This move marked the end of a twenty-year-old split in organized labor. Quoted in news reports February 10, 1955.

"In the next forty years we will accomplish so much more than in the past forty that people will wonder why we didn't do more in the first forty."

Thomas Watson, Jr., president of International Business Machines, news reports of February 15, 1955.

"The faults of advertising are only those common to all human institutions. If advertising speaks to a thousand in order to influence one, so does the church. And if it encourages people to live beyond their means, so does matrimony. Good times, bad times, there will always be advertising. In good times, people want to advertise; in bad times, they have to."

Bruce Barton, chairman of the board of Batten, Barton, Durstine & Osborne, New York advertising agency; Town & Country, Madison Avenue issue, February 1955.

"Advertising did not invent the products or services which called forth jobs, nor inspire the pioneering courage that built factories and machinery to produce them. What advertising did was to stimulate ambition and desire—the craving to possess, which is the strongest incentive to produce. To satisfy this craving the little factory was impelled to turn itself into a growing factory; and then, by the pressure of mass demand, into many factories. Mass production made possible mass economies, reflected in declining prices, until the product that began as the luxury of the rich became the possession of every family that was willing to work."

Bruce Barton, "Advertising: Its Contribution to the American Way of Life," Reader's Digest, April 1955 (the first issue of the Digest to carry advertisements); reprinted by permission.

"In my long and cheerful years of marriage my wife superintended the remodeling and redecorating of five houses and one apartment. In every case she sat down in advance with the architect, and brought to the conference a huge bundle of clippings which she had garnered from the magazines devoted to home building and decoration. The so-called women's magazines were her inspiration for our better living, better eating, better health and better parenthood. No money estimate can ever measure the contribution of their influence on the American way of life."

Bruce Barton. Ibid.

". . . The trade and professional publications are the post-graduate universities of the doctor, the lawyer, as well as the engineer, the executive and the plumber. . . ."

Bruce Barton. Ibid.

"Advertising is of the very essence of democracy. An election goes on every minute of the business day across the counters of hundreds of thousands of stores and shops where the customers state their preferences and determine which manufacturer and which product shall be the leader today, and which shall lead tomorrow."

Bruce Barton. Ibid.

"Let's try to enjoy our good fortune and reject once and for all time the idea that planned scarcity is the way to prosperity."

Henry Ford II, addressing a meeting of publishers and editors in New York, news reports, April 29, 1955.

"I am impatient with the slavish and stereotyped thinking which has led some businessmen to consider security a bad word and to brand all concern for human and social progress as Communism or creeping socialism. I'm all for chasing the sacred cows out of business."

Henry Ford II answers charges that he "sold out to labor," News-week, June 20, 1955.

"The establishment of this federation through the merger of the American Federation of Labor and the Congress of Industrial Organizations is an expression of the hopes and aspirations of the working people of America.

"We seek the fulfillment of these hopes and aspirations through democratic processes within the framework of our constitutional government and consistent with our institutions and traditions.

"At the collective bargaining table, in the community, in the exercise of the rights and responsibilities of citizenship, we shall responsibly serve the interests of all the American people.

"We pledge ourselves to the more effective organization of working men and women; to the securing to them of full recognition and enjoyment of the rights to which they are justly entitled; to the achievement of ever higher standards of living and working conditions; to the attainment of security for all the people; to the enjoyment of the leisure which their skills make possible; and to the strengthening and extension of our way of life and the fundamental freedoms which are the basis of our democratic society.

"We shall combat resolutely the forces which seek to undermine the democratic institutions of our nation and to enslave the human soul. We shall strive always to win full respect for the dignity of the human individual whom our unions serve.

"Grateful for the fine traditions of our past, confident of meeting the challenge of the future, we proclaim this constitution."

Preamble of constitution for a combined American Federation of Labor and Congress of Industrial Organizations, formulated for the consolidation of the AF of L and the CIO, Washington, May 2, 1955.

"It isn't as if the Pittsburgh Pirates won a ball game."

Roger Blough, refusing to celebrate his appointment as chairman of the board of U. S. Steel, news summaries, May 4, 1955.

"Pink represents a mood of sentimentality, good times and luxury."

A Chicago firm reports on the popularity of pink in clothes and decorating in America during the mid-1950s, Time, May 9, 1955.

". . . Most executives are, by nature, healthy, strong, and adaptable. But even for the neurotic executive—as for everyone else—work has great therapeutic value; it is generally his last refuge, and deterioration there marks the final collapse of the man; his marriage, his social life, and outside interests—all have suffered beforehand. The true influence of work in the crack-up of an executive comes down to this: a neurotic individual encounters in his work a special stress (or a series of stresses) that at some point unbearably intensifies the conflicts in his own personality; then he goes to pieces . . . though success can be the result of a strong neurotic drive, the neurosis will eventually make trouble for the individual."

Richard Austin Smith, "The Executive Crack-Up," Fortune, *May 1955, copyright 1955 Time, Inc.; reprinted by permission.*

"Practically all problems in the realm of judgment, in the realm of operating a business involving men and women, in the realm of government, whether executive, legislative or judicial, can be handled more efficiently by a man and wife, in our estimation. The American people, in our judgment, if they had sense, would elect a man president and a wife as vice-president."

Mr. and Mrs. Bruce Gould, in a statement to the Wall Street Journal, *June 17, 1955, on twenty years spent in joint editorship of the* Ladies' Home Journal.

"Beware of inherited wealth. The job of getting is better than spending. I have often marveled at the fact that so many large eastern businesses are headed by western boys. Is it because the son of the well-to-do eastern family is exposed to social temptations which sap his energies and dull his perceptions, thus causing him to be outrun in life's race despite his heritage of accomplishment and family connections? A debutante party is certainly not a fitting prelude to a busy day, nor is a night at the Stork Club. The western boy at work in New York, bolstered, perhaps, by a little quiet homework, keen and fresh each morning, has proved himself tough competition for the man who wears the club tie. This business of how a young man spends his evenings is a part of that thin area between success and failure. . . ."

Robert R. Young, chairman of the board of the New York Central Railroad, in an address to the graduating class of Culver Military Academy, Newsweek, *June 20, 1955.*

"After the first million, it doesn't matter. You can only eat three meals a day—I tried eating four and I got sick. You can't sleep in more than one bed a night. Maybe I have twenty suits, but I can only wear one at a time, and I can't use more than two shirts a day. Money comes easy to me—like breathing. I want to do something useful with it."

Joseph Hirshhorn, American multimillionaire in uranium, gold, and oil mining, comment on his collection of art, Time, July 25, 1955.

"The American executive in his office is a familiar figure; he is, typically, decisive, somewhat aloof, and generally regarded by his employees with a certain awe. In the life he leads outside his office, however, he is a much less familiar character; the occasional pictures painted of him by fiction writers tend to be romantic, or even lurid, and with the possible exception of John Marquand's heroes, the fictional executive is rarely a man you have met. Yet millions of Americans diligently aspire to the life of a top executive, coveting his opportunities for pleasure while, actually, they have only the faintest notion of what his life is really like or of what he does when he goes home."

Duncan Norton-Taylor, "How Top Executives Live," Fortune, July 1955, copyright 1955 by Time, Inc.; reprinted by permission.

"There are in the U.S. approximately 30,000 executives with incomes of $50,000.00 or more."

Fortune. *Ibid.*

"The successful American executive, for example, gets up early—about 7 A.M.—eats a large breakfast, and rushes to his office by train or auto. It is not unusual for him, after spending from 9 A.M. until 6 P.M. in his office, to hurry home, eat dinner, and crawl into bed with a briefcase full of homework. He is constantly pressed for time, and a great deal of the time he spends in his office is extraneous to his business. He gets himself involved in all kinds of community work, either because he wants to or because he figures he has to for the sake of public relations."

Fortune. *Ibid.*

"The business executive is by profession a decision maker. Uncertainty is his opponent. Overcoming it is his mission. Whether the outcome is

a consequence of luck or of wisdom, the moment of decision is without doubt the most creative and critical event in the life of the executive."
John McDonald, "How Businessmen Make Decisions," Fortune, August 1955, copyright 1955 by Time, Inc.; reprinted by permission.

"Whenever I think, I make a mistake."
Roger Stevens, New York real estate and theatre executive, quoted in "How Businessmen Make Decisions," Fortune, August 1955.

"One of the tragedies of this business is that these days the young geologist hesitates to go out and get his hands dirty. He wants to wear a white collar and sit behind a desk, make a down payment on a Buick and buy a house he can't afford. I try to tell him that if it's money he's interested in, prospecting is the most remunerative business in the world. You don't even need to be literate. But you can't find metals behind a desk."
Franc Renault Joubin, prospector and uranium executive of Blind River, Canada, Life, August 8, 1955.

"They came to scoff and stayed to pray."
Dale Carnegie, comment on early days of his Institute for Effective Speaking and Human Relations, founded in 1912, Newsweek, August 8, 1955.

"The ideas I stand for are not mine. I borrowed them from Socrates. I swiped them from Chesterfield. I stole them from Jesus. And I put them in a book. If you don't like their rules, whose would you use?"
Dale Carnegie, comment on his book, How to Win Friends and Influence People. *Ibid.*

"When I've had a rough day, before I go to sleep I ask myself if there's anything more I can do right now. If there isn't, I sleep sound."
L. L. Colbert, president, Chrysler Corporation, Newsweek, August 22, 1955.

"After all the meetings are over, the phones have stopped ringing and the vocalizing has died down, somebody finally has to get out an ad, often after hours. Somebody has to stare at a blank piece of paper. This is probably the very height of lonesomeness. Out of the recesses of his mind must come words which interest, words which persuade, words which inspire, words which sell. Magic words. I regard him as the man of the hour in our business today."

Lee Burnett, advertising executive, address to annual Eastern Conference, American Association of Advertising Agencies, news reports of October 19, 1955.

"This is the most important aviation development since Lindbergh's flight. In one fell swoop we've shrunken the earth."

Juan Trippe, president, Pan American World Airways, comment on placing 269-million-dollar order for forty-five jet transports, beginning of commercial aviation's venture into age of jet travel, news summaries of October 24, 1955.

"Well, yes. You could say we have independent means."

John D. Rockefeller III, reply to an Indianapolis newspaper reporter who asked, "Are you a multimillionaire?", news summaries of October 24, 1955.

"No girl in her right mind should deliberately set out to become a model."

John Robert Powers, This Week Magazine, November 20, 1955, copyright 1955, United Newspapers Magazine Corporation.

"We have gone completely overboard on security. Everything has to be secured, jobs, wages, hours—although the ultimate in security is jail, the slave labor camp and the salt mine."

Cola Parker, president, National Association of Manufacturers, address to the NAM's sixtieth annual Congress of American Industry, news reports of December 9, 1955.

WINSTON CHURCHILL

"They must sometimes have felt . . . like a shipwrecked sailor on a raft who had to burn up one of his planks every day to cook his dinner."
Sir Winston Churchill announces a new program of construction in Britain, sympathizes with bricklayers who work themselves out of a job as they complete a building, news reports of January 26, 1955.

"It doesn't matter so much to old people; they are going soon anyway, but I find it poignant to look at youth in all its activity and ardor and, most of all, to watch little children playing their merry games, and wonder what would lie before them if God wearied of mankind."
Churchill, address to Commons on the hydrogen bomb, news reports of March 2, 1955.

"Our renowned grain and shipping market was founded in a coffee house—with not too strict an interpretation of the word coffee. There is no need for you to be abashed at that. The Cabinet began as a dinner party and was continued at occasional dinner parties—business was not so pressing in those days—at which matters were discussed not only on the table but under the table."
Churchill, address at the laying of cornerstone for Baltic Exchange Building, London, news reports of March 3, 1955.

". . . It may be that we shall by a process of sublime irony have reached a stage in this story where safety will be the sturdy child of terror, and survival the twin brother of annihilation."
Churchill, comment on danger of hydrogen bomb to large nations as well as small ones. Ibid.

"All deterrents will improve and gain authority during the next ten years. By that time, the deterrent may well reach its acme and reap its final reward, [enabling] tormented generations to march forth serene and triumphant over the hideous epoch in which we have to dwell. Meanwhile, never flinch, never weary, never despair."

Churchill. Ibid.

"I have the honor of proposing a toast which I used to enjoy drinking during the years when I was a cavalry subaltern in the reign of Your Majesty's great-great-grandmother, Queen Victoria.

"Having served in office or in Parliament under the four sovereigns who have reigned since those days, I felt, with these credentials, that in asking our Majesty's gracious permission to propose a toast I should not be leading to the creation of a precedent which would often cause inconvenience.

"Madame, I should like to express the deep and lively sense of gratitude which we and all your people feel to you and to His Royal Highness, the Duke of Edinburgh, for all the help and inspiration we receive in our daily lives, and which spreads with ever-growing strength throughout the British realm and the Commonwealth and Empire.

"Never have the august duties which fall upon the British monarchy been discharged with more devotion than in the brilliant opening of Your Majesty's reign. We thank God for the gift He has bestowed upon us and vow ourselves anew to the sacred causes and wise and kindly way of life of which Your Majesty is the young, gleaming champion."

A toast to Queen Elizabeth II at dinner attended by the Queen at No. 10 Downing Street on eve of Sir Winston's resignation as Prime Minister, news reports of April 4 and 5, 1955.

London, April 5, 1955, by United Press:
"Iron entered the spirit of the British people when Winston Churchill became Prime Minister in this country's darkest hour—1940.

"Seldom since Shakespeare had an Englishman struck such fire from the language. Britons said Sir Winston mobilized the English language. Following are some of the words that brought tears of pride to the eyes of men throughout the English-speaking world. . . ."

United Press dispatch on retirement of Sir Winston Churchill as Prime Minister, introduction to quotation of his best-known statements; reprinted by permission.

"The twenty-eight-year-old Queen and the eighty-year-old statesman each knew what was in the other's mind when they met today. He knew in advance what she would offer and she knew what his reply would be. But Elizabeth and Sir Winston, both exemplars of tradition in a tradition-loving land, observed the forms and courtesies due between the sovereign and a retiring counselor and friend."

Benjamin Welles of The New York Times, *report from London on Churchill's last call at Buckingham Palace as Prime Minister; he tendered his resignation and declined a dukedom in order to remain in the House of Commons;* The New York Times, *April 6, 1955.*

Churchill's best-known statements, recalled on the occasion of his retirement as Prime Minister:

Account of being struck by a taxicab on Fifth Avenue, New York, in 1932 (dictated from his sickbed a few days later):

"There was one moment—I cannot measure it in time—of a world aglare, of a man aghast. I certainly thought quickly enough to achieve the idea, 'I am going to be run down and probably killed.' Then came the blow.

"I felt it in my forehead and across the thighs. But besides the blow there was an impact, a shock, a concussion indescribably violent. It blotted out everything except thought.

"A friend of mine of mathematical predilections has been kind enough to calculate the stresses involved in the collision.

"The car weighed some 2400 pounds. With my evening coat on I could not have weighed much less than two hundred pounds. Taking the rate of the car at thirty miles an hour—I think a moderate estimate—I had actually to absorb in my body six thousand footpounds.

"It was the equivalent of falling thirty feet into a pavement.

"The energy absorbed, though not, of course, the application of destructive force, was the equivalent of stopping ten pounds of buckshot dropped six hundred feet, or two charges of buckshot at point-blank range.

"I do not understand why I was not broken like an eggshell or squashed like a gooseberry.

"I certainly must be very tough, or very lucky, or both."

New York Herald Tribune, *and other news reports, April 6, 1955.*

"I would say to the House, as I have said to those who have joined this government: I have nothing to offer but blood, toil, tears and sweat. You ask what is our policy? I will say it is to wage war—by sea, land and air, with all our might and with all the strength that God can give us; to wage war against a monstrous tyranny never surpassed in the dark lamentable catalogue of human crimes. That is our policy."
Churchill, May 13, 1940. Ibid.

"After this battle for France abates its force there will come a battle for our island; for all that Britain is, and all that Britain means. That will be the struggle. In that supreme emergency we shall not hesitate to take every step, even the most drastic, to call forth from our people the last ounce and the last inch of effort of which they are capable. The interests of property and the hours of labor are nothing compared with the struggle for life and honor, for life and freedom to which we have vowed ourselves."
Churchill, May 19, 1940. Ibid.

"Even though large tracts of Europe and many old and famous states have fallen or may fall into the grip of the Gestapo and all the odious apparatus of the Nazi rule, we shall not flag or fail. We shall go on to the end. We shall fight in France, we shall fight on the seas and oceans, we shall fight with growing confidence and growing strength in the air. We shall fight on the beaches, we shall fight on the landing grounds, we shall fight in the fields and in the streets, we shall fight in the hills. We shall never surrender."
Churchill, June 4, 1940. Ibid.

"The whole fury and might of the enemy must very soon be turned on us. Hitler knows that he will have to break us in this island or lose the war. If we can stand up to him all Europe may be free, and the life of the world may move forward into broad sunlit uplands; but if we fail, then the whole world, including the United States, and all that we have known and cared for will sink into the abyss of a new dark age, made more sinister and perhaps more prolonged by the lights of a perverted science. Let us therefore address ourselves to our duty and so bear our-

selves that if the British Commonwealth and Empire last for a thousand years men will still say: 'This was their finest hour!' "
Churchill, June 18, 1940. Ibid.

"And now it has come to us to stand alone in the breach and face the worst that the tyrants' might and enmity can do. Bearing ourselves humbly before God, but conscious that we serve an unfolding purpose, we are ready to defend our native land against the invasion by which it is threatened. We are fighting by ourselves alone. But we are not fighting for ourselves alone. Here in this strong city of refuge, which enshrines the title deeds of human progress, and is of deep consequence to Christian civilization; here, girt about by the seas and oceans where the Navy reigns, shielded from above by the prowess and devotion of our airmen, we await undismayed the impending assault. Perhaps it will come tonight. Perhaps it will come next week. Perhaps it will never come. We must show ourselves equally capable of meeting a sudden, violent shock, or, what is perhaps a harder test, a prolonged vigil. But be the ordeal sharp or long, or both, we shall seek no terms, we shall ask no parley. Should the invader come, there will be no placid lying down of the people in submission. We shall defend every village, every town and every city. The vast mass of London itself, fought street by street, could easily devour an entire hostile army, and we would rather see London laid in ruins and ashes than that it should be tamely and abjectly enslaved."
Churchill, July 14, 1940. Ibid.

"The gratitude of every home in our island, in our Empire and indeed throughout the world, except in the abodes of the guilty, goes out to the British airmen, who, undaunted by odds, unwearied in their constant challenge and mortal danger, are turning the tide of world war by their prowess and their devotion. Never in the field of human conflict was so much owed by so many to so few."
Churchill, Autumn 1940. Ibid.

"Our qualities and deeds must burn and glow through the gloom of Europe until they become the veritable beacon of its salvation."
Churchill, October 8, 1940. Ibid.

"This bloodthirsty guttersnipe must launch his mechanical armies upon new fields of slaughter, pillage and devastation. . . . Any man or state who fights against Nazidom will have our aid. Any man or state who marches with Hitler is our foe."

Churchill, June 1941. Ibid.

"Give us the tools and we will finish the job."

Churchill, February 9, 1941. Ibid.

"This whipped jackal, Mussolini, who to save his own skin has made of Italy a vassal state of Hitler's empire, is frisking up by the side of the German tiger. . . . I am sure there are a great many millions who will find a new object in life if in making sure when we come to the final reckoning this absurd impostor will be abandoned to public justice and universal scorn."

Churchill, 1940. Ibid.

"When we think of the insane ambition and insatiable appetite which have caused this vast and melancholy extension of the war we can only feel that Hitler's madness has affected the Japanese mind. . . . We have at least four-fifths of the population of the globe upon our side. We are responsible for their safety and for their future. In the past we have had a light which flickered, in the present we have a light which flames, and in the future there will be a light which shines over all the land and sea."

Churchill, December 1941. Ibid.

"Beware, I say, time may be short. A shadow has fallen upon the scene so lately lighted by Allied victory. From Stettin in the Baltic to Trieste in the Adriatic, an Iron Curtain has descended across the continent. Behind that line lie all the capitals of the ancient states of central and eastern Europe. These are somber facts. . . . But we should be most unwise not to face them squarely while time remains. I do not believe that Soviet Russia desires war. What they desire is the fruits of war and the indefinite expansion of their power and doctrine."

Churchill, March 5, 1946. Ibid.

"That's only fair. We had them the last time."
Churchill, remark to Joachim von Ribbentrop, German ambassador to Great Britain, when von Ribbentrop said Italy would surely join Germany in World War II. Ibid.

"Just before dawn I awoke suddenly with a sharp stab of almost physical pain. A hitherto unconscious conviction that we were beaten broke forth and dominated my mind."
Churchill, comment on the eve of his defeat by Clement Attlee, Labor party leader, July 5, 1945. Ibid.

"Is it really true that nobody, but nobody, undersells Gimbels?"
Churchill, inquiry about a famous American advertising slogan. Ibid.

"I married and lived happily ever after . . . with a being incapable of an ignoble thought."
Winston Churchill, comment on his forty-fifth wedding anniversary in 1953. Ibid.

"Once upon a time all the animals in the Zoo decided that they would disarm, and they arranged to have a conference to arrange the matter. So the Rhinoceros said when he opened the proceedings that the use of teeth was barbarous and horrible and ought to be strictly prohibited by general consent. Horns, which were mainly defensive weapons, would, of course, have to be allowed. The Buffalo, the Stag, the Porcupine, and even the little Hedgehog all said they would vote with the Rhino, but the Lion and the Tiger took a different view. They defended teeth and even claws, which they described as honorable weapons of immemorial antiquity. The Panther, the Leopard, the Puma, and the whole tribe of small cats all supported the Lion and the Tiger. Then the Bear spoke. He proposed that both teeth and horns should be banned and never used again for fighting by any animal. It would be quite enough if animals were allowed to give each other a good hug when they quarreled. No one could object to that. It was so fraternal, and that would be a great step towards peace. However, all the other animals were very offended with the Bear, and the Turkey fell into a perfect panic. The discussion got so hot and angry, and all those animals began thinking so much about horns and teeth and hugging when they argued about the peaceful intentions that had brought them together that they began to look at one another in a very nasty way. Luckily the keepers were able to calm them down and persuaded them to go back quietly to their cages, and they began to feel quite friendly with one another again."

Churchill, fable published in 1928, reprinted at time of Big Four Conference, Geneva, July 1955, from The Second World War, *by Winston Churchill, used by permission of the publisher, Houghton Mifflin Company.*

"This conference should not be overhung by a ponderous or rigid agenda or led into mazes of technical details, zealously contested by hordes of experts and officials drawn up in a vast cumbrous array."

Sir Winston Churchill, comment on what the "summit conference" should not be, recalled at time of the conference in Geneva, news reports of July 20, 1955.

CRIME

"The thought that I had cut off an innocent young life and the knowledge of the grief I had caused both his family and mine has been present in my consciousness every day of every year for the past quarter century. It is not, gentlemen, an easy thought to live with. At any time in the past twenty-five years I would have welcomed joyously the chance to take Bobby Franks' place—to lay down my life if it would restore his."

Nathan Leopold, letter to the Illinois State Parole Board seeking release from a life sentence for the murder of a Chicago boy, Bobby Franks. The appeal was rejected, news reports of March 18, 1955.

"The hardest thing about being in prison is just doing time. Being idle, doing nothing constructive, nothing that means anything. Very shortly I realized I had to make up my mind whether to do this life sentence or not—whether it is worth going through what you have to go through in order to have a bare existence, or whether it's better to take a parole off ten-gallery (suicide). I thought it through very carefully. The reasons on both sides were so strong I couldn't reach a sound decision because I didn't have enough data. So I decided to put the decision off for six months to nine months. There was a second question: If I did decide to do my time, how would I do it? What could I do toward trying to overcome my environment? About all you could do was read and study or lie on the bed and count the cracks in the wall."

Nathan Leopold, "Murder on His Conscience," by John Bartlow Martin, The Saturday Evening Post (published as Leopold neared his thirtieth anniversary in prison). © *1955, The Curtis Publishing Company; reprinted by permission of Harold Ober Associates.*

"It was just one long gob of nothing. Complete monotony. The same thing every day. Weaving fiber chair bottoms. Drudgery. No hope, reward or advancement. Spiritually it was as bleak and empty as it is possible to imagine."

Nathan Leopold, on his first year in prison. Ibid.

"The first tub in a year, boy did that water feel wonderful. Then they gave me a real bath towel, and they took me down to a real bed with two white sheets, not one yellowish one, and I even had a nightgown. I'll never forget it. The sun was just coming up and I could hear larks and robins. I could smell grass and clover. For a moment I wasn't sure I hadn't died."

Nathan Leopold, comment on being taken to the prison hospital during first year of his sentence. Ibid.

"Ever since I can remember, I have heard how bright I was."

Leopold, comment on his IQ of 206 to 210. Ibid.

"Banks are an almost irresistible attraction for that element of our society which seeks unearned money."

J. Edgar Hoover, chief of the Federal Bureau of Investigation, comment in a warning sent to bankers, news reports of April 7, 1955.

"We are a fact-gathering organization only. We don't clear anybody. We don't condemn anybody. Just the minute the FBI begins making recommendations on what should be done with its information, it becomes a Gestapo."
J. Edgar Hoover. Look, *June 14, 1956.*

"Instead of shooting a man, you finesse him."
Patrolman Arthur Fegan, crack marksman of New York City police force, marks twenty-four years of duty without once shooting a man, news reports of June 26, 1955.

"I usually start with a repulsive character and go on from there."
Chester Gould, creator of the Dick Tracy comic strip, interview in New York Daily News, Sunday Magazine, *December 18, 1955.*

DEFINITIONS

"The spirit of liberty is the spirit which is not too sure that it is right; the spirit which seeks to understand the minds of other men and women; the spirit which weighs their interests alongside its own without bias; the spirit of Him who, nearly two thousand years ago, taught mankind that lesson it has never learned, but has never quite forgotten—that there may be a Kingdom where the least shall be heard and considered side by side with the greatest."
Judge Learned Hand, news reports of January 4, 1955.

"An economist is an unemployed financier with a Phi Beta Kappa key on one end of his watch chain and no watch on the other."
Senator Alben Barkley, news reports of January 7, 1955.

"Egotism is the anesthetic that dulls the pain of stupidity."
Frank Leahy, former Notre Dame football coach, Look, *January 10, 1955.*

"An optimist is a person who sees a green light everywhere, while the pessimist sees only the red stop light. . . . But the truly wise person is color-blind."
Dr. Albert Schweitzer, news summaries of January 14, 1955.

"Dialogue is just lyrics that don't rhyme."
Nat "King" Cole, news summaries of January 15, 1955.

"Sir James Barrie once said that charm is a sort of bloom on a woman, but it seems to me that glamour is a sort of gloss on a woman, and every housewife knows you cannot create the bloom on a peach, but for a high gloss, it just takes elbow grease and will power."
Rhea Talley in a lecture on "Behind the Scenes in Glamour," quoted in news reports of January 15, 1955.

"Revenge is a dish that should be eaten cold."
King Victor Emmanuel II of Italy, words recalled by Time *in a report on an Italian Communist's trial, January 31, 1955.*

". . . There is a vast difference. A hobo is a vagabond, a foot-loose wanderer whose address is everywhere. But he will work to live, if necessary, and he makes a fetish of cleanliness. A bum is a forsaken man, a man without hope."
Roger Payne, Cambridge-educated writer known as "the world's most educated hobo," recalled in obituaries reporting his death, news reports of February 24, 1955.

"Texas . . . is a sitting duck for the hunter of humor."
Fred Allen, "Analysis of the Boffolo Texensis," The New York Times Magazine, *March 20, 1955.*

"Comets are the nearest thing to nothing that anything can be and still be something."
National Geographic Society, announcement of discovery of a comet visible only by telescope, March 31, 1955.

"Bohemians are people who sit on the floor and drink black coffee when all the while there are chairs and cream in the room."
Beatrice Lillie, news summaries of April 1, 1955.

"Bop is just Stravinsky played on an empty stomach."
Florian Zabach, violinist, news summaries of April 19, 1955.

"Science is like art. You have to work at it or you go stale fast."
Willard Frank Libby, nuclear scientist, member of U. S. Atomic Energy Commission, news summaries of May 2, 1955.

"Courage is fear that has said its prayers."
Karle Baker, quoted by Margaret Blair Johnstone, Better Homes and Gardens, *June 1955.*

"The Senior Prom is the point at which we learn how well we are doing thus far. A date means we are popular with at least one other person and therefore, we are potentially lovable. Reassured, we press on."
Julian Huxley, English biologist, "All About Love," Look, *July 12, 1955.*

"Glamour is what makes a man ask for your telephone number. But it also is what makes a woman ask for the name of your dressmaker."
Lilly Daché, Woman's Home Companion, *July 1955.*

". . . Adventure is something you seek for pleasure, or even for profit, like a gold rush or invading a country; for the illusion of being more alive than ordinarily, the thing you *will* to occur; but experience is what really happens to you in the long run; the truth that finally overtakes you."
Katherine Anne Porter, "Adventure in Living," Mademoiselle, *August 1955.*

" 'Queuemania' is an ailment that afflicts people with a compulsive urge to line up behind someone or something, even a lamp-post. . . . Usually it is used to describe disparagingly the alleged British inclination to line up in sheeplike fashion for any reason or no reason at all."

Thomas P. Ronan, British correspondent for The New York Times, The New York Times, *August 23, 1955.*

"Business is like riding a bicycle. Either you keep moving or you fall down."

John David Wright, president, Thompson Products, Inc., Cleveland, Ohio, Fortune, *September 1955.*

"Success is that old ABC—ability, breaks and courage."

Charles Luckman, manufacturing executive and architect, quoted by Mary Margaret McBride, New York Mirror, *September 19, 1955.*

"The ideal woman is one with whom a particular man has the fortune to be in love at a particular moment. The same conditions of time and place also determine the ideal man."

Clare Boothe Luce, U. S. ambassador to Italy, news summaries of September 27, 1955.

"Life is like a B-picture script. It is that corny. If I had my life story offered to me to film, I'd turn it down."

Kirk Douglas, motion picture actor, Look, *October 4, 1955.*

"A neurotic is the man who builds a castle in the air. A psychotic is the man who lives in it. And a psychiatrist is the man who collects the rent."

Lord Webb-Johnson, British surgeon, Look, *October 4, 1955.*

"A fox is a wolf who sends flowers."

Ruth Weston, actress, quoted by Leonard Lyons, New York Post, *November 8, 1955.*

"Tenterhooks are the upholstery of the anxious seat."
> *Robert Sherwood, playwright-author, quoted in obituaries reporting his death, news reports of November 15, 1955.*

"A jay is a bird of the crow family, which can be found in fields and meadows. A jaywalker, on the other hand, is a bird of the Schmoe family who can be found in traffic jams and morgues."
> *Phyllis Battelle, "Assignment: America,"* New York Journal-American, *November 28, 1955.*

"A kiss can be a comma, a question mark or an exclamation point. That's basic spelling that every woman ought to know."
> *Mistinguette, French vaudeville star,* Theatre Arts, *December 1955.*

"An atheist is a man who has no invisible means of support."
> *Bishop Fulton Sheen,* Look, *December 14, 1955.*

"Voting is like the waves on the beach. They come higher and higher and then there's one that doesn't come as high—but then it is usually followed by one that comes up even higher still."
> *Former British Prime Minister Clement Attlee, comment after the Labor party, for the first time in twenty-four years, had failed to add to its popular vote in an election, news summaries of December 31, 1955.*

"Platonic love is love from the neck up."
> *Thyra Samter Winslow, novelist, used on radio program and in interview with James Simpson.*

> "Four is too big for his breeches,
> Knows infinitely more than his mother,
> Four is a matinee idol
> To Two-and-a-Half, his brother.
> Four is a lyric composer,
> Raconteur extraordinaire,
> Four gets away with murder,

Out of line, and into hair.
Where Four is, there dirt is also,
And nails and lengths of twine,
Four is Mr. Fix-it
And all of his tools are mine.
Four barges into everything
(Hearts, too) without a knock.
Four will be five on the twelfth of July,
And I wish I could stop the clock."
Elise Gibbs, poem entitled, "Four," copyright 1955, the Curtis Publishing Company, reprinted by permission.

EDUCATION

"If a man has good manners and is not afraid of other people, he will get by—even if he is stupid."
Sir David Eccles, Britain's Minister of Education, Look, January 10, 1955.

"After such a long dearth, lovers of the humanities may be excused if their hearts leap up inordinately at the sight of such slight rainbows."
Nathan Pusey, president of Harvard University, reporting a rise of interest and enrollment in the humanities—languages, literature, philosophy, music, and fine arts. Students following these courses had decreased for twenty-five years as compared to enrollment in the natural and social sciences, news reports of January 25, 1955.

"The American male at the peak of his physical powers and appetites, driving a hundred and sixty big white horses across the scenes of an increasingly open society, with week end money in his pocket and with little prior exposure to trouble and tragedy, personifies 'an accident going out to happen.' He is not always a college undergraduate, and not all undergraduates are trouble-prone, but I am sure that any close observer

144

of the campus will agree that there is no more vulnerable human combination than an undergraduate."

John Sloan Dickey, president, Dartmouth College, "Conscience and the Undergraduate," Atlantic Monthly, April 1955, reprinted by permission.

"The college undergraduate is a lot of things—many of them as familiar, predictable, and responsible as the bounce of a basketball, and others as startling (and occasionally as disastrous) as the bounce of a football."

John Sloan Dickey. Ibid.

"The focus of that total experience which we call 'going to college' is the day-to-day relationship between the undergraduate as a person and the college as an institutional embodiment of other people's purposes."

John Sloan Dickey. Ibid.

"We're trying to show that we're not a little bit of England in America, but a place for Americans to gain a better perspective on their own history. All the fundamental concepts which make up the kind of people we are today had their modern conception in the Tudor and Stuart periods. For us, that's the milk in the coconut."

Louis Booker Wright, director of Folger Shakespeare Library, Washington, news summaries of May 9, 1955.

"The drums of Africa still beat in my heart. They will not let me rest while there is a single Negro boy or girl without a chance to prove his worth."

Mrs. Mary McLeod Bethune, head of Bethune-Cookman College and other movements to improve Negro education, quoted in obituaries reporting her death, at the age of seventy-nine, news reports of May 19, 1955.

"A distinguished member since 1948 of the 'most exclusive gentlemen's club in the world,' Senator Smith reaffirms the growing realization, wisely recognized by her astute constituents, that ability and proven performance, rather than sex, provide the reasonable standards for political selection."

> *Columbia University citation accompanying the award of an honorary Doctorate of Letters to Senator Margaret Chase Smith of Maine, news reports of June 2, 1955.*

"Discoverer of the vaccine for the prevention of poliomyelitis, that scourge which has caused dread in the hearts of every family, not only in America, but throughout the world; his is a name that will go down in history and will be spoken amongst men in words of wonder and gratitude."

> *Columbia University citation accompanying the award of an honorary degree of Doctor of Science to Jonas Edward Salk. Ibid.*

"Physician extraordinary to the body politic, skilled in diagnosis, bold in prognosis, forthright in prescription, buoyant of bedside manner and articulate in professional discourse; a scholarly statesman who, like Demosthenes of old in an age not dissimilar to our own, speaks eloquently of the noble purpose of democracy and the urgency of unity in the great cause of peace."

> *Columbia University citation accompanying the award of an honorary Doctorate of Letters to Adlai Stevenson. Ibid.*

"While I am not in favor of maladjustment, I view this cultivation of neutrality, this breeding of mental neuters, this hostility to eccentricity and controversity with grave misgiving. One looks back with dismay at the possibility of a Shakespeare perfectly adjusted to bourgeois life in Stratford, a Wesley contentedly administering a country parish, George Washington going to London to receive a barony from George III, or Abraham Lincoln prospering in Springfield with nary a concern for the preservation of the crumbling Union."

> *Adlai Stevenson, commencement address at Smith College, news reports of June 7, 1955.*

"Post quinquaginta annos amicitiae mutuae, alumni Universitatis Yalensis hic in Novo Portu congregati classi simili Harvardensi salutem plurimam dicimus."
Telegram sent by Yale Class of 1905, celebrating its fiftieth anniversary, to reunion class of 1905 at Harvard. Translation:
"After fifty years of mutual friendship, we alumni of Yale University assembled here in New Haven express affectionate greetings to the corresponding class of Harvard."
News summaries of June 15, 1955.

"Please crush a tiny leaf, then smell it."
Braille lettering on cards given to blind visitors to Brooklyn Botanic Gardens, news summaries of June 27, 1955.

"Never get up with the lark. Get up only for a lark."
Lord Boyd-Orr, Nobel Prize winner and chancellor of Edinburgh University, reply when asked about his spryness at the age of seventy-five, quoted by Leonard Lyons, Boston Herald, July 1, 1955.

"Too often people think our purpose is to educate cheaply, when rather it is to release the potentialities of young people for the good of the country. Perhaps the 'Berea idea' can best be described as educational implementation of values that support belief in the perfectability of man. That is why we believe at this century mark that Berea has a meaning for international problems besetting the common humanity."
Dr. Francis Hutchins, president of Berea College, opening the centennial celebration of the Kentucky institution noted for educational pioneering, news summaries of July 11, 1955.

"The scramble to get into college is going to be so terrible in the next few years that students are going to put up with almost anything, even an education."
Barnaby C. Keeney, president, Brown University, Time, August 29, 1955.

"It is true that the academic body has been in serious danger of losing its independence. The reason is that nobody can understand why it should have it. And the reason why nobody can understand this is that the colleges and universities of this country have, in their desire for popularity and money, gladly responded to every pressure and every demand. They have insisted on their dependence; they have become folk institutions, reflecting the whims, no matter how frivolous or temporary, of those whose support they hope to gain. . . ."

Dr. Robert Hutchins, former president of the University of Chicago and head of foundation known as The Fund for the Republic, address to American College of Hospital Administrators, Atlantic City, N.J.; news reports of September 20, 1955.

"Most foundations, unlike the Fund for the Republic, have very general purposes, such as the welfare of mankind. The decision as to what expenditures will promote the real welfare of mankind is so difficult, it involves such a tremendous intellectual effort, which at best can result only in a guess, that a natural desire is to give nearly everybody something for nearly everything in the hope that some interesting entries will emerge for the annual report."

Dr. Robert Hutchins. Ibid.

"Most suburban schools in America are incredibly good, compared to any sort of school in the past. . . . The people seem to vacillate between complacency at these gains and exaggerated horror at weaknesses which have not yet been overcome."

Sloan Wilson, executive of White House Conference on Education, news summaries of September 26, 1955.

"I was well beaten myself, and I am the better for it."

Field Marshal Viscount Montgomery, "Education for Leadership," in a lecture given at Teachers College, Columbia University, says that corporal punishment in schools will help end juvenile delinquency, news reports of November 8, 1955.

"Teaching is not a lost art, but the regard for it is a lost tradition."

Jacques Barzun, dean, Graduate School, Columbia University, Newsweek, *December 5, 1955.*

"Although in recent years not more than one boy in one hundred has been educated in the private schools of the United States, those schools have . . . educated approximately as many leaders as all the public schools combined."

Arthur Traxler, executive director, Educational Records Bureau, news reports of December 31, 1955.

AMERICAN GOVERNMENT

"Not Chiang Kai-shek, not Chinese Nationalist officials, no admiral and no officer of the line will decide how we shall protect Formosa. It will be a personal decision of the President of the United States. I believe the President of the United States is a good man, dedicated to a peaceful world. I believe what he says."

Senator Walter George of Georgia, one-minute statement on the floor of the Senate, which helped prepare way for almost unanimous approval of President Eisenhower's special message on Formosa, news reports of January 25, 1955.

". . . Old reformers never die. They get thrown out."

Herbert Hoover, comment on Hoover Commission for the study of government, address to Silver Quill Award Dinner of National Business Publications, news reports of January 30, 1955.

"We have recently completed the first part of a report on paper work in the government. This does not sound like much. You would understand it better if it were called 'The Birth Control of Federal Documents.'"

Herbert Hoover. Ibid.

"Our recommended methods of saving 250 million dollars is perhaps peanuts as government expenditures go these days."

Herbert Hoover. Ibid.

"One lasted thirty-six years and lost money nearly every year."

Herbert Hoover, citing an example of "extraordinary longevity" of a government bureau, news reports of May 20, 1955.

"At the Washington level, the use of water is more a political, ideological and emotional problem than it is an engineering problem—I suggest that the urgent need for development of our resources requires more cement and less ideology and less emotion."

Herbert Hoover, defending Hoover Commission report on water resources and power, news reports of June 30, 1955.

"I do not see any way of realizing our hopes about world organization in five or six days. Even the Almighty took seven."

Winston Churchill, message to President Roosevelt prior to Yalta Conference, quoted in Yalta Papers made public by U. S. State Department in March 1955.

"No more let us falter. From Malta to Yalta. Let nobody alter."

Winston Churchill, message to President Roosevelt on completion of plans for Malta meeting prior to Yalta Conference. Ibid.

"Churchill protested: 'We must consider the phantom of a starving Germany, and who is going to pay for that . . . ? If you wish a horse to pull a wagon you will at least have to give it fodder.' Retorted Stalin: 'Care should be taken to see that the horse does not turn around and kick you.'"

State Department Report. Ibid.

"He [Stalin] said the Germans were savages, and seemed to hate with a sadistic hatred the creative work of human beings. The President agreed. . . ."

State Department Report. Ibid.

"The Russians have given in so much at this conference that I don't think we should let them down. Let the British disagree if they want to."

Harry Hopkins, note given to President Roosevelt during Yalta Conference. Ibid.

"I have three kings waiting for me in the Near East."

President Roosevelt, comment on his impatience to leave Yalta. Ibid.

"I think that the end of this war may well prove to be more disappointing than was the last."

Winston Churchill, cable to Franklin Roosevelt near the end of World War II. Ibid.

"Every person high in public life proposes a toast a little sweeter than the preceding one on Soviet-British-American friendship. It is amazing how those toasts go down past the tongues in the cheeks."

Major General John Deane, head of U. S. military mission to Moscow from 1943 to 1945, writing to Secretary of War Henry Stimson regarding diplomatic life in Moscow prior to Yalta Conference. Ibid.

"On Stalin's night to play host at dinner, 'The atmosphere,' says the record, 'was most cordial and forty-five toasts in all were drunk.' Under sparkling chandeliers at Yusupovsky Palace sat the men casually engaged in reshaping the globe. Marshal Stalin, the cobbler's son who was on the way to inheriting a quarter of the earth, proposed a toast to the Prime Minister of Great Britain: 'The bravest governmental figure in the world . . . fighting friend, and a brave man.' Winston Churchill, the pink-cheeked giant of Western statesmen, who was about to be ousted from power, raised a glass to Marshal Stalin, who, 'in peace no less than in war, will continue to lead his people from success to success.' Stalin drank to the health of the President of the U.S., 'the chief forger of the instruments [for] mobilization of the world against Hitler.' Franklin Delano Roosevelt, gentleman by birth and democrat by career, who was soon to die, offered his toast, to 'give every man, woman, and child on this earth the possibility of security and well-being.' "

"Unguarded Moments," report on toasts at Yalta Conference, reprinted from Time, March 28, 1955, copyright 1955, Time, Inc.

"I tell her that when she goes to bed, she should just say her prayers, tell everybody to go to hell and then go to sleep."

Douglas McKay, Secretary of the Interior, advice to his wife on how to live with criticism, Reader's Digest, May 1955.

"History teaches us that previous experience of great powers negotiating in the absence of very small allies does not reflect great credit upon the large nations and has been disastrous to the small ones."

Senator William Knowland of California, The New York Times, May 12, 1955.

"The road to appeasement is not the road to peace, only surrender on the installment plan."

Senator William Knowland, addressing the U. S. Conference of Mayors, news reports of May 21, 1955.

"Good man."

Franklin D. Roosevelt, message to British Minister Neville Chamberlain on day before Munich Conference, September 28, 1939; the two-word secret message was a part of collection of diplomatic papers made public by the State Department, news reports of May 15, 1955.

"It's futile to talk too much about the past—something like trying to make birth control retroactive."

Charles E. Wilson, Secretary of Defense, news summaries of May 22, 1955.

"I believe it's possible to put these fellows on their honor. I've found most of them trustworthy and they pay their bills a hell of a lot better than some of their critics. There have been prostitutes since the days of Christ. Christ couldn't prevent it so why should I try?"

George Roy Clough, mayor-elect of Galveston, Texas, announcement of plans to put gambling and prostitution on "honor code" of conduct in Galveston, news summaries of May 23, 1955.

"That's one wrong impression I can correct for you right away. I have been a bricklayer and housepainter. I think I had just as much connection with the working class as you have. I'm a country boy."

James Riddleberger, U. S. ambassador to Russia, reply to Soviet Communist party chief Nikita Khrushchev who had told him,

"You are an American ambassador. You have no connection with the working class." News reports of May 29, 1955.

"Our people have always been endowed with a sense of mission in the world. They have believed that it was their duty to help men everywhere to get the opportunity to be and do what God designed."
John Foster Dulles, Secretary of State, baccalaureate address at Indiana University, news reports of June 13, 1955.

"The task of statesmanlike diplomacy is to realize to the full the opportunities while avoiding the hazards."
John Foster Dulles, report to the American people on Geneva conference, news reports of July 27, 1955.

"War is an awful thing. God grant that we have seen the last of it. But war in this case made the people of our two countries know each other as never before."
John Foster Dulles, Secretary of State, toast to Japanese Foreign Minister Mamoru Shigemitsu, news summaries of September 3, 1955.

"Indeed, the government is, among other things, the largest electric-power producer in the country, the largest insurer, the largest lender and the largest borrower, the largest landlord and the largest tenant, the largest holder of grazing land and the largest holder of timberland, the largest owner of grain, the largest warehouse operator, the largest shipowner and the largest truck-fleet operator. For a nation which is the citadel and the world's principal exponent of private enterprise and individual initiative, this is a rather amazing list."
Rowland Hughes, U. S. Budget Director, Collier's, July 8, 1955.

"Today, we stand on one of the crests of our upward climb. The struggle for recognition has given way to success. The Air Force has come of age."
Harold Talbott, Secretary of the Air Force, comment on dedication of Air Force Academy, news reports of July 12, 1955.

"What?—The best man in the Cabinet?"

> *Treasury Secretary George Humphrey, comment when told by President Eisenhower that Oveta Culp Hobby would soon submit her resignation as Secretary of Health, Education, and Welfare, news reports of July 14, 1955.*

"It's an Army that's tried and trusted, reliable and ready and shall ever be. In land battles, that is the force on which we will depend."

> *Wilbur Brucker, comment on being sworn in as Secretary of the Army, news reports of July 22, 1955.*

" 'I received them coldly and did not ask them to sit down,' Mr. Hull wrote in his memoirs. After having read the Japanese note, he said to the Japanese who stood expressionless before him: 'In all my fifty years of public service I have never seen a document that was more crowded . . . with falsehoods and distortions on a scale so huge that I never imagined until today that any government on this planet was capable of uttering them.' [Then, Mr. Hull noted:] 'Nomura seemed about to say something. His face was impassive, but I felt he was under great emotional strain. I stopped him with a motion of my hand. I nodded toward the door. . . .' "

> *Cordell Hull, Secretary of State from 1933 to 1944, comment on receiving the two Japanese envoys, Kichisaburo Nomura and Saburo Kurusu, at the hour that Pearl Harbor was being bombed; remark recalled in obituaries reporting the death of Mr. Hull, news reports of July 24, 1955.*

"If I had my way, I would take Hitler, Mussolini and Tojo and the archaccomplices and bring them before a drumhead court-martial. And at sunrise on the following day there would occur a historic incident."

> *Cordell Hull, remark to Soviet officials during meeting in Moscow, October, 1943. Ibid.*

"This department has got a great future. It is only starting."

> *Mrs. Oveta Culp Hobby, prediction made a few days before leaving her post as the first secretary of the new department of Health, Education and Welfare, news reports of July 28, 1955.*

"It's all so solemn. Somebody will get up and say: 'I thank the gentleman for his contribution,' when all the guy did was belch or gargle. Now I'm all for back-scratching, but I'd like to see a wink once in a while."

> *Representative James Tumulty, of New Jersey, comment after his first year in the House of Representatives, news reports of July 30, 1955.*

"Blessed are they who run around in Circles, for they shall be called Wheels."

> *Sinclair Weeks, Secretary of Commerce, quotation on favorite office plaque given to him by a friend, news reports of July 30, 1955.*

"Conferences at the top level are always courteous. Name-calling is left to the Foreign Ministers."

> *Averell Harriman, former U. S. ambassador to Russia, comment on hearing of conclusion of Geneva conference, news summaries of August 1, 1955.*

"A successful diplomat should speak very frankly, very firmly, in words people cannot fail to understand."

> *John Peurifoy, State Department career diplomat, comment recalled in obituaries reporting his death while U. S. ambassador to Thailand, news reports of August 13, 1955.*

"All is booming except the guns."

> *Senator Karl Mundt, Republican, South Dakota, comment describing conditions brought about by his party, news summaries of August 15, 1955.*

"Stone by stone, he built the foundation of our constitutional structure, and he constructed it sufficiently strong to support everything we have since built upon it."

> *Chief Justice Earl Warren, statement regarding John Marshall, Chief Justice of the United States from 1801 to 1835,* The New York Times Magazine, *August 21, 1955.*

"I don't think we can rest on our oars . . . to encourage young people to go into science. . . . We are not developing young scientists and engineers commensurate with the demands that the atomic age will make. We've got to have many more of them."

Lewis Strauss, chairman, Atomic Energy Commission, comparison of U. S. scientific training program with that of Russia, news reports of August 23, 1955.

". . . Although poverty was the worst problem our family had to face, not one of the seven children ever lacked the sense of being entirely secure. Which, I guess, is as fine a tribute as anyone could ever pay to his parents."

Ivy Baker Priest, Treasurer of the U.S., Guideposts, September 1955.

"Gentlemen, as we all know, it is a custom of the Cabinet to open with a silent prayer. While this has not been the practice of the Security Council, may I propose a moment of silent prayer of thanksgiving for the marvelous record of recovery the President has made up to this hour."

Richard Nixon, U. S. Vice-President, on calling to order a meeting of the National Security Council following President Eisenhower's heart attack; quotation constitutes first public announcement ever made by the Council, news reports of October 1, 1955.

"This is a weapon of war dedicated to peace."

Charles Thomas, Secretary of the Navy, at dedication of the supercarrier Forrestal, news reports of October 3, 1955.

"We are not the bosses of taxpayers. They are ours."

T. Coleman Andrews' order to investigators after changing name of department from Internal Revenue Bureau to Internal Revenue Service, news reports of October 24, 1955.

"There is something wrong with any law that causes that many people to quit their jobs and spend a day trying to find out how to comply."

T. Coleman Andrews, comment on report that twelve million taxpayers in 1954 sought help from Internal Revenue Service in filling out income tax forms, news reports of October 24, 1955.

"Bean Soup has been a featured item on the menu of the House of Representatives Restaurant since long before that day in 1904 when the then Speaker of the House, Joseph Cannon, of Illinois, came into the House Restaurant and ordered Bean Soup. Then, as now, Bean Soup was a hearty, zesty, and filling dish; but it was typically hot and humid in Washington that day, and, therefore, Bean Soup had been omitted from the menu. 'Thunderation,' roared Speaker Cannon, ' I had my mouth set for Bean Soup' and, he continued, 'From now on, hot or cold, rain, snow, or shine, I want it on the menu every day.' And so it has been —Bean Soup on the menu every single day since."

Back cover of menu for House of Representatives Restaurant, U. S. Capitol Building, Washington.

FOREIGN GOVERNMENTS

"My life has been spent in crowds. I feel isolated if bodyguards come between me and the crowds."

Jawaharlal Nehru, Prime Minister of India, news summaries of January 24, 1955.

"Let there be wrong decisions, but quick ones."

Prime Minister Nehru deplores delayed trials in India. Ibid.

"We speak in a soft voice and I hope a gentle voice, for that is the tradition of India."

Prime Minister Nehru, response to a toast proposed during a banquet in the Kremlin, news reports of June 10, 1955.

"The situation is one something like living with your wife. Sometimes it is difficult and even irritating to live with her but it is always impossible to live without her."

Lester Pearson, Canadian Secretary of State for External Affairs, defines Canadian attitude toward U.S., news summaries of March 15, 1955.

"It is a period described in North America as one when politicians go around shooting from the lip. It therefore behooves outsiders, even though friendly to all parties involved, to avoid not only participating in the shooting but keeping out of the line of fire."

Lester Pearson, advice to persons visiting the British Isles during national elections, news reports of May 17, 1955.

"I want you to make a revolution in the country. I want a revolution. I believe we have to make it before others seize the chance to make one. If we don't, they will. If you cannot perform the heavy task I assign you, I will fire you."

The Shah of Iran, instructions to a Cabinet appointed without the customary consultation with his Parliament, news reports of April 10, 1955.

"You belong to us. We belong to you. . . . You can always rely on us, in common with the free world, never to rest until human rights have also been restored to you."

Konrad Adenauer, a proclamation broadcast to the eighteen million Germans in East Germany, on occasion of end of ten-year Allied occupation of West Germany, news reports of May 6, 1955.

"There is only one place for us in the world. That is at the side of the free peoples. Our goal is: A free and united Germany in a free and united Europe."

Konrad Adenauer, Chancellor of West Germany, statement as West Germany became a free nation and an equal member of the North Atlantic Treaty Organization, news reports of May 10, 1955.

"The danger of German militarism has disappeared. It is not there any more."

> Konrad Adenauer, comment during a visit to Washington, news reports of June 15, 1955.

". . . The time will come when senators and representatives will be picked for their beauty, and God help the country then."

> Robert Menzies, Prime Minister of Australia, discusses the U.S. during a visit to Washington, news reports, May 17, 1955.

"Few young men of conscription age have any idea what NATO means. They think it's some sort of new toothpaste."

> Sir David Kelly, former British ambassador to Russia, Look, May 17, 1955.

"At the present time this Britain of ours is selling more, earning more, buying more, saving more, exporting more, and eating more than it has at any time in the history of the country."

> Sir Anthony Eden, campaign speech while seeking re-election as member of Parliament, news reports of May 22, 1955.

"It seems that the country has said to us, 'Get on with the job.'"

> Sir Anthony Eden, comment when his party was returned to power, news reports of May 27, 1955.

"We have only to stretch out our hand and the human race can enter an age of prosperity such as has never been known."

> Sir Anthony Eden, opening speech at Big Four Geneva Conference, news reports of July 19, 1955.

"I liked the last statement of Eisenhower at his press conference—not all of it. I must tell the truth: There were right things and wrong things. I think that in any case what he said was a fresh stream of ozone."

> Nikita Khrushchev, comment during surprise appearance at Independence Day party at U. S. Embassy, Moscow, news reports of July 5, 1955.

"They pay little attention to what we say and prefer to read tea leaves."
Nikita Khrushchev, comment on press interpretations of Soviet attitudes. Ibid.

"I know that we do not want war and I know that you do not. If there must be a war, let's be on the same side."
Nikita Khrushchev, speaking to a military attaché of U. S. Embassy. Ibid.

"Let's all go. Things are different now."
Nikita Khrushchev, comment at Geneva Conference inviting Americans to visit Russia, news reports of July 20, 1955.

"I know what I say at times is not very diplomatic."
Nikita Khrushchev, comment at Geneva Conference. Ibid.

"Those who wait for that must wait until a shrimp learns to whistle."
Nikita Khrushchev, declaration that Russia will never abandon Communism; address at Kremlin dinner honoring East German delegation visiting Russia, news reports of September 18, 1955.

"I have heard a lot of opinions about the life of Russian women and the way they are dressed. But the worst work for a woman is prostitution. . . . In Paris you cannot walk down the street without having a woman accost you in order to subsist. Here in Russia, if a woman works like a man, she is at least not in a degrading situation but honestly earns her living."
Nikita Khrushchev, on Russian women, news summaries of October 3, 1955.

"We remain atheist, and we do everything we can to liberate a certain part of the people from the opium attraction of religion which still exists. But every person can practice the religion that pleases him, and care is taken never to annoy priests. Now that Soviet power has become so great, most priests have stopped their opposition to the Soviet Government."

Nikita Khrushchev, on religion, news summaries of October 3, 1955.

"Don't address us as gentlemen. Call us comrades."

Nikita Khrushchev, Soviet party chief, interrupting a salutation being given by Marshal Tito during a visit of Russian leaders to Yugoslavia, news summaries of December 31, 1955.

"It was publicity for myself. You see, I'm getting old now and I'd like the people—including the American people—to think of me as something more than a man who says 'no.'"

V. M. Molotov, Soviet Foreign Minister, comment on why he permitted himself to be photographed wearing a ten-gallon Western hat presented him during a visit to the U.S., news reports of July 20, 1955.

"Prior to the revolution, I imagined that the whole nation . . . awaited the advance of the vanguard and the storming of the outside walls for it to pour down in a solid phalanx, marching faithfully to the great goals. After the revolution I was shocked by the reality. The walls of the fort of tyranny had been stormed; Farouk had been forced to abdicate. But the mission of the vanguard had not ended. In fact it was just beginning. We needed discipline but found chaos behind our lines. We needed unity but found dissensions. . . . Every fresh success of the revolution also laid unwittingly a heavy burden on my shoulders."

Lieutenant Colonel Gamal Abdel Nasser, Egyptian Government head, comment on third anniversary of Cairo revolution and abdication of King Farouk, This Week Magazine, July 24, 1955; copyright 1955, United Newspaper Magazine Corporation.

"Oh, my men, stand in your places. Oh, free men, stand. I revolted for your sake. I taught you dignity and self-respect. Oh, my citizens, my men, I brought to this country dignity and freedom, and I fought for your sons. Oh, free men, stand."

> *Gamal Abdel Nasser, speech quieting crowd after assassination attempt on him during appearance in Alexandria, news summaries of September 26, 1955.*

"There ain't gonna be no war."

> *Harold Macmillan, British Foreign Secretary, comment on return to England from Geneva Conference, news reports of July 25, 1955.*

". . . We are not bossy and don't let us introduce the bossy element among us."

> *Lord Llewellin, opposition to admitting women to the House of Lords, news reports of September 16, 1955.*

"This time we won't even hear them."

> *Antoine Pinay, French Foreign Minister, comment on plans of new West German army to wear rubber-soled shoes, news summaries of December 31, 1955.*

HOLLYWOOD

"Oscar means about an added million dollars to the gross of a picture."

> *Samuel Goldwyn, Hollywood producer, on value of statuette awarded annually by Academy of Motion Picture Arts and Sciences, news summaries of February 26, 1955.*

"He is gentle, as all real men are gentle: without tenderness, a man is uninteresting."

> *Marlene Dietrich, on Ernest Hemingway as "the most fascinating man I know." News summaries of April 4, 1955.*

162

"The reason good women like me and flock to my pictures is that there is a little bit of vampire instinct in every woman."

Theda Bara, on her many roles as a "vamp"; quoted in obituaries reporting her death, news reports of April 8, 1955.

"To understand those days, you must consider that people believed what they saw on the screen. Nobody had destroyed the grand illusion. They thought the stars of the screen were the way they saw them. Now they know it's all just make-believe."

Theda Bara. Ibid.

"The goal is to make pictures reasonably accepted by reasonable people."

Eric Johnston, president, Motion Picture Association of America, Time, May 30, 1955.

"I don't know how much I'm making, but I have a faint idea of how much I'm spending, and it's more than I can afford."

Broderick Crawford, actor, comment as lawyers attempted to work out financial settlement for his estranged wife, quoted by Dorothy Kilgallen, New York Journal-American, September 30, 1955.

"Obviously the modern girl wears just as many clothes as her grandma did—but never at the same time."

Van Johnson, comment on autumn fashions of 1955, news summaries of October 2, 1955.

"I have never made a gangster picture. I always deal with the man in the street; the innocent fellow getting involved in something he can't control. This is the basis of true suspense. The audience is Terribly Worried because it could happen to them."

Alfred Hitchcock, news summaries of December 26, 1955.

"There is another word for being a good trouper, a word that show business would think too grand to use. That word is dedication. And that word, I think, is Mary Pickford's secret, as it is the secret of anyone who succeeds at anything. Most of us serve our ideals by fits and starts. The person who makes a success of living is the one who sees his goal steadily and aims for it unswervingly. That is dedication."

> *Cecil B. de Mille, introduction to* Sunshine and Shadow, *the autobiography of Mary Pickford, copyright 1955 by Mary Pickford Rogers, reprinted by permission of Doubleday & Company, Inc.*

"I'm thirteen years old, and at the crossroads of my life. I've got to make good between now and the time I'm twenty, and I have only seven years to do it in. I'm the father of my family, and I've got to earn all the money I can."

> *Mary Pickford, comment during her first conference with Producer David Belasco, recounted in* Sunshine and Shadow. *Ibid.*

MEDICINE

"Extensive interviews show that not one alcoholic has ever actually seen a pink elephant."

> *Yale University Center of Alcohol Studies, news summaries of January 1, 1955.*

"On the first sign of a cold, go to bed with a bottle of whisky and a hat. Place hat on left-hand bedpost. Take a drink of whisky and move hat to right-hand post. Take another drink and shift it back again. Continue until you drink the whisky but fail to move the hat. By then the cold is probably cured."

> *Richard Gordon, M.D., "The Common Cold," Atlantic Monthly, January 1955, favorite suggestion for cure, reprinted by permission.*

"The brain is viewed as an appendage of the genital glands."

> *Carl Jung, Swiss psychoanalyst, commenting on Freud's theory that the infantile parricide-and-incest wish (Oedipus complex) is crucially important in all humans; reprinted from* Time, *February 14, 1955, copyright 1955, Time, Inc.*

"Both Freud and Adler say to everything, 'You are nothing but. . . .' They explain to the sufferer that his symptoms come from here or there and are 'nothing but' this or that. . . . Sexuality, it is true, is always and everywhere present; the instinct for power certainly does penetrate the heights and the depths of the soul: but the soul itself is not solely either the one or the other, or even both together. . . . A person is only half understood when one knows how everything in him came about. Only a dead man can be explained in terms of the past. . . . Life is not made up of yesterdays only. . . ."

Carl Jung. Ibid.

"I could not say I believe. I know! I have had the experience of being gripped by something that is stronger than myself, something that people call God."

Carl Jung, when asked if he believed in God. Ibid.

"Our heart glows, and secret unrest gnaws at the roots of our being. . . . Dealing with the unconscious has become a question of life for us. . . . I have treated many hundreds of patients. . . . Among [those] in the second half of life—that is to say, over thirty-five—there has not been one whose problem in the last resort was not that of finding a religious outlook on life. . . ."

Carl Jung. Ibid.

"The neurosis contains the soul of the sick person, or at least a considerable part of it, and if the neurosis could be taken out like a decayed tooth, in the rationalistic way, then the patient would have gained nothing and lost something very important, much as a thinker who loses his doubt of the truth of his conclusions. . . . The individual [must] choose his own way consciously and with conscious moral decision."

Carl Jung. Ibid.

"Individuation means to become what one is really meant to be. In Zen Buddhism they have a saying: 'Show your natural face.' I think I have shown my natural face, often to the bewilderment of my time. Yes, I've attained individuation—thank heavens! Otherwise I would be very neurotic, you know."

Carl Jung. Ibid.

"So the battle must go on. We won't stop until all polio is just a dark word in history."

Basil O'Connor, head of the National Foundation for Infantile Paralysis, comment that bulbar polio remains unconquered although a vaccine has been developed for spinal polio, news summaries of April 23, 1955.

"If a man is good in his heart, then he is an ethical member of any group in society. If he is bad in his heart, he is an unethical member. To me, the ethics of medical practice is as simple as that."

Elmer Hess, M.D., president of the American Medical Association, "Do Doctors Charge Too Much?," an article appearing in The American Weekly, *April 24, 1955.*

"There is no greater reward in our profession than the knowledge that God has entrusted us with the physical care of His people. The Almighty has reserved for Himself the power to create life but He has assigned to a few of us the responsibility of keeping in good repair the bodies in which this life is sustained."

Elmer Hess, M.D. Ibid.

"It was just another job to be done in a field in which I was interested."

Dr. Jonas Salk, explaining why he devoted three years to perfecting the Salk anti-polio vaccine, news summaries of April 25, 1955.

"I have the courage of my convictions. I couldn't do it unless I was more critical of myself than others are of me. It is courage based on confidence, not daring, and it is confidence based on experience."

Dr. Jonas Salk, recollection of administering the anti-polio vaccine, in 1953, for the first time to persons who had never had polio—with himself, his wife, and their three sons among the first, news summaries of May 9, 1955.

"You find yourself projected into a set of circumstances for which neither your training nor your talents have prepared you. It's very difficult in some respects, but it's a transitory thing and you wait till it blows over. Eventually people will start thinking, 'That poor guy,' and leave me alone. Then I'll be able to get back to my laboratory."

Dr. Jonas Salk, comment three months after announcement that he was the discoverer of successful anti-polio vaccine, news summaries of June 20, 1955.

"Medicine has made more progress in the first half of the twentieth century than in the six thousand previous years."

L. H. McDaniel, M.D., chairman of Section on General Practice, American Medical Association convention, news reports of June 9, 1955.

"In spite of all our learning and scientific approach that we will have on December 31, 1999, we still will need a physician with a sober and investigative mind and a kind and understanding heart, just as a sane pilot is necessary in spite of all the plane safety gadgets yet discovered, for most air tragedies in the final analysis revert back to the human element. We still will need to treat people with sympathy and pain with drugs."

L. H. McDaniel, M.D. Ibid.

"Boxing journalists are apt to write with pained surprise about the poor showing made in some particular fight by a hitherto stout-hearted pugilist. If only they would learn a few elementary facts about the anatomy and physiology of the brain, the explanation would readily emerge. Better still, let them attend a few post-mortem examinations upon those who succumb to boxing, so that they can see what havoc may be wrought upon the lobes of a repeatedly hammered brain."

Dr. James Hamilton Doggert, medical officer in charge of the orthopedic department of Moorfields Eye Hospital, London, speaking at American Medical Association convention, news reports of June 9, 1955.

The following footnote to history appeared in the Temple University Medical Center *Bulletin* in July 1955, thirty-one years after occurrence of the event it describes. It was written by Dr. John Kolmer, professor of medicine at Temple, attending physician when Calvin Coolidge, Jr., sixteen-year-old son of President Coolidge, died in Washington in 1924, a few days after scratching his toe while playing tennis on the White House tennis courts:

"About two hours before death it was decided to administer oxygen. The wrong valves were accidentally opened on the oxygen tank with the result that a glass container exploded. A fragment of glass struck the President at the bedside on the forehead, but, fortunately, with slight injury. A very large fragment just missed my head. During the last two hours of life the patient was attended by me alone, in the presence of President and Mrs. Coolidge and a nurse. From time to time, I examined the heart and was astounded by the President requesting that he be permitted to listen to hear the sounds. At about 10 P.M., I announced the boy was rapidly dying. The President sprang from his chair and took his dying son in his arms, shouting hysterically into his ears that he would soon join him in the Great Beyond and requesting that young Calvin so inform his grandmother (the mother of the President). A medallion of the grandmother was also placed in the hands of the dying boy. Mrs. Coolidge joined the President in this hour of terrific grief. The boy died at 10:20 P.M. It is commonly stated that President Coolidge was 'cold as ice,' but I had the opportunity of seeing him in this hour of grief and so know quite otherwise. Indeed, it was the most touching and heart-rending experience of my whole professional career."

"When the personality pattern is dominated by this inhibition of expression, we advise the patient to go back to his job, but not just sit there quietly in the corner. We want them to go back and blow their stacks—or at least, talk it over with their bosses."

Dr. David Gelfand, head, Cardiac Work Evaluation Unit, Philadelphia General Hospital, comment on heart trouble among persons with supposedly quiet, mild personalities, news reports of July 15, 1955.

"Of all the traps and pitfalls in life, self-disesteem is the deadliest, and the hardest to overcome; for it is a pit designed and dug by our own hands, summed up in the phrase, 'It's no use—I can't do it.' . . . It is that good hard second look—taken not just for one's own sake but everyone else's too—that very often reveals that the 'impossible' task is quite possible after all."

Maxwell Maltz, M.D., noted plastic surgeon and author, "You Can Do the Impossible," This Week Magazine, July 24, 1955; copyright 1955 by United Newspapers Magazine Corporation.

"The species of the country doctor is not extinct. With urban life, paved roads, and the automobile, he has changed his name to that of the family doctor. He is better equipped to fight disease and accident, but the family doctor has the same qualities of moral strength, friendship, and family guidance as of old."

Herbert Hoover, address at dedication as a national shrine of the Newberg, Oregon, home in which he was reared by his uncle, Dr. Henry John Minthorn, news reports of August 11, 1955.

"It fulfills a most important function in propagation of the human species and is all the more interesting because it is involuntary and shows a readiness to be courted."

Dr. Joseph Sandler, research psychologist, address at Tavistock Clinic, London, comment on blushing, news reports of September 9, 1955.

"I don't use the word 'incurable.' I say 'inoperable.' When patients ask me questions I say, 'Your case is an exception.' Oh, I can lie like a trooper. But I don't think I'm doing wrong, do you?"

Mrs. Catherine McParlan, comment on her one hundredth birthday, after more than half a century of caring for a total of fifteen thousand cancer cases as the founder of a New York City hospital known as the House of Calvary; news reports of September 12, 1955.

"In some cases the act of killing may in itself be therapeutic, in so far as it may relieve anxieties, conscious or unconscious, and remove tension."

Dr. J. A. Hobson, chief, Psychiatric Department, Middlesex Hospital, London, address at third International Congress on Criminology; news reports of September 14, 1955.

"The moment of health is the moment of unconscious creative synthesis, when, without thinking about it at all, we know that we make sense to ourselves and to others. . . . When such simplicity amid complexity has been achieved, I think that two new and important [feelings] come into the individual's experience: 1) the feeling that one is free and that life and its outcome are in one's own hands; 2) . . . a deeper sense of relaxed participation in the present moment. . . . Life ceases to be a course between birth and death, and becomes instead a fully realized experience of change. . . ."

Dr. Frank Barron, University of California psychologist, paper prepared for delivery to American Psychological Association; Time, September 26, 1955.

"The type of person who never should be President is a worrier. Mr. Roosevelt and Mr. Truman weren't. Mr. Eisenhower isn't. He would have had the heart attack had he not been President."

Dr. Ross T. McIntire, personal physician to Presidents Roosevelt and Truman, news summaries of September 30, 1955.

"I said the country will be very pleased—the country is so bowel-minded anyway . . . and it is important."

Dr. Paul Dudley White, heart specialist, comment on making public all details of President Eisenhower's condition following heart attack; news summaries of October 10, 1955.

"Striving to outdo one's companions on the golf course and tennis court or in the swimming pool constitutes several socially acceptable forms of suicide."

Dr. George Griffith, professor of medicine, University of Southern California, comment on weekend athletics by men over forty years of age; news summaries of October 21, 1955.

"If you had taken all the funds you gave to surgeons and hospitals and had spent them instead on vacations or help around the house, you would have been better off."

Dr. Walter C. Alvarez, authority on nervous indigestion and nationally-syndicated columnist, quoted in "Alvarez, Everybody's Family Doctor," by G. Williams, in Harper's, October 1955.

"Never call in a tiger to chase away a dog."
Dr. Walter Alvarez, comment on over-concern for minor ailments. Ibid.

"Death keeps taking little bites of me."
Dr. Walter Alvarez, quoting an ageing woman patient. Ibid.

"We should never notice slights. If we are wise, we shall not expect much consideration from others. We can go through life easily and happily if we will only like people and show it."
Dr. Walter Alvarez. Ibid.

". . . there is no time at which a woman is more apt to go to pieces than when she is engaged in decorating her home. . . . Decorating a home puts a woman under tremendous psychic pressure and, in doing so, brings to the surface her underlying weaknesses."
Milton R. Sapirstein, Paradoxes in Everyday Life, in collaboration with Alis De Sola, copyright 1955 by Milton R. Sapirstein; reprinted by permission of Random House, Inc.

MUSIC

"You can't know how, as a youngster, I dreamed of the Met—how I once saved money to go, only to find that I didn't even have enough for half of the cheapest ticket."
Marian Anderson, comment to newsmen the night that she became the first Negro ever to sing in the Metropolitan Opera House, news reports of January 8, 1955.

"I guess the nicest thing anyone has ever said to me was what the doorman at the Metropolitan Opera House said the first time I arrived: 'Welcome home, Miss Anderson.' 'But,' I protested, 'this isn't my home.' The doorman replied, 'It should have been.'"
Marian Anderson, news summaries of June 9, 1955.

"Any song that moves you to joy or tears has greatness. Everything in life should be enjoyed for what it is."

Marguerite Piazza, Metropolitan Opera star and entertainer, news reports of January 19, 1955.

"Genius is an overused word. The world has known only about a half dozen geniuses. I have achieved only a medium approach to my ideal in music. I got only fairly near."

Fritz Kreisler, on the eve of his eightieth birthday, news summaries of February 2, 1955.

"Art is a complex riddle of life. You can't define it, the complexity of things. Every day the artist is a different man. He may be better or worse. If he tries to tell you what he is, he isn't being honest. For he doesn't know himself. I have never even been able to say if I did or didn't play well."

Fritz Kreisler. Ibid.

"I never play now except for my own pleasure, and there's not much pleasure in playing for yourself."

Fritz Kreisler, five years after he stopped playing concerts at seventy-five. Ibid.

"This story is not hard to follow. It's merely the tale of a strong boy called Samson, who needed a haircut, and a sweet dish known as Dalila, who knew her way around with a pair of clippers. . . . Samson is playing on the Israelite team and Dalila is pitching for the Phillies, which makes it bad at the shove-off. . . . This dame Dalila knows just what it takes to get a man's mind off of light, water, and gas bills, groceries, and city taxes, and she throws the result of years of study on the subject at the poor lug in the long-hair wig. . . ."

Reuben Bradford, Dallas, Texas, businessman, broadcasts his Damon Runyonesque analysis of Samson and Dalila *by Saint-Saëns;* Newsweek, *February 7, 1955.*

"It's the story of a dame in Paris who had a very bad cough. Also, a nice business of her own and doing all right, too. 'La Traviata' . . . means, they tell me, 'the strayed one.' That title seems to be O.K. with everyone, as the gal really did some plain and fancy straying and in the right paths, with the right boys. . . . On this particular opening evening, Violette, that's the babe's name, is throwing a super wingding. Among those present is a new face, a lad from the sticks called Alfredo."

Reuben Bradford, on La Traviata. *Ibid.*

"We listen too much to the telephone and we listen too little to nature. The wind is one of my sounds. A lonely sound, perhaps, but soothing. Everybody should have his personal sounds to listen for—sounds that will make him exhilarated and alive, or quiet and calm. . . . As a matter of fact, one of the greatest sounds of them all—and to me it is a sound —is utter, complete silence."

André Kostelanetz, conductor, on returning to New York from a tour in which he recorded noises for a record album to be called, "Sounds of the World," comment in interview with Phyllis Battelle, New York Journal-American, *February 8, 1955.*

"To me, 'God Bless America' was not just a song but an expression of my feeling toward the country to which I owe what I have and what I am."

Irving Berlin, comment to President Eisenhower on receiving a gold medal, voted by Congress, for contributions to American music during two world wars, news reports of February 19, 1955.

"My sole inspiration is a telephone call from a producer."
Cole Porter, news summaries of February 28, 1955.

"I hand him a lyric and get out of his way."
Oscar Hammerstein II, comment on his partnership with Richard Rodgers, news summaries of May 12, 1955.

"In old music you stand alone, alone and naked, and every note you play has got to be perfect. No one notices in modern music how many wrong notes you play. The cry today is 'Down with Mozart, to hell with anyone who can write a tune. Give us discord.'"

> *Sir Thomas Beecham, addressing the Bath Music Festival, news summaries of May 21, 1955.*

"If an opera cannot be played by an organ-grinder—as Puccini's and Verdi's melodies were played—then that opera is not going to achieve immortality."

> *Sir Thomas Beecham. Ibid.*

". . . Dance is the only art of which we ourselves are the stuff of which it is made. I never go on stage without saying, 'Here I am, Lord, use me.' I have had almost a vocation from childhood to be a religious. . . . The dance is religion. It is the finest symbol of the activity of God that we have in this world."

> *Ted Shawn, veteran leader in ballet theatres; Time, July 25, 1955.*

"I feel as if I were hearing this piece for the first time."

> *Olin Downes, comment on trying not to be jaded or weary of concert going in his many years as music critic of* The New York Times, *quotation included in obituaries of August 23, 1955, reporting his death.*

"Give me thirty competent performances of the 'Eroica' in thirty days and I will find something to say—in fact, that demands saying—about each one."

> *Olin Downes. Ibid.*

"I'm going to do as I please. I don't need anybody in the world. I did it all myself."

> *Frank Sinatra, on his way of life; Time, August 29, 1955.*

"Man, I'm buoyant. I feel about eight feet tall."
Frank Sinatra, comment on the fact that he is certain to pay income tax for 1955 of nearly one million dollars, news summaries of November 20, 1955.

"A musical talent is like having six fingers on one hand. You're born with it, you're different because of it, you can't do a thing about it except put it to use."
Florian Zabach, violinist; Tempo, September 20, 1955.

"Our singers work for art's sake—and maybe a few flowers. Perhaps she will have a few more flowers."
Rudolf Bing, general manager, Metropolitan Opera, reply to report that the Met had given in to alleged demand by soprano Maria Meneghini Callas that she be the highest paid member of any company in which she sings; Time, November 21, 1955.

". . . When Helen Traubel sings, 'Suzy Is a Good Thing' in *Pipe Dream* it seems to me that she does a great deal more good to the average human being, and the species in general, than she ever did in the clanking armor of her Wagnerian roles."
Bob Considine, columnist, New York Journal-American, December 2, 1955.

". . . Jazz may be thought of as a current that bubbled forth from a spring in the slums of New Orleans to become the main stream of the twentieth century."
Henry Pleasants, critic, news summaries of December 30, 1955.

PERSONALITIES

"If you haven't struck oil in five minutes, stop boring."
George Jessel, advice to after-dinner speakers, Look, January 10, 1955.

"I don't care what people call me. I've been called everything. But I instructed the White House staff always to call Mr. Hoover 'Mr. President' and I did myself. . . ."

Harry Truman expresses the belief that ex-Presidents should always be addressed as "Mr. President." He gave this opinion in an interview with etiquette expert Amy Vanderbilt, news summaries of January 23, 1955.

"I would have been much happier if I could have served out the term as Vice-President and probably have gone back to the Senate from the great state of Missouri."

Harry Truman, former U. S. President, comment on the tenth anniversary of death of President Roosevelt and Mr. Truman's succession to the presidency, news reports of April 13, 1955.

"Any man who has had the job I've had and didn't have a sense of humor wouldn't still be here."

Mr. Truman, testimony before the Senate Foreign Relations Committee on United Nations Charter revisions, news reports, April 19, 1955.

"I like people and I believe in treating them now as I would if running for office."

Mr. Truman, comment to newsmen on the eve of his seventy-first birthday, news reports of May 6, 1955.

"I always like the home town better than any other place I know of."

Mr. Truman, in a television interview with his daughter, "Person to Person," CBS-TV, May 27, 1955. Margaret Truman substituting for Edward R. Murrow.

"Well, I have been through a similar experience on two or three occasions and I had come to the conclusion that when the people know the facts and they know that you are telling the truth and stand for the things that are for their best interests they will vote for you and I was very well assured if I could see enough people I could be elected. That is what I did and this is the way it came out."

> *Mr. Truman, recalling his election of 1948. Ibid.*

"I have found the best way to give advice to your children is to find out what they want and then advise them to do it."

> *Mr. Truman. Ibid.*

"Hell, no. I'm glad to be rid of it. One really can't enjoy being President of the greatest republic in the history of the world. It's just too big a job for any one man to control it."

> *Mr. Truman, when asked by newsmen at Shrine convention in Chicago if he missed living in the White House, news reports of July 12, 1955.*

"Just say I'm going to raise a mite of hell."

> *Harry Truman, summing up his intentions to go on a speech-making tour aimed at putting the Democrats back into the White House in 1956. Ibid.*

The following quotations are from the first volume of Mr. Truman's autobiography, *Year of Decisions,* and are reprinted by courtesy of the author and *Life Magazine,* © 1955, Time, Inc.:

"I knew at once that something unusual had taken place. Mrs. Roosevelt seemed calm in her characteristic, graceful dignity. She stepped forward and placed her arm gently about my shoulder. 'Harry,' she said quietly, 'the President is dead.' For a moment I could not bring myself to speak. . . . 'Is there anything I can do for you?' I asked at last. I shall never forget her deeply understanding reply. 'Is there anything we can do for you?' she asked. 'For you are the one in trouble now.' "

> *Mr. Truman, recollection of how he learned of the death of Franklin Roosevelt. Ibid.*

"Boys, if you ever pray, pray for me now. I don't know whether you fellows ever had a load of hay fall on you, but when they told me yesterday what had happened, I felt like the moon, the stars, and all the planets had fallen on me. I've got the most terribly responsible job a man ever had."

Mr. Truman, statement to newsmen on his first visit to Capitol after becoming President. Ibid.

"But though his voice is silent, his courage is not spent, his faith is not extinguished. The courage of great men outlives them to become the courage of their people and the peoples of the world. It lives beyond them and upholds their purposes and brings their hopes to pass."

Mr. Truman, tribute to Franklin Roosevelt in first proclamation Mr. Truman signed as President. Ibid.

"Back in Washington that evening I felt that an epoch had come to an end. A great President, whose deeds and words had profoundly affected our times, was gone. Chance had chosen me to carry on his work, and in these two days I had already experienced some of the weight of its unbelievable burdens. As I went to bed that night, I prayed I would be equal to the task."

Mr. Truman, recollection of his return from Franklin Roosevelt's funeral. Ibid.

"At this moment I have in my heart a prayer. As I have assumed my heavy duties, I humbly pray to Almighty God in the words of King Solomon, 'Give therefore Thy servant an understanding heart to judge Thy people that I may discern between good and bad; for who is able to judge this Thy so great a people?' I ask only to be a good and faithful servant of my Lord and my people."

Mr. Truman, first congressional address as President. Ibid.

"I can't really be glad he is President, because I'm sorry that President Roosevelt is dead. If he had been voted in, I'd be out waving a flag, but it doesn't seem right to be very happy or wave a flag now."

Mrs. Martha Truman, comment to newsmen when her son became President, recalled in Harry Truman's memoirs. Ibid.

"It is often helpful for a President to judge, from questions put to him by the reporters, what is going on in the minds of the people."

Mr. Truman, comment on recalling his first news conference as President. Ibid.

"I felt as if I had lived five lifetimes in my first five days as President."

Mr. Truman. Ibid.

"We must build a new world, a far better world—one in which the eternal dignity of man is respected."

Mr. Truman, address at charter signing of the United Nations. Ibid.

"It is a terrible—and I mean terrible—nuisance to be kin to the President of the United States."

Mr. Truman, letter to his mother and sister a few weeks after becoming President. Ibid.

"We went to Sunday school, public school from the fifth grade through high school, graduated in the same class and marched down life's road together. For me she still has the blue eyes and golden hair of yesteryear."

Mr. Truman, comment on his wife, Bess Wallace Truman. Ibid.

"I was beginning to realize—forty years before I had any thought of becoming President of the United States—that almost all current events in the affairs of governments and nations have their parallels and precedents in the past."

Mr. Truman. Ibid.

"Although I was nearly fifty-one years old at the time, I was as timid as a country boy arriving on the campus of a great university for his first year."

Mr. Truman, recollection of his first day as a U. S. senator, January 3, 1935. Ibid.

"Don't start out with an inferiority complex. For the first six months you'll wonder how you got here, and after that you'll wonder how the rest of us got here."

Senator Ham Lewis of Illinois, advice to Harry Truman during Mr. Truman's first days as a U. S. senator. Ibid.

"Now you behave yourself."

Mrs. Martha Truman, advice to her son on his inauguration as Vice-President of the United States. Ibid.

"The Charter of the United Nations which you have just signed is a solid structure upon which we can build a better world. History will honor you for it. Between the victory in Europe and the final victory in Japan, in this most destructive of all wars, you have won a victory against war itself."

Mr. Truman, address at signing of the United Nations charter. Ibid.

"That's what happens when a man overreaches himself."

Mr. Truman, comment on visiting the Reich Chancellery where Adolf Hitler died. Ibid.

"I was surprised at Stalin's stature—he was not over five feet, five or six inches tall. When he had pictures taken, he would usually stand on the step above me. Churchill would do the same thing. They were both shorter than I."

Mr. Truman. Ibid.

"I expressed the hope that our next meeting together might be in Washington. Someone said, 'God willing.' It was Stalin."

Mr. Truman, recollection of conclusion of Potsdam Conference. Ibid.

"We could hope for a miracle, but the daily tragedy of a bitter war crowded in on us. We labored to construct a weapon of such overpowering force that the enemy could be forced to yield swiftly once we could resort to it."

Mr. Truman, on preparations for use of the first atomic bomb. Ibid.

"This is the greatest thing in history. It's time for us to get home."

Mr. Truman, comment at sea, August 6, 1945, on learning of detonation of first atomic bomb. Ibid.

"We are now prepared to obliterate more rapidly and completely every productive enterprise the Japanese have above ground in any city. We shall destroy their docks, their factories, and their communications. Let there be no mistake; we shall completely destroy Japan's power to make war."

Mr. Truman, first public announcement on atomic bomb. Ibid.

"Our global victory has come from the courage and stamina and spirit of free men and women united in determination to fight."

Mr. Truman, proclamation declaring end of war with Japan. Ibid.

"The opportunities afforded by the vice-presidency, particularly the presidency of the Senate, do not come—they are there to be seized. Here is one instance in which it is the man who makes the office, not the office the man."

Mr. Truman, comment on the vice-presidency. Ibid.

"I always considered statesmen to be more expendable than soldiers."

Mr. Truman, on expendability. Ibid.

Clare Boothe Luce, U. S. ambassador to Italy, quoted in a "profile" published by *Newsweek*, January 24, 1955, reprinted by permission:

On sex: "I never try to act masculine, but on the other hand, I never made a point of being a woman."

On fame and critics: "Public life with all its attendant censure has no horrors for the man who . . . has once been taken naked over the live coals by a group of professional theater critics. It is the quickest way I know to acquire a spiritual elephant hide."

On Democrats: "They are 'troubadours of trouble and crooners of catastrophe.'"

On Pius XII: "If there could be such a thing in this modern age as a Saint of Public Relations, he is this Pope."

On Communism: "The opiate of the intellectuals . . . but no cure, except as a guillotine might be called a cure for a case of dandruff."

On contrasting careers: "Being a playwright and casting plays is really excellent preparation for diplomacy. I watch a man's inflections, his gestures, his manner of speaking—and try to determine what his inner convictions really are—very much in the way that a playwright casts the characters for one of his plays."

". . . It is not unlikely that the human race will cease to exist before the end of the present year."
> *Bertrand Russell, a prediction of what would happen unless the Far Eastern situation of early 1955, the protection of Formosa from the Chinese Communists, was resolved, news reports, January 30, 1955.*

"We are speaking on this occasion, not as members of this or that nation, continent or creed but as human beings, members of the species man, whose continued existence is in doubt."
> *Bertrand Russell, a statement warning against nuclear weapons; he obtained the signatures of nine of the world's leading scientists including Albert Einstein, who signed the statement the week he died, news reports of July 10 and 11, 1955.*

"We have found that the men who know most are the most gloomy. Here then is the problem which we present to you, stark and dreadful and inescapable: Shall we put an end to the human race: Or shall mankind renounce war?"
> *Bertrand Russell. Ibid.*

"The tour which is to take me across the world seems as wonderful as any fairy tale. I only hope that, with all the help my friends are giving me, I shall meet my adventures and hard work with flying colors."

Helen Keller, on eve of forty thousand mile world-wide journey, message typed out on conventional typewriter during interview with newspaperman, news reports of February 5, 1955.

"It's wonderful to climb the liquid mountains of the sky. Behind me and before me is God and I have no fears."

Helen Keller, at seventy-four, contemplates world trip, much of which was to be made by air. Ibid.

"Never bend your head. Always hold it high. Look the world straight in the face."

Helen Keller, words to a five-year-old blind child, daughter of a U. S. Army officer, brought to meet her in Tokyo, news reports, May 31, 1955.

"Self-pity is our worst enemy and if we yield to it, we can never do anything wise in the world."

Helen Keller, a few days before her seventy-fifth birthday, news reports of June 26, 1955.

"Retire? Never! My work is unfinished. I'm sure when we cross the River Styx, over which the dead are taken, the boatman Charon will tell us: 'Excuse me, but you're not ready for this trip yet.'"

Helen Keller, in an interview one week before her seventy-fifth birthday. Ibid.

"Life is an exciting business and most exciting when it is lived for others."

Helen Keller. Ibid.

"It gives me a deep comforting sense that 'things seen are temporal and things unseen are eternal.'"
Helen Keller, on reading the Bible daily. Ibid.

"It has been a happy life. My limitations never make me sad. Perhaps there is just a touch of yearning at times. But it is vague, like a breeze among flowers. Then, the wind passes, and the flowers are content."
Helen Keller. Ibid.

"These boys are such different individuals with such different interests that if they had all lived in New York City and not been brothers, they would never have met."
Anna Rosenberg, former Assistant Defense Secretary, comment on her friends—Winthrop, Laurance, John, David, and Nelson Rockefeller, Fortune, February 1955.

"My mother was given to a typical question: 'We have always done this. Why should we do anything else?' But my wife's typical question was 'We have always done this. Why not do it in another way or, better still, why not do something else?'"
John D. Rockefeller, Jr. Ibid.

"I'm always looking for a new idea that will be vastly more productive than its cost."
Laurance Rockefeller. Ibid.

"In my enterprises, you need a calendar, not a stop-watch. They're geared to a ten-year cycle."
Laurance Rockefeller. Ibid.

"American men are the most gallant husbands in the world. American women should always marry American men."
Christian Dior, interview with columnist Inez Robb, New York World Telegram & Sun, March 21, 1955.

"I am the humble servant of women. I merely try to guess what they want."
Christian Dior. Ibid.

"My dream is to save them from nature."
Christian Dior, comment on desire to make all women look beautiful, Collier's, *June 10, 1955.*

"Women are most fascinating between the age of thirty-five and forty after they have won a few races and know how to pace themselves. Since few women ever pass forty, maximum fascination can continue indefinitely."
Christian Dior. Ibid.

"A woman does not really need chic until the animal has lost some of its spring and the mind begins to prowl. That is the time for masking. *Merveilleux!*"
Christian Dior. Ibid.

"To manufacture emotion a man must have a working agreement with madness."
Christian Dior. Ibid.

"My vigor, vitality, and cheek repel me. I am the kind of a woman I would run from."
Lady Astor, comment during a visit to Washington, news reports of March 29, 1955.

"A real celebrity never dies."
Earl Blackwell, founder of the international Celebrity Service for information on famous people, The Saturday Evening Post, *April 2, 1955.*

"I assert that the cosmic religious experience is the strongest and the noblest driving force behind scientific research."
Albert Einstein, in an article in The New York Times, *November 9, 1930; quotations recalled in obituaries reporting his death, April 19, 1955.*

"The most incomprehensible thing about the world is that it is comprehensible."
Albert Einstein. Ibid.

"My passionate interest in social justice and social responsibility has always stood in curious contrast to a marked lack of desire for direct association with men and women. I am a horse for single harness, not cut out for tandem or team work. I have never belonged wholeheartedly to country or state, to my circle of friends, or even to my own family. These ties have always been accompanied by a vague aloofness, and the wish to withdraw into myself increases with the years."
Albert Einstein. Ibid.

"Ach! The world is not ready for it."
Albert Einstein, when told by a newspaper reporter of the atomic bombing of Hiroshima. Ibid.

"I cannot believe that God plays dice with the cosmos!"
Albert Einstein. Ibid.

"God is subtle but He is not malicious."
Albert Einstein. Ibid.

"The supreme task of the physicist is to arrive at those universal elementary laws from which the cosmos can be built up by pure deduction. There is no logical path to these laws; only intuition, resting on sympathetic understanding of experience, can reach them."
Albert Einstein, on physicists. Ibid.

"The man of science . . . suffers a truly tragic fate. Striving in great sincerity for clarity and inner independence, he himself, through his sheer superhuman efforts, has fashioned the tools which are being used to make him a slave and to destroy him also from within. He cannot escape being muzzled by those who have the political power in their hands. As a soldier he is forced to sacrifice his own life and to destroy the lives of others even when he is convinced of the absurdity of such sacrifices. He is fully aware of the fact that universal destruction is unavoidable since the historical development has led to the concentration of all economic, political, and military power in the hands of national states. He also realizes that mankind can be saved only if a supra-

national system, based on law, would be created to eliminate for good the methods of brute force."
Albert Einstein, on scientists. Ibid.

"I am absolutely convinced that no wealth in the world can help humanity forward, even in the hands of the most devoted worker in this cause. The example of great and pure individuals is the only thing that can lead us to noble thoughts and deeds. Money only appeals to selfishness and irresistibly invites abuse. Can anyone imagine Moses, Jesus, or Gandhi armed with the moneybags of Carnegie?"
Albert Einstein, on wealth. Ibid.

"The true value of a human being is determined primarily by the measure and the sense in which he has attained liberation from the self."
Albert Einstein. Ibid.

"Of what is significant in one's own existence one is hardly aware, and it certainly should not bother the other fellow. What does a fish know about the water in which he swims all his life?"
Albert Einstein. Ibid.

"The bitter and the sweet come from the outside, the hard from within, from one's own efforts. For the most part I do the thing which my own nature drives me to do. It is embarrassing to earn so much respect and love for it. Arrows of hate have been shot at me too; but they never hit me, because somehow they belonged to another world, with which I have no connection whatsoever. I live in that solitude which is painful in youth but delicious in the years of maturity."
Albert Einstein. Ibid.

"It is in fact nothing short of a miracle that the modern methods of instruction have not entirely strangled the holy curiosity of inquiry; for this delicate little plant, aside from stimulation, stands mainly in need of freedom. Without this it goes to wreck [sic] and ruin without fail."
Albert Einstein, on education. Ibid.

"My life is a simple thing that would interest no one. It is a known fact that I was born and that is all that is necessary."
Albert Einstein. Ibid.

"Pipe smoking contributes to a somewhat calm and objective judgment in our human affairs."
Albert Einstein. Ibid.

"There may be men who can live without political rights and without opportunity of free individual development, but I think this is intolerable for most Americans."
Albert Einstein, on becoming a U. S. citizen in Trenton, New Jersey, in 1940. Ibid.

"War seems to me a mean, contemptible thing. I would rather be hacked to pieces than take part in such abominable business."
Albert Einstein. Ibid.

"The discovery of nuclear chain reaction need not bring about the destruction of mankind any more than the discovery of matches."
Albert Einstein. Ibid.

"I would not try to become a scientist or scholar or teacher. I would rather choose to be a plumber or a peddler in the hope to find that modest degree of independence still available under present circumstances."
Albert Einstein, when asked how he would relive his life. Ibid.

"When a man sits with a pretty girl for an hour, it seems like a minute. But let him sit on a hot stove for a minute—and it's longer than any hour. That's relativity."
Albert Einstein. Ibid.

"Do you know that I am the only man in Princeton who never saw a football game?"
Albert Einstein, on sports. Ibid.

"I think and think for months and years. Ninety-nine times, the conclusion is false. The hundredth time I am right."

Albert Einstein. Ibid.

"If A equals success, then the formula is A equals X plus Y plus Z. X is work. Y is play. Z is keep your mouth shut."

Albert Einstein, defining success during a newspaper interview. Ibid.

"The word 'imposition' is never used where there is love."

Albert Einstein, admonition for a friend who said it was "an imposition" for the scientist to visit the bedside of the sick friend. Ibid.

"Love your children with all your hearts, love them enough to discipline them before it is too late. A child should know discipline by the age of three. Forget little things they do wrong that are not important. Praise them for important things, even if you have to stretch them a bit. Praise them a lot. They live on it like bread and butter and they need it more than bread and butter."

Mrs. Lavina Christensen Fugal, Pleasant Grove, Utah, named by the American Mothers Committee as 1955 Mother-of-the-Year, news reports of May 3, 1955.

". . . Novelty is mistaken for Progress. Of steel and glass we have aplenty; but what of the imaginative and creative powers which makes of these glittering materials structures responsible to the needs of the Human Individual? What of Real Sun, Real Air, Real Leisure?"

Frank Lloyd Wright, "The Future of the City," Saturday Review, May 21, 1955.

"Clear out eight hundred thousand people and preserve it as a museum piece."

Frank Lloyd Wright, a suggestion for disposal of Boston, Massachusetts, during a lecture in Boston, The New York Times Magazine, November 27, 1955.

"New York: Prison towers and modern posters for soap and whisky. Pittsburgh: Abandon it."
Frank Lloyd Wright. Ibid.

"Automobiles: Ferryboats coming down the street gnashing their teeth."
Frank Lloyd Wright. Ibid.

"Centralization: If it keeps up, man will atrophy all his limbs but the push-button finger."
Frank Lloyd Wright. Ibid.

"Civilization: Art and religion are the soul of our civilization. Go to them, for there love exists."
Frank Lloyd Wright. Ibid.

"The two moments when New York seems most desirable, when the splendor falls all around about and the city looks like a girl with leaves in her hair, are just as you are leaving and must say good-by, and just as you return and can say hello. We had one such moment of infatuation not long ago on a warm, airless evening in town, before taking leave of these shores to try another city and another country for a while. There seemed to be a green tree overhanging our head as we sat in exhaustion. All day the fans had sung in offices, the air-conditioners had blown their clammy breath into the rooms, and the brutal sounds of demolition had stung the ear—from buildings that were being knocked down by the destroyers who have no sense of the past. Above our tree, dimly visible in squares of light, the city rose in air. From an open window above us, a whiff of perfume or bath powder drifted down startlingly in the heavy night, somebody having taken a tub to escape the heat. On the tips of some of the branches, a few semiprecious stars settled themselves to rest. There was nothing about the occasion that distinguished it from many another city evening, nothing in particular that we can point to to corroborate our emotion. Yet we somehow tasted New York on our tongue in a great, over-powering draught, and felt that to sail away from so intoxicating a place would be unbearable, even for a brief spell."

"Talk of the Town" column, June 11, 1955, reprinted by permission, copyright 1955, The New Yorker Magazine, Inc.

"A trial is still an ordeal by battle. For the broadsword there is the weight of evidence; for the battle-axe the force of logic; for the sharp spear, the blazing gleam of truth; for the rapier, the quick and flashing knife of wit."

Lloyd Paul Stryker, noted trial lawyer, quoted in obituaries reporting his death, news reports of June 22, 1955.

"Trying a case the second time is like eating yesterday morning's oatmeal."

Lloyd Paul Stryker. Ibid.

"I know, that obscure as I am, my name is making a considerable deal of fuss in the world."

Davy Crockett, writing in 1834; words frequently recalled during spring and summer of 1955 when a popular song about the frontiersman swept the country, news summaries of June 25, 1955.

"Some women are wonderful and some of them are she-devils. Well, what are you going to do? You can't do with them, you can't do without them."

Bernarr MacFadden, comment on being jailed at eighty-six for failure to pay alimony to his forty-nine-year-old wife, news summaries of June 30, 1955.

"How much do we know about love? The first thing we know about love is that, for most of us, it is the most absorbing and interesting subject in existence. There is an enormous range of meanings in this one little word 'love.' There are mother love and self-love, father love and children's love for their parents; there are brotherly love and love of one's home and one's country; love of money and love of power; making love and loving food; there are music lovers, sports lovers, bird lovers, sun lovers. Preachers insist that we should love God; Jesus adjures us to love our enemies. Love clearly includes all these usages: but the love in which one can *be* is the pre-eminent love for most of us."

Julian Huxley, English biologist, "All About Love," Look, July 12, 1955, copyright 1955 by Cowles Magazines, Inc.

"I propose to anybody. I say it to a hat-check girl. I say it to anybody,— a sort of form of introduction."

Tommy Manville, news summaries of July 14, 1955.

"Asthma doesn't seem to bother me any more unless I'm around cigars or dogs. The thing that would bother me most would be a dog smoking a cigar."

Steve Allen, television comedian, news summaries of July 15, 1955.

"Many a man has fallen in love with a girl in a light so dim he would not have chosen a suit by it."

Maurice Chevalier, French entertainer, news summaries of July 17, 1955.

"Here they come! Here they come! The Russians are coming!"

Iowa farm hand shouts arrival of twelve visiting Russian farm experts, news reports of July 19, 1955.

"Oh boy, real Russians!"

Iowa farm boy. Ibid.

"No government could survive without champagne. Champagne in the throat of our diplomatic people is like oil in the wheels of an engine."

Joseph Dargent, French champagne bottler, New York Herald Tribune, July 21, 1955.

"We have a power mower and I spent the better part of last summer trying to induce Mr. Truman to use it. Finally he did. Eleven o'clock of a Sunday morning, with all the Methodists and Baptists going by our house on the way to church. Mr. Truman got out on our front lawn in his shirt sleeves and began cutting the grass. When I looked out of the window and saw him, I was horrified. 'Harry! Come in here this minute,' I called to him. 'You know what those churchgoers are saying.' There's no doubt in my mind he planned the whole thing deliberately to save himself from ever touching that mower again. And he hasn't."

Bess Wallace Truman, wife of former President Truman, "Do I Miss the White House?," This Week Magazine, July 24, 1955, copyright 1955, United Newspapers Magazine Corporation.

"The most tiresome of all tasks were the big receptions, where hundreds and hundreds of strange hands had to be shaken, and sometimes there were afternoon receptions and evening receptions on the same day. I do not miss them one bit. . . . The mountain of daily mail that had to be answered with the help of my secretary and her staff—that task is scarcely regretted. The day-in day-out schedule of appointments that kept me living by the clock—not missed at all. I was recently asked whether, when I now read in the papers about some function taking place in the White House, or when I see a photo of Mrs. Eisenhower engaged in some activity which I once performed, I sometimes feel a twinge of nostalgia. No, I most certainly do not."

Bess Wallace Truman. Ibid.

"When my husband and I recently returned to Washington for a brief visit, I was reminded how much I enjoy and how much I miss the physical beauty of the city. The wide, tree-lined avenues, the splendid buildings, the thrilling monuments—they lifted my heart the way they did the first time I saw them."

Bess Wallace Truman. Ibid.

"For the truth is, I have two loves, and I would be happiest if I could live half-time in Washington, and half-time in Independence. My husband and I lived in the Capital too long for us not to miss it fondly when we are away from it."

Bess Wallace Truman. Ibid.

"John Steinbeck was in a while back and when Louis Bromfield was here, he opened and shut the place. Tennessee Williams was in this morning and Truman Capote comes in whenever he's in town. The big difference is that people don't spend money any more, honey. In Paris in the old days, with just four tables, with maybe the Prince of Wales at one and Cole Porter at another, and everybody drinking champagne—even if they were drinking whisky, they had to pay for champagne—why, I could make as much in one night as I make in a month here. People don't have as much fun any more. Of course, in those days, people didn't have nothing to think about."

Bricktop, the international hostess, compares Paris of the 1920s with Rome of the 1950s, reported in Time, *July 25, 1955, copyright 1955, Time, Inc.*

"You should crawl in space before you fly."

Dr. Athelstan Spilhaus, member of U. S. National Committee for the International Geophysical Year, reply when asked possibility of man following earth satellites into outer space, news reports of July 30, 1955.

"To me, old age is always fifteen years older than I am."

Bernard M. Baruch, comment on his eighty-fifth birthday, news reports of August 20, 1955, and news summaries of August 29, 1955.

"At eighteen friendship is the buoyant acceptance of those who play and work and laugh and dream together. Some of those early friendships remain to the end. At eighty-five, a man is fortunate to keep his old friends. His new ones have been drawn to him by common interests, and a respect for their character and dependability, though their opinions may differ. As a man gets older he wants friends to stimulate him, to keep his mind active and young."

Bernard M. Baruch. Ibid.

"Age is only a number, a cipher for the records. A man can't retire his experience. He must use it. Experience achieves more with less energy and time."

Bernard M. Baruch. Ibid.

"Let unswerving integrity ever be your watchword."
Bernard M. Baruch, recalling his "most enduring lesson" from his father. Ibid.

"I am quite sure that in the hereafter she will take me by the hand and lead me to my proper seat. I always have a great reverence for teachers. For teachers, both lay and clerical, and for nurses. They are the most underpaid people in the world for what they do."
Bernard M. Baruch, recalling one of his early teachers. Ibid.

"I love kings and queens more than anybody in the world, but they don't have any money to spend ashore."
Elsa Maxwell, barring royalty from a cruise she planned, quoted by Art Buchwald, New York Herald Tribune, *September 11, 1955.*

"One hundred and twenty accepted invitations. A lot of the girls are pregnant right now and couldn't come."
Elsa Maxwell. Ibid.

"People who get seasick will be fined, and I've added another innovation. If a person wears his hat on the side of his head, that means he doesn't want anyone to talk to him."
Elsa Maxwell. Ibid.

"Thank God for giving me the talent."
Sharon Kay Ritchie, comment, as Miss Colorado, when named Miss America of 1956, news summaries of September 19, 1955.

"Who was that little girl 'Peaches'? I hardly know her."
Frances Heenan Browning Hynes Wilson, comment twenty-eight years after she made divorce trial headlines as "Peaches" Browning; New York Post, *September 20, 1955.*

"Sometimes I think I'll look up the old clippings but then I'm afraid."
"Peaches" Browning. Ibid.

"If a little nobody like me and a little nobody son of mine can arouse people as you have been aroused, then it is God's work and he hasn't died in vain."

> *Mrs. Mamie Bradley, address to eight thousand Harlem residents assembled to protest Mississippi murder of her Negro son, Emmett Louis Till, news reports of September 26, 1955.*

"Nobody can live in the past or the future without being something of a nut. I live for the Everlasting Now."

> *Evelyn Nesbit, figure in famed Thaw-White murder case of forty-nine years ago, statement when her life story was made into a motion picture biography; news summaries of September 26, 1955.*

"There is nothing so fine as to be twenty-one and an American. One is for a fleeting instant—and the other is forever. So live—decently, fearlessly, joyously—and don't forget that in the long run it is not the years in your life but the life in your years that counts!"

> *Adlai Stevenson, "If I Were Twenty-One,"* Coronet Magazine, *December 1955; reprinted in* New York Post, *December 4, 1955.*

"If there is a single quality that is shared by all great men, it is vanity. But I mean by 'vanity' only that they appreciate their own worth. Without this kind of vanity they would not be great. And with vanity alone, of course, a man is nothing."

> *Yousuf Karsh, internationally known Canadian photographer;* Cosmopolitan, *December 1955.*

"The name of the subspecies, then, is Exurbanite; its habitat, the Exurbs. The exurb is generally further from New York than the suburb on the same railway line. Its houses are more widely spaced and generally more various and more expensive. The town center tends to quaintness and class, rather than modernity and glass, and the further one lives from the station the better."

> *A. C. Spectorsky,* The Exurbanites, *© 1955 by A. C. Spectorsky, published by J. B. Lippincott Company; reprinted by permission.*

"There are some who still, after ten or fifteen years of exurban life, insist with utmost vehemence that they are coursing down the one-way autobahn to happiness, that they would not change their way of life no matter what the Devil offered them. But the passion with which they deny that their dream is limited or tainted or corrupted suggests that they themselves may feel misgivings, that there are times when even happiness—or barbiturates, gin, or sheer fatigue—can't get them by that four A.M. spell of insomnia when a man faces himself with something akin to sober horror."

A. C. Spectorsky. Ibid.

"Next to reading somebody else's love letters, there's nothing quite so delightful as being privy to the facts of his financial life, especially if they tend toward the disastrous."

A. C. Spectorsky. Ibid.

"When two bridge players get together, they can no more avoid talking about the game than women can stop talking about clothes."

Ely Culbertson, comment after calling on President Eisenhower at the White House, news summaries of December 30, 1955.

"People think of the inventor as a screwball, but no one ever asks the inventor what he thinks of other people."

Charles Kettering, developer of a workable automobile self-starter and of the two-cycle Diesel engine, retired research chief for General Motors, news summaries of December 30, 1955.

"When it comes to flying, there is no difference between the sexes. It doesn't require any brawn and . . . the more sensitive and gentle you are with a plane, the better you can fly. Perhaps women can't compete with men in tennis, golf, swimming, or things like that, but flying is a matter of intelligence and tenacious courage."

Jacqueline Cochran, famed woman flyer; news summaries of December 31, 1955.

"I did insult your city and I have come to make a public apology. And now that I have seen your city and your magnificent city hall, there is no doubt about it that the city is indeed the cat's whiskers."

Field Marshal Viscount Montgomery, apology to Buffalo, N.Y., for his question, "Where's Buffalo?," during a talk about possible atom-bomb targets in the U.S.; news summaries of December 31, 1955.

"I have left the world. . . . Every cell, fluid, muscle of my body is acutely awake. Perception is enormously exaggerated—black is blacker, white is whiter. Silence is more acute. . . . Fear seems to be independent, a ghost sitting on my shoulder. . . . Time is now. Nothing but this experience is significant. . . . It is intensely bright outside. . . . There seems to be no reflection; it is all black or white, apparent or non-apparent. No half-tones. . . . I roll to the right and there it is. Out of the tiny window slits there is the earth, wiped clean of civilization. . . . The earth curves to the south. It is as if I am the only living thing connected to this totally strange, uninhabited planet fifteen miles below me."

William Bridgeman, test pilot, description of sensations of establishing an altitude record, The Lonely Sky, by William Bridgeman and Jacqueline Hazard, copyright 1955 by Henry Holt and Company, Inc.; reprinted by permission of the publisher.

". . . That blank wall is an appalling thing to look at. The wall of a museum—a canvas—a piece of film—or a guy sitting in front of a typewriter, and you start out to do something—that vague thing called creation. It kind of strikes awe within you."

Edward Steichen, noted photographer, interview on "Elder Wise Men" series, NBC-TV, printed by permission.

"I had a feeling, a hangover from the last war, that if we could really photograph war as it was, if war could be photographed in all its monstrous actuality, that that would be a great deterrent for war."

Edward Steichen. Ibid.

"Actors and actresses are most difficult to photograph. The thing that makes photography wonderful is getting models to be themselves. Well, actors can't do that. All actors can do is act."
Edward Steichen. Ibid.

". . . There is love. That is the same all over the world. That has always been there . . . the one thing we have really learned the importance of . . . and unless we have the element of love dominating this entire exhibition, we better take it down before we put it up."
Edward Steichen, comment on giant exhibition of his work entitled, "The Family of Man." Ibid.

"Man has survived everything, and we have only survived it on our optimism, and optimism means faith in ourselves, faith in the everydayness of our lives, faith in our universal qualities, and above all, faith in love."
Edward Steichen. Ibid.

THE PRESIDENCY

"We shall have much to do together. I am sure that we shall get it done, and that we shall do it in harmony and good will."
President Eisenhower, opening remark in State of the Union message to Congress, January 6, 1955.

"Let the general good be our yardstick on every great issue of our time."
President Eisenhower. Ibid.

"Nineteen fifty-four was one of the most prosperous years in our history. Business activity surges with new strength. Production is rising. Employment is high. Toward the end of last year average wages in manufacturing were higher than ever before. Personal income after taxes is at a record level. So is consumer spending. Construction activity is reaching new peaks. Export demand for our goods is strong. State and local government expenditures on public works are rising. Savings are high

and credit is readily available. So, today, the transition to a peacetime economy is largely behind us. The economic outlook is good."
President Eisenhower. Ibid.

"If as a people we act wisely, our annual national output can rise, within a decade, from its present level of about 360 billion to 500 billion, measured in dollars of stable buying power."
President Eisenhower. Ibid.

"Americans want a good standard of living—not simply to accumulate possessions, but to fulfill a legitimate aspiration for an environment in which their families may live meaningful and happy lives. Our people are committed, therefore, to the creation and preservation of opportunity for every citizen, opportunity to lead a more rewarding life. They are equally committed to our alleviation of unavoidable misfortune and distress among their fellow citizens."
President Eisenhower. Ibid.

"The aspirations of most of our people can best be fulfilled through their own enterprise and initiative without government interference. This Administration, therefore, follows two simple rules: First, the federal government should perform an essential task in this field only when it cannot be adequately performed; and second, in performing that task, our government must not impair the self-respect, the freedom and incentive of the individual. So long as these two rules are observed, the government can and must fully meet its obligations without creating a dependent population or a domineering bureaucracy."
President Eisenhower. Ibid.

"Farm production is gradually adjusting to markets, markets are being expanded and stocks are moving into use. We can now look forward to an easing of the influences depressing farm prices, to reduced government expenditures for purchase of surplus products, and to less federal intrusion into the lives and plans of our farm people. . . . I urgently recommend to the Congress that we continue resolutely on this road."
President Eisenhower. Ibid.

"A decade ago, in the death and desolation of European battlefields, I saw the courage and resolution, I felt the inspiration of American youth. In these young men, I felt America's buoyant confidence and irresistible will-to-do. In them I saw, too, a devout America, humble before God. And so I know in my heart, and I believe all Americans know, that despite the anxieties of this divided world, our faith and the cause in which we all believe will surely prevail."

President Eisenhower. Ibid.

"There was a man from the United States, a political figure—and I am not going to name him because he is still alive—we had just cleaned up North Africa, and this man came to me and said he hoped I knew that no American general could have a success of that scope and kind and fail to be considered for the presidency. I kicked him out of the office."

President Eisenhower, story related at close of news conference, January 13, 1955.

"I would never admit failure to anything, as long as it is going on. . . . That would be just as incomprehensible as to admit defeat in a battle as long as you have got one man on the firing line."

President Eisenhower, comment on UN negotiations to secure release of American airmen imprisoned in Communist China at news conference, January 19, 1955.

". . . The outlook, certainly from the standpoint of our individual economy, is good, and I know of no better measure . . . than to say, how do people feel today as to the way they felt then."

President Eisenhower, comment on eve of second anniversary of his inauguration. Ibid.

". . . A suitable congressional resolution would clearly and publicly establish the authority of the President as Commander in Chief to employ the armed forces of this nation promptly and effectively for the purposes indicated if in his judgment it became necessary. It would make clear the unified and serious intentions of our government, our Congress and our people. Thus it will reduce the possibility that the Chinese Communists, misjudging our firm purpose and national unity, might be disposed to challenge the position of the United States, and precipitate a major crisis which even they would neither anticipate nor desire."

> *President Eisenhower, message asking Congress to pass a resolution supporting him in whatever he felt must be done to protect Formosa and the Pescadores from Communist attack; he won almost unanimous support after delivery of the message, January 24, 1955.*

"The United Nations is working on this, and I don't see how any statement of mine could do anything more than muddy the water."

> *President Eisenhower, reply to question on possible U.S. action in Far East unrest, news conference, February 2, 1955.*

"Unless education continues to be free—free in its response to local community needs, from any suggestion of political domination, and free from impediments to the pursuits of knowledge by teachers and students —it will cease to serve the purposes of free men."

> *President Eisenhower, message to Congress on state of American education, February 8, 1955.*

". . . The finest buildings, of themselves, are no assurance that the pupils who use them each day are better fitted to shoulder the responsibilities, to meet the opportunities, to enjoy the rewards that one day will be their lot as American citizens. Good teaching and good teachers made even the one-room crossroads school of the nineteenth century a rich source of the knowledge and the enthusiasm and patriotism, joined with spiritual wisdom, that mark a vigorously dynamic people."

> *President Eisenhower. Ibid.*

"Education is really bread and butter to citizenship."

> *President Eisenhower, comment at news conference, February 9, 1955, the day after sending to Congress message on state of American education.*

"As quickly as you start spending federal money in large amounts, it looks like free money. The shibboleth of free money from Washington can certainly damage."

President Eisenhower, citation of one of the reasons he approves of initiative of state and local governments. Ibid.

"When I asked him to visit our country, I was acting as the agent of my government which desired me to do so; and more than that, arrangements had been made once. My plane had been put at his disposal and my son had been detailed as his aide. And I remember he made the remark, 'Well, I shall certainly be very safe, with your plane and your son.' We were good friends and we could talk in that fashion. Now I explained to him how absolutely impossible it was for a democracy to organize a surprise aggression against anybody. Our processes are open. Every time you get money or you change anything in your military affairs, you go to Congress. It is debated. There is no possibility of a country such as ours producing a completely surprise attack on any other."

President Eisenhower, recollection of invitation to Marshal Zhukov in 1945 when they were serving together in Berlin; recalled the day it was revealed that Zhukov had been named Soviet defense minister. Ibid.

"Rich people can buy equities, can afford to invest in equities, and as the dollar goes, cheapens, the amount of dollars that they have invested goes up and up. But the fixed income group, the man who is buying an insurance policy . . . or looking forward to living on his pension, is the one that is hurt. We simply cannot have this kind of thing in responsible government."

President Eisenhower, comment on possible controls of the cost of living, news conference, February 23, 1955.

"He has been invited, as has every other Democratic leader, to bring to me anything by reaching for a telephone and calling me up, just as any leader of the Republican party has."

President Eisenhower, reference to Speaker Sam Rayburn, comment on accessibility which leaders have to the President. Ibid.

"We do not cease our efforts in research in cancer, nor do we abolish the laboratories in which the research goes on merely because of lack of success, and we have had a tremendous lack of success. Here is a laboratory where nations come together and they talk. . . . Here is something for which mankind has had a yearning ever since the dawn of history and I am not going to give up in my time on it."

President Eisenhower, comment on the United Nations. Ibid.

"If they have found a practical way to accomplish something along this line, I am going to design some new type of medal for them. . . . It is the hardest thing in the world."

President Eisenhower, comment on Hoover Commission's recommendations to reduce paper work in government. Ibid.

". . . As to His Holiness, the Pope, [on] his seventy-ninth birthday, a man that I have had the honor of visiting personally, admiring him greatly, and particularly because of his unbroken record of opposition to all forms of fascism and communism, I am quite certain that America, all America, would wish this great spiritual leader a very happy day today, and many more of them."

President Eisenhower, tribute to Pope Pius XII, at opening of news conference, March 2, 1955.

"There comes a time, possibly, when a lead is not significant in the defensive arrangements of a country. If you get enough of a particular type of weapon, I doubt that it is particularly important to have a lot more of it."

President Eisenhower, comment on manufacture of the hydrogen bomb. Ibid.

"Good faith is the ingredient that must be implicit in any plan that is finally adopted. . . ."

President Eisenhower, comment on various plans for world disarmament. Ibid.

". . . Just as a personal opinion as to what good might come out of it, these two people, these two representatives of agriculture getting together, I would say it would be good and good only."

President Eisenhower, comment on visit to U.S. by Russian farmers. Ibid.

". . . It will be done under scientists and for the development and benefit of the world, nothing else."

President Eisenhower, explanation of an American research expedition to the Antarctic. Ibid.

"Did you ever think of what a fate civilization would suffer if there was such a thing as an indispensable man? When he went the way of all flesh, what would happen? It would certainly be a calamity, wouldn't it? I don't think we need fear that."

President Eisenhower, reply when told that the Republican party depended on him to win the 1956 election. Ibid.

"I rather think it is a good thing to shift around from one city to another . . . instead of always going back to the same place—switch around in this country. It is a big country and if the place can accommodate all members of the convention . . . let's go there once in a while."

President Eisenhower, on selection of sites for nominating convention. Ibid.

". . . I think the American people, in their individualistic selves, are very independent, and I would doubt any organization can just set itself up and be in all phases of their political and economic and cultural life, the bosses of any great number of Americans."

President Eisenhower, on possibility of a labor monopoly in merger of AF of L and CIO. Ibid.

". . . I have talked to a number of what I thought promising young people, people who are establishing themselves, about the possibility of them getting into government and I find that, particularly with respect to jobs that bring them to Washington, the economic factor has a very important bearing on their decisions, and frequently they must simply decline. . . . They must keep a home in their own places, in their own districts if they hope to be re-elected—incidentally, which, I think, is a mistake, I would like to see a four-year term for them—and then they have to set up a new home here and, as you know, they do have unusual expenses."

President Eisenhower, comment approving pay increase for congressmen. Ibid.

". . . We will get half of it back, don't forget that!"

President Eisenhower, comment on taxes of $7500 congressional pay increase. Ibid.

". . . That was not the biggest battle that ever was, but for me it always typified one thing—the dash, the ingenuity, the readiness at the first opportunity that characterizes the American soldier."

President Eisenhower, comment on the tenth anniversary of World War II Battle of the Ramagen Bridgehead, March 8, 1955.

"In spite of all the publicity gimmicks, all the shrewd recruiting systems, there is one thing that will bring Republican party recruits—fine programs for all America, and real work in putting them over."

President Eisenhower, comment on building political strength, news conference, March 16, 1955.

"Would it be allowable to just say, 'Hurrah'?"

President Eisenhower, comment on Senate vote rejecting proposed income tax cut. Ibid.

". . . I have said time and again there is no place on this earth to which I would not travel, there is no chore I would not undertake if I had any faintest hope that, by so doing, I would promote the general cause of world peace."

President Eisenhower, comment at news conference, March 23, 1955.

"Now, international meetings have a number of purposes, and one of them, let us not forget, is just sheer propaganda. Nevertheless, we must never abandon the hope that in some new conference some constructive step will be taken and start this weary world at last on the path that could lead hopefully and definitely toward a better agreement."

President Eisenhower. Ibid.

". . . The most changeable factor in war is human nature, in its day-by-day manifestation; but the only unchanging factor in war is human nature. . . . The next thing is that every war is going to astonish you in the way it occurred, and in the way it is carried out."

President Eisenhower. Ibid.

". . . [Do] not try to say, 'They are going to attack me today; therefore, I shall attack them yesterday. . . .' "

President Eisenhower, comment on danger of being overly prepared for war at news conference, March 30, 1955.

". . . The last thing that I would ever ask any man that I appoint to a high office is what are going to be his decisions in specific cases. If any man would pledge to me that he was going to make a certain decision because I asked him, he would never be appointed."

President Eisenhower, comment on his view of the work of his appointees. Ibid.

"They have a freedom I would personally dearly love."

President Eisenhower, comment on White House squirrels. Ibid.

"All of us in the free world can respect your decision, Sir Winston, to retire from official office, to live now a somewhat more serene life than has been possible in a position of such great responsibility as yours. But we shall never accept the thought that we are to be denied your counsel, your advice. Out of your great experience, your great wisdom, and your great courage, the free world yet has much to gain."

President Eisenhower, message to Sir Winston Churchill on his retirement as Prime Minister of Great Britain, April 5, 1955.

"Today, a man to do his duty in the military services must study humanity first of all—what makes humans tick. Not only as regards your own companies, to be for them the leader and the model, but since you must be one of the principal apostles of peace you must try to understand other people. You must try to understand the heart of America and how to translate that heart to other peoples. You must know something of economics, and of course, your profession will make you know something of law and engineering, and many of the sciences. But above all, we come back to it: You must try to understand people. How else, I ask you, are we to achieve peace in this world, unless there be a magnificent growth of understanding?"

President Eisenhower, address on receiving an honorary LL.D. from The Citadel, Charleston, South Carolina, April 12, 1955.

"No other man contributed so much to the vast expansion of twentieth century knowledge."

President Eisenhower, tribute on the death of Albert Einstein, April 18, 1955.

"In this wealthiest of nations, where per capita income is the highest in the world, more than one-fourth of the families who live on American farms still have cash incomes of less than one thousand dollars per year."

President Eisenhower, Farm Message to Congress, April 27, 1955.

"Curtailed opportunity begets an economic and social chain reaction which creates unjustified disparity in individual reward. Participation diminishes in community, religious, and civic affairs. Enterprise and hope give way to inertia and apathy. Through this process all of us suffer. This problem calls for understanding and for action."

President Eisenhower. Ibid.

". . . When it comes to talking about the affairs that involve our ally bound to us by treaty we are not going to talk behind their backs."

President Eisenhower, comment on negotiations involving Nationalist China, news conference, April 27, 1955.

". . . A trained Intelligence system can get a terrific source of information out of the combined documents that can be procured on the newsstands and the libraries of the United States. Now, that is as it should be because to inform ourselves, we have to be ready to inform others. But we do not need to turn out such things as an airplane being able to fly straight up or do some other things that seem to be a strong new principle."

President Eisenhower, comment on publication of confidential government information. Ibid.

"Of course, I think we knew six weeks before that victory was certain and was coming very quickly. It . . . merely became a question of the day. But I think May 8 represented for a great many people in Europe at that time practically the realization of all their dreams and you might say, their ambitions. Certainly I thought it marked for me . . . the end of my military career. I saw a nice farm over the other side of the ocean —and it is still a long ways away at least. . . . I do believe this: I believe that there was in the hearts of all the fighting men, all of the people that were in uniform in Europe on that day, I believe there was a genuine desire for peace, and the hope that there would be no more war. That hope has not been realized. And it has encountered its defeats, but I still believe it is a mighty force in the world. . . . I wish that in the cold war we could now get some victory that would make us feel as good as we felt that day of May 1945."

President Eisenhower, comment on approach of tenth anniversary of end of war in Europe. Ibid.

". . . After men's minds have become persuaded of the truth of something, though it be wrong, they can support that idea, if they believe it to be true."

President Eisenhower, on communist propaganda given the Russian people. Ibid.

". . . I have warned you people plenty of times that when you go to begin a search for the initiation of an idea . . . the memory can play you very, very sad tricks."

President Eisenhower, on origination of idea for atom-powered peace ship. Ibid.

". . . I take their words with reservation, but with hope."
President Eisenhower, on Chinese Communists' statement of desire for peace. Ibid.

". . . I am not above saying that I often need friendly treatment."
President Eisenhower, on his relationship with the press. Ibid.

"For some two years and three months I have been plagued by inexplicable, undiscovered leaks in this government. But we mustn't be too astonished when we recognize that [there are] great numbers of people in this town who necessarily know details of one kind or another. . . . The kind of thing that foreign Intelligence systems spend thousands and thousands of dollars to get, unless we give it to them for nothing and since we don't get it for nothing, I don't believe in that kind of a trade!"
President Eisenhower, on leaking government secrets. Ibid.

"There will never be a child in the United States denied this emergency protection for want of ability to pay."
President Eisenhower, statement on Salk anti-polio vaccine at opening of news conference, May 4, 1955.

". . . I believe that women are better apostles than men. Men are engrossed in many kinds of activities. They earn the living. They are engaged in business all day, and they are very apt, at times, to lose that great rounded concept of man that women almost always have before them: that he is a spiritual and intellectual and a physical being. He is not merely someone trying to get a higher wage. He wants a higher wage for a purpose, to give greater opportunity in all three of these fields to his family. Because women think of these things in their process of homemaking, think of them in terms of children and the family, I believe that their influence in spreading the basic doctrines of this kind is more profound than that of men."
President Eisenhower, address to Republican Women's National Conference, Washington, May 10, 1955.

". . . This is what I believe in giving away: I think today to hold secret any documents of the world war, including my own mistakes, except only when they are held there by some past agreement with a foreign nation that has not yet been abrogated, that is foolish. Everything ought to be given out that helps the public of the United States to profit from past mistakes, to make decisions of the moment."
President Eisenhower. Ibid.

"It is rather erratic in its [rate of] output."
President Eisenhower, comment on work of Congress at news conference, May 11, 1955.

"There are a number of things wrong with Washington. One of them is that everyone has been too long away from home."
President Eisenhower. Ibid.

The following is a transcript of significant portions of a televised dialogue between John Foster Dulles, Secretary of State, and President Eisenhower, reporting on a European trip made by Mr. Dulles; broadcast from the White House, May 17, 1955:

Mr. Dulles: "The meeting of the Western European Union and the meeting of NATO, into which Germany walked in the presence of the great Chancellor Adenauer, whom you know so well and we all admire so much, walked into that room and it was a very significant and historic occasion. . . . There was a sense of a great event as the Free German Republic took its place there. And then you saw, because you see France and Germany come together in the alphabet, France and Germany sat side by side. And you saw these two countries sitting there side by side as allies. And you felt that a new page had been opened on European history and that the vision which so many people have had for so many years of the united Europe had actually started to come to pass."

Mr. Dulles: ". . . During these eight years we have had no less than 379 meetings . . . at one level or another with the Soviet representatives about this Austrian treaty. And often times we'd be just so close to getting it through that we'd think it was just around the corner. But the corner seemed to be an interminable series of corners."

President Eisenhower: "It proves in this business you must not be easily discouraged."
(*Exchange of remarks on signing of the Austrian treaty*)

Mr. Dulles: "I don't think for a minute that they've got religion or been converted. But it just may be as a practical matter they may think that they can get along better by conforming to some of these rules and practices which normally govern the civilized community."
(*Comment on change in Soviet policies*)

President Eisenhower: "In a word, we will stay strong and we'll stay vigilant, but we're not going to extinguish the hope that a new dawn may be coming, even if the sun rises very slowly."
(*Conclusion to dialogue*)

"I believe that the greatest honor, the greatest distinction, that can come to any American is to feel that in his own niche he has been of service to the United States of America."
President Eisenhower, address at a Republican "kick-off for 1956" dinner, Washington, May 23, 1955.

"We must grow up with this great force, assuring the freedom of people to express their proper opinions, with the whole industry governed by the same rules that govern newspapers, the normal rules of decency and good taste. As long as those are observed, any proper opinion—any opinion—can be expressed before the public."
President Eisenhower, informal talk to National Association of Radio and Television Broadcasters, Washington, May 24, 1955.

"There is a tremendous responsibility here—in some way, I think, transcending that that is placed before the publisher. The publisher puts in your home a piece of print. It is essentially cold—although, of course, we admit that some writers have an ability to dress it up and make even disagreeable facts at times look fairly pleasant. But with the television or with the radio, you put an appealing voice or an engaging personality in the living room of the home, where there are impressionable people from the ages of understanding on up. In many ways, therefore, the effect of your industry in swaying public opinion, and I think, particularly

about burning questions of the moment, may be even greater than the press. . . ."
President Eisenhower. Ibid.

"I once heard an expression with respect to newspaper standards: The newspaper columns belong to the public, and the editorial page belongs to the paper. And, for myself, I find that an easy standard to follow and to apply as I examine a newspaper. I should think that some such standard could be developed by you."
President Eisenhower. Ibid.

"Never was it so important as it is today that the American public is informed. . . . It is absolutely essential that the Americans know the actual facts of these problems. Moreover, that they be helped to gain an understanding of the relationship between these facts, because knowledge alone, necessarily—always remember—is not sufficient. We must understand. We must understand the relationship between the farmer working in Kansas in a wheat field, and the need for wheat in far-off Pakistan or some other country."
President Eisenhower. Ibid.

"I think everybody in the television and radio professions has a right to think of himself as a man bearing a great responsibility as a crusader, and help to do this job of education, of ourselves and others about us, and to bring home here an understanding of what goes on in the rest of the world."
President Eisenhower. Ibid.

". . . The term 'politics' as such seems to be one of those words that means many things to many people. We so often use it in a derogatory sense. And I think in the general derogatory sense you can say that, of course, that I do not like politics. Now, on the other hand, any man who finds himself in a position of authority where he has a very great influence in the efforts of people to work toward a peaceful world, toward international relationships that will eliminate or minimize the chances of war, all that sort of thing, of course, it is a fascinating business. It is a kind of thing that would engage the interest, intense interest, of any man alive. There are in this office thousands of unique opportunities to meet especially interesting people, because the government here in Washington has become the center of so many things that, again, you have a very fascinating experience in meeting scientists, people that are leaders in culture, in health, in governmental action, and from all over the world. There are many things about the office and the work, the work with your associates, that are, well, let's say, at least intriguing, even if at times they are very fatiguing. But they are and it is a wonderful experience. But the word 'politics' as you use it, I think the answer to that one, would be, no. I have no great liking for that."

President Eisenhower, reply to a question, "How do you like the game of politics after three years?" at news conference, May 31, 1955.

". . . Bad deportment is never to be confused with strength of character. If a man is sure of himself and the integrity of the processes he has used to reach his decisions, he can be strong but he can be mild. In the life that we find outside of the armed services there seems to be a prevalent notion that if you call enough names, if you hammer enough desks, that you are a great leader. Happily, this Academy has never subscribed to any such false belief."

President Eisenhower, address to his fellow members of West Point Class of 1915, during class reunion at West Point, June 6, 1955.

"Leadership is something of the heart and of the head. It is not merely of a fluent and wicked tongue."

President Eisenhower. Ibid.

"We prepared ourselves in the lessons and the experiences of the past for a future that we complacently felt was clearly predictable in pattern and design. None among us could have realized that the world in which our fathers and we had lived was at that moment disappearing."

President Eisenhower, recollection of his own cadet days, commencement address at West Point, June 7, 1955.

"By the calendar, exactly forty years separates my class from this one of nineteen fifty-five. Yet, by the changes mine has seen—in the weapons of combat and the tools of peace, in the balance of international power, in the thinking of men—there might as easily be forty as four decades separating us."

President Eisenhower. Ibid.

"Of all the nations of today the future will say that there were two kinds: those that were intelligent, courageous, decisive and tireless in their support of high principle—and those that disappeared from the earth. The true patriots of today are those who are giving their best to assure that our own country will always be found in the first of these two categories."

President Eisenhower. Ibid.

"All of us gratefully acknowledge, as our fathers did before us, our dependence on the guidance of a Divine Providence. But this dependence must not tempt us to evade our personal responsibility to use every one of our individual and collective talents for the better discharge of our lifetime missions. Working and living in this spirit, you as soldiers will make yourselves and the Army a professional counterpart of the American way—jealously conserving principle; forceful in practice; courageous and calm in present crises; steadfast and patient in the long campaign for a secure and peaceful world; stout of faith in yourselves, your Alma Mater, your country and your God."

President Eisenhower. Ibid.

". . . As we look at the probable face of future warfare, if ever we must face that tragedy, we acknowledge that every hamlet and important city in the United States is likely to be in the front lines."

President Eisenhower, comment on need for a trained civilian reserve, news conference, June 8, 1955.

"Do you suppose for one minute that if I am ready to pick up and go from any place from Timbuctoo to the North Pole to do something about this question of peace, that I am going to stand on twenty-four hours?"

President Eisenhower, comment on limiting a Big Four meeting to four or five days. Ibid.

"Human relations—the art of getting along with people who work beside you and with those who live thousands of miles away—does not change in its essence with the centuries. But the age of nuclear energy, in its industrial and economic aspects, will likely bear no more resemblance to the age of steam than a jet-powered plane to an old-fashioned box kite. Indeed, the social pattern of living may be transformed beyond recognition."

President Eisenhower, commencement address at Pennsylvania State University, June 11, 1955.

". . . The people of the United States instinctively reject any thought that their greatest scientific achievement can be used only as a weapon. Our increasing progress in its peaceful applications is evidence of that fact. While we build atomic-powered ships for war—because we must —we have the desire, the determination to build atomic-powered ships for peace. And build them we shall. The first atomic-powered merchant ship, and its ports of call, will be a laboratory demonstration that man can harness this unlimited energy for normal, peaceful, prosperous life. While we design bombs that can obliterate great military objectives— because we must—we are also designing generators, channels, and reservoirs of atomic energy so that man may profit from this gift which the Creator of all things has put into his hands. And build them we shall."

President Eisenhower. Ibid.

". . . As nuclear and other technological achievements continue to mount, the normal life span will continue to climb. The hourly productivity of the worker will increase. How is the increase in leisure time and the extension of life expectancy to be spent? Will it be for the achievement of man's better aspirations or his degradation to the level of a well-fed, well-kept slave of an all-powerful state? Indeed, merely to state that question sharply reminds us that in these days and in the years ahead the

need for philosophers and theologians parallels the need for scientists and engineers."
President Eisenhower. Ibid.

"What I should like first to say to you—this is my deepest impression of this exercise: The most devout daily prayers that any of us has should be uttered in the supplication that this kind of disaster never comes to the United States."
President Eisenhower, report to the nation on "Operation Alert," a mock air raid alarm in which the executive branch of the government was evacuated from Washington, June 17, 1955.

"I pay respectful tribute to you whose faith, and patience, and courage, and wisdom have brought the United Nations through ten tumultuous, frequently discouraging, sometimes terrifying—but often rewarding—years. That there have been failures in attempts to solve international difficulties by the principles of the Charter, none can deny. That there have been victories, only the willfully blind can fail to see. But clear it is that without the United Nations the failures would still have been written as failures into history. And, certainly, without this organization the victories could not have been achieved; instead, they might well have been recorded as human disasters. These, the world has been spared."
President Eisenhower, address on the tenth anniversary of signing of United Nations Charter, San Francisco, June 20, 1955.

"The summer of 1955, like that one of 1945, is another season of high hope for the world. There again stirs in the hearts of men a renewed devotion to the work for the elimination of war. Each of us here is witness that never in ten years has the will of many nations seemed so resolved to wage an honest and sustained campaign for a just and lasting peace. . . . The heartfelt longings of countless millions for abundance and justice and peace seem to be commanding, everywhere, a response from their governments. These longings have strengthened the weak, encouraged the doubtful, heartened the tired, confirmed the believing. Almost it seems that men, with souls restored, are, with faith and courage, resuming the march toward the greatest human goal."
President Eisenhower. Ibid.

217

"Only a few moments ago, I had the first opportunity of my life to look at the Old Man of the Mountain. The natural question asked me was, 'What did you think of it, Mr. President?' I answered, as anyone would in polite conversation, and said: 'Remarkable, wonderful, interesting.' The real thought that crossed my mind was: what does the Old Man of the Mountain think of us?"

President Eisenhower, address at Franconia Notch, New Hampshire, June 24, 1955.

"If we are sufficiently devoted to the cause of peace, the kind of progress of which I speak, we will be strong, and then we will be able to cooperate with others, because only strength can cooperate—weakness cannot cooperate, it can only beg; and we will be able to cooperate and to help lead the world toward that promised goal."

President Eisenhower. Ibid.

"I know that Americans everywhere are the same, in their longing for peace, a peace that is characterized by justice, by consideration for others, by decency, above all by its insistence on respect for the individual human being as a child of his God."

President Eisenhower speaking to the Vermont Dairy Festival at Rutland, Vermont, June 21, 1955.

"We know we must be determined. We know we must not sacrifice principle for mere expediency. But do we know also that the responsibility is on us to attempt to understand others as we think they should understand us? Do we even make the mistake of assuming that the rest of the world knows us, knows our peaceful intentions, knows that we want nobody else's land?"

President Eisenhower. Ibid.

"It is probably a pity that every citizen of each state cannot visit all the others, to see the differences, to learn what we have in common, and to come back with a richer, fuller understanding of America—in all its beauty, in all its dignity, in all its strength, in support of moral principle."

President Eisenhower. Ibid.

"We will remain strong always, but always in one hand will be the olive branch held out to all who will take it in honesty and in integrity."
President Eisenhower. Ibid.

". . . You possibly saw my friends along the roads, and we don't know who was behind in the alleys."
President Eisenhower, comment on crowds which apparently wanted him to seek re-election, news conference of June 28, 1955.

". . . I don't know of any two people in the world who agree on this subject in its details, and I have personally been studying it for forty years."
President Eisenhower, comment on international disarmament. Ibid.

"This is vital. Why are we fooling around about it?"
President Eisenhower, comment on proposed reserve bill for strengthening the Armed Forces. Ibid.

"What I am trying to do as one of the peace-movers in this world is to convince the world . . . that here is a science that can mean practically the doubling, let us say, of living standards within a reasonable space of time. Here is a great science opening up opportunities in every way."
President Eisenhower, comment on peacetime uses of the atom. Ibid.

"Actually, I am delighted that the city of Memphis or any other local community, when it comes to the simple building of a power station through steam plant methods, and with no flood control or navigation or other factors in it, do it themselves. I believe we should do it ourselves. So I am not really concerned as to who is claiming political victories. This is in accordance with the philosophy in which I believe."
President Eisenhower, praising the independence of municipalities, presidential news conference, July 6, 1955.

"I wouldn't want to have anything I now say taken as authoritative for the simple reason that the more one studies intensively this problem of disarmament, the more he finds himself in sort of a squirrel's cage. He is running around pretty rapidly, and at times he has a feeling that he is merely chasing himself."

President Eisenhower. Ibid.

". . . Never sacrifice the basic principle that the human being is the most important thing on this planet. . . . Don't ever let anyone tell you you are licked."

President Eisenhower, informal address to a group of American Field Service students in White House rose garden, July 13, 1955.

". . . It is natural for a people steeped in a religious civilization when they come to moments of great importance—maybe even crises, such as now we face—to turn to the Divine Power that each has in his own heart, believes in in his own heart, for guidance, for wisdom, for some help in doing the thing that is honorable and is right. I have no doubt that tonight throughout this country, and indeed throughout the free world, such prayers are ascending. This is a mighty force. And this brings to me the thought that through prayer we could also achieve a very definite and practical result at this very moment."

President Eisenhower, address to the nation an hour before departing for Big Four Conference at Geneva, July 15, 1955.

"Some eleven years ago, Mr. President, I came to Europe with an Army, a Navy, an Air Force, with a single purpose: to destroy Nazism. I came with the formations of war, and all of the circumstances of war surrounded that journey at that time. This time I come armed with something far more powerful: the good will of America—the great hopes of America—the aspirations of America for peace."

President Eisenhower, greeting to President Max Petitpierre of Switzerland on arrival in Geneva for Big Four Conference, July 16, 1955.

"The problems that concern us are not inherently insoluble. . . . They seem insoluble under conditions of fear, distrust, and even hostility. . . . If those conditions can be changed, then much can be done. . . . It is not always necessary that people should think alike and believe alike before they can work together."

President Eisenhower, opening address at Geneva Conference, July 21, 1955.

"Gentlemen, since I have been working on this memorandum to present to this conference, I have been searching my heart and mind for something that I could say here that could convince everyone of the great sincerity of the United States in approaching this problem of disarmament. I should address myself for a moment principally to the delegates from the Soviet Union because our two great countries admittedly possess new and terrible weapons in quantities which do give rise in other parts of the world, or reciprocally, to the fears and dangers of surprise attack. I propose, therefore, that we take a practical step, that we begin an arrangement, very quickly, as between ourselves—immediately. These steps would include: To give to each other a complete blueprint of our military establishments, from beginning to end, from one end of our country to the other: lay out the establishments and provide the blueprints to each other. Next, to provide within our countries facilities for aerial photography to the other country—we to provide you the facilities within our country, ample facilities for aerial reconnaissance, where you can make all the pictures you choose and take them to your own country to study; you to provide exactly the same facilities for us and we to make these examinations, and by this step to convince the world that we are providing as between ourselves against the possibility of great surprise attack, thus lessening danger and relaxing tensions. Likewise, we will make more easily attainable a comprehensive and effective system of inspection and disarmament, because what I propose, I assure you, would be but a beginning."

President Eisenhower, statement to Big Four Conference, Geneva, afterwards considered the keynote address of parley, July 21, 1955.

"The successful working out of such a system would do much to develop the mutual confidence which will open wide the avenues of progress for all our peoples. The quest for peace is the statesman's most exacting duty. Security of the nation entrusted to his care is his greatest responsibility. Practical progress to lasting peace is his fondest hope. Yet in pursuit of his hope he must not betray the trust placed in him as guardian of the people's security. A sound peace—with security, justice, well-being, and freedom for the people of the world—can be achieved, but only by patiently and thoughtfully following a hard and sure and tested road."

President Eisenhower. Ibid.

"We make long speeches—some of them dull—in the big sessions; but in the refreshment room we really think. You get to know a man a little in there."

President Eisenhower, aside remark during Geneva Conference, July 23, 1955.

"If our peoples, in the months and years ahead, broaden their knowledge and their understanding of each other, as we, during this week, have broadened our knowledge of each other, further agreement between our governments may be facilitated. May this occur in a spirit of justice. May it result in improved well-being, greater freedom and less of fear or suffering or distress for mankind. May it be marked by more of good will among men. These days will then indeed be ever remembered. I came to Geneva because I believe mankind longs for freedom from war and rumors of war. I came here because of my lasting faith in the decent instincts and good sense of the people who populate this world of ours. I shall return home with these convictions unshaken, and with the prayer that the hope of mankind will one day be realized."

President Eisenhower, final address at Geneva Conference, July 23, 1955.

"I brought my paints and brushes to Geneva. I saw the beautiful colors around my villa and the changing colors of the lake. I longed to paint them, but I never had a chance."

President Eisenhower, aside remark after end of Geneva Conference.

222

". . . We must never be deluded into believing that one week of friendly, even fruitful negotiations can wholly eliminate a problem arising out of the wide gulf that separates so far East and West. A gulf as wide and deep as the difference between individual liberty and regimentation, as wide and deep as the gulf that lies between the concept of man made in the image of his God and the concept of man as a mere instrument of the state."

President Eisenhower, broadcast upon return from Geneva Conference, July 25, 1955.

". . . There is great pressure to advance constructively, not merely to re-enact the dreary performances—the negative performances—of the past. We all of us, individually and as a people, now have possibly the most difficult assignment of our nation's history. Likewise we have the most shining opportunity ever possessed by Americans. May these truths inspire, never dismay us. I believe that only with prayerful patience, intelligence, courage and tolerance, never forgetting vigilance and prudence, can we keep alive the spark ignited at Geneva. But if we are successful in this then we will make constantly brighter the lamp that will one day guide us to our goal, a just and lasting peace."

President Eisenhower. Ibid.

". . . If I can go from great nationalistic subjects, public subjects, to something that concerns only me and my family—and this may not be news—but I got home to be greeted by my daughter-in-law with the statement that if all goes well, I will be a grandfather for the fourth time next Christmas which, of course, was a happy ending to the week."

President Eisenhower, opening comment in first news conference held after returning from Geneva.

"It cannot rest on any record, no matter how good."

President Eisenhower, comment on economic activity in U.S., presidential news conference, August 4, 1955.

"There is always present the two twin dangers of deflation and inflation. And the function of government so far as it affects this matter at all is to be watchful, to be vigilant and alert, and to take measures from time to time that tend to move in one direction if the signs are we are moving in another."

President Eisenhower. Ibid.

Text of the code of conduct for war prisoners which President Eisenhower ordered put into effect by the armed services, August 17, 1955:

1. I am an American fighting man. I serve in the forces which guard my country and our way of life. I am prepared to give my life in their defense.
2. I will never surrender of my own free will. If in command I will never surrender my men while they still have the means to resist.
3. If I am captured I will continue to resist by all means available. I will make every effort to escape and aid others to escape. I will accept neither parole nor special favors from the enemy.
4. If I become a prisoner of war, I will keep faith with my fellow prisoners. I will give no information or take part in any action which might be harmful to my comrades. If I am senior, I will take command. If not I will obey the lawful orders of those appointed over me and will back them up in every way.
5. When questioned, should I become a prisoner of war, I am bound to give only name, rank, service number, and date of birth. I will evade answering further questions to the utmost of my ability. I will make no oral or written statements disloyal to my country and its allies or harmful to their cause.
6. I will never forget that I am an American fighting man, responsible for my actions, and dedicated to the principles which made my country free. I will trust in my God and in the United States of America.

"No American prisoner of war will be forgotten by the United States. Every available means will be employed by our government to establish contact with, to support and to obtain the release of all our prisoners of war. Furthermore, the laws of the United States provide for the support and care of dependents of members of the armed forces including those who become prisoners of war. I assure dependents of such prisoners that these laws will continue to provide for their welfare."

President Eisenhower, statement attached to new code of conduct for war prisoners, August 17, 1955.

"The heart of America is not going to stand still while other Americans are in distress and in need of help."

President Eisenhower, comment regarding relief and funds needed to aid flood damage in Northeast after Hurricane Diane in August, 1955; quoted in news summaries of August 23, 1955.

"We must not think of peace as a static condition in world affairs. That is not true peace, nor in fact can any kind of a peace be preserved that way. Change is the law of life, and unless there is peaceful change, there is bound to be violent change."

President Eisenhower, address to seventy-eighth annual convention of American Bar Association, Philadelphia, August 24, 1955.

"Today when our nation needs every skilled worker available, we cannot afford to squander our manpower through a prejudice which obscures the values of maturity, responsibility, and constancy found in older workers."

President Eisenhower, Labor Day message appealing for employment of workers over forty-five, September 4, 1955.

". . . Humans are frail—and they are mortal. Finally—you never pin your flag so tightly to one mast that if a ship sinks you cannot rip it off and nail it to another. It is sometimes good to remember that."

President Eisenhower, address to breakfast of forty-eight Republican state chairmen meeting in Denver, September 10, 1955.

"Misfortune, and particularly the misfortune of illness, brings to all of us an understanding of how good people are."

President Eisenhower, remark on being discharged November 11, 1955, from Fitzsimmons Army Hospital, Denver, after recovery from a heart attack.

"It has been a little longer stay than we had planned but the circumstances you will understand. I am happy that the doctors have given me at least a parole if not a pardon, and I expect to be back at my accustomed duties, although they say I must ease my way into 'em and not bulldoze my way into them."

President Eisenhower, comment on return to Washington, November 11, 1955, seven weeks after suffering heart attack in Denver.

"I know that no setback, no obstacle to progress will ever deter this government and our people from the great effort to establish a just and durable peace. Success may be long in coming, but there is no temporal force so capable of helping achieve it as the strength, the might, the spirit of 165 million free Americans."

President Eisenhower, comment to nation on hearing reports of failure of Foreign Ministers' Conference and possible resumption of the "cold war"; November 19, 1955.

"We know that education, centrally controlled, finally would lead to a kind of control in other fields which we don't want and will never have. So we are dedicated to the proposition that the responsibility for educating our young is primarily local."

President Eisenhower, opening address for White House Conference on Education, November 28, 1955; the President went further than at any previous time in his appeal for limited federal aid to education.

"In the world struggle some of the finest weapons for all Americans are these three simple tenets of free labor. . . . Man is created in the Divine Image and has spiritual aspirations that transcend the material; second, the real interests of employers and employes are mutual; third, unions and employers can and should work out their own destinies. As we appreciate and practice that message without ceasing, we will wage a triumphant crusade for prosperity, freedom, and peace among men."

President Eisenhower, address by telephone to unification meeting of the American Federation of Labor and Congress of Industrial Organizations, New York, December 5, 1955.

". . . This Christmas is, nevertheless, brighter in its background and its promise for the future than any we have known in recent years. I think it is even better than last year, and you will remember that Christmas was the first one in many years that was not marred by the tragic incidents of war."

President Eisenhower, Christmas address broadcast to the nation, December 18, 1955, from Gettysburg, Pennsylvania.

"Well, it worked!"

President Eisenhower, spontaneous comment heard across the nation when he lighted the national community Christmas tree in Washington by remote control from Gettysburg, Pennsylvania, December 18, 1955.

"To Mamie, For never-failing help since 1916—in calm and in stress, in dark days and in bright. Love—Ike. Christmas 1955."

President Eisenhower, message engraved on a gold medallion presented to his wife as a Christmas gift, December 25, 1955.

THE PRESS

"The reason I talk fast is that if I talk slowly people will be able to hear what I say and find out how dull and unimportant it really is."

Walter Winchell, comment on his reported broadcast delivery speed of an average of 215 words per minute, news summaries of January 28, 1955.

"The newspaper is an institution developed by modern civilization to present the news of the day, to foster commerce and industry, to inform and lead public opinion, and to furnish that check upon government which no constitution has ever been able to provide."

Colonel Robert McCormick, publisher of The Chicago Tribune, definition of a newspaper, quotation recalled in obituaries reporting his death, news reports of April 2, 1955.

"To hell with the Marshall Plan. It's really a snob plan."

Colonel Robert McCormick. Ibid.

"I think America is four times as important as I thought before I left. It is ten times as important as the average man thinks, and one hundred times as important as the average New Yorker thinks."

Colonel Robert McCormick, returning from a 1948 European trip. Ibid.

"[The British] aristocracy continues to direct the foreign policy of the United States and thereby rules the world. . . . Ancestry [there] is more important than accomplishment."

Colonel Robert McCormick. Ibid.

"Last week Professor Einstein trudged no more in the grounds of his beloved institute. A lingering gall-bladder infection sent him to the hospital. Blood began to escape from his aorta, the main artery. Shortly after midnight he muttered a few sentences in German. The night nurse could not understand, and the last words of the modern world's greatest scientist were lost. At 1:15 A.M., Albert Einstein, seventy-six, died in his sleep.

". . . Words could not convey the feelings of a world in which the many unquestioningly accepted Einstein's genius while only the few—and they, of scientific training—adequately understood what he had contributed to knowledge. In person, Albert Einstein was diffident, almost childlike. As a man of scientific thought, he strode boldly with history's handful: Pythagoras and Archimedes, Copernicus and Newton.

"Einstein's only instruments were a pencil and scratch-pad; his laboratory was under his cap. Yet he saw farther than a telescope, deeper than a microscope. Einstein traveled in lonely splendor to the crossroads of the visible and the invisible, expressing each in terms of the other. He came close to proving by mathematicians' logic what men of religion had long accepted on philosophers' reasoning or faith: that the laws which move the tiniest unseen electrons must also govern the microcosms of intergalactic space. Einstein's scratch-pad theorems broke through the thought barriers of knowledge and rewrote the basic scientific law of the universe. The now-mundane miracle of clouds of atomic fission and hydrogen fusion are his unwanted monuments; mankind's chance to turn earth-shaking force into good is his legacy."

Time, May 2, 1955, report on the death of Albert Einstein, April 18, 1955, copyright 1955, Time Inc.; reprinted by permission.

"Paris, May 5, 1955—French fashion designers today faced up to the facts of life and agreed to scrap the 'Flat Look' of designer Christian Dior. Even Mr. Dior himself appeared to be ready to admit defeat by Mother Nature. The rest of the French fashion experts revolted en masse against continuing their unpopular attempts to suppress the feminine bosom. Their patrons were pleased."

United Press dispatch on passing of the "Flat Look," reprinted by permission.

"It was an extraordinary moment. What all the imagination and discussion by diplomats, what all the destruction of the war in Korea had been unable to do was all of a sudden produced by an air of complete frankness and a rare combination of simplicity and greatness. The psychological iron curtain that separates the two worlds much more effectively than the political and economic iron curtain was all of a sudden pierced. The words reached the depths of the souls to which they were addressed. With much emphasis, Bulganin responded, saying simply: 'We believe you.'"

Le Monde, Paris "neutralist" newspaper, appraisal of President Eisenhower's direct appeal for peace with Russia at Geneva Conference, quoted by New York Herald Tribune, July 21, 1955.

"Race or gang fight stories will be filed as advisory notes during the active stage of trouble in order to help prevent a minor disturbance from exploding into a major conflict. . . . It is hoped that this method of treatment . . . will prevent hundreds of racists from concentrating at the trouble scene, and yet provide the assurance that the basic news is reported to the public."

Isaac Gershman, managing editor, Chicago City News Bureau, comment on new confidential advisory code devised by him for radio and television news editors; news reports of July 24, 1955.

". . . The repository for washed-away cares? It must lie somewhere in the ocean, for nothing can vanish as completely as cares seem to vanish, just beyond the breakers. There is a twisting, slithering mass of them somewhere, perhaps in a dark cavern, many fathoms down. The spot should be discovered and then charted, so that no chance voyager might

accidentally stumble upon it. All the cares of the world is better as a
figure of speech than it would be as a reality. . . . On vacation, and
out beyond the breakers, all men are millionaires, at least for the time.
It is good to turn over out there, and float, and to think about those
vanished cares, wherever they may be."

*"Topics of The Times," The New York Times, August 1, 1955,
reprinted by permission.*

"Some of the society women of Chicago are drinking themselves silly.
'Round the clock they go, lapping it up from high noon till they reach
another high at midnight. By their own admission some of them are
consuming from twelve to twenty ounces a day. . . . I love society and
I don't like to think there are any lady lushes in society. [But] some
women who lead brisk social lives can consume . . . nearly a gallon a
week."

*Athlyn Deshais, society editor, Chicago Daily News, news sum-
maries of August 1, 1955.*

"We hoped that other publications would be attracted by the common
sense and etymological rightness of sherif and tarif for example, but
this hope has been disappointed."

*The Chicago Tribune, editorial announcing discontinuation of
tradition of phonetic spelling in Tribune editorial columns, August 21, 1955.*

"It was like combining a psychoanalysis with a fraternity initiation."

*Colonel John Paul Stapp, Air Force space researchist, comment
on being interviewed for a Time "cover story," Time, September
26, 1955.*

"We have had, in the history of the Internal Security Subcommittee, wit-
nesses from most of the professions. We have gotten more cooperation
from newspapermen than from any other group in the country."

*Senator James Eastland of Mississippi, news reports of October
18, 1955.*

"If we ever get rid of the ups and downs of business, it will be because people now are reading much more about it and are acting on what they've learned by reading."

Barney Kilgore, publisher, the Wall Street Journal, Time, *November 14, 1955.*

RADIO AND TELEVISION

"I would think that television is the most important vehicle for the dissemination of art that has ever come to hand. I think it is just as important as the invention of printing was in the fifteenth century."

Francis Henry Taylor, director, Metropolitan Museum of Art, New York City, comment in interview with Edward R. Murrow, "Person to Person," CBS-TV, January 7, 1955.

"We are in the twentieth century—the second part."

James Hagerty, White House press secretary, reply to critics who expressed belief that television cameras would disturb presidential news conferences, The New York Times, *February 13, 1955.*

"The White House must have control over the spoken word of the President. There are too many unpredictable consequences that can flow from the slightest off-hand remark."

James Hagerty, comment on plans to edit films of presidential news conferences before releasing films to television stations. Ibid.

"It is a kaleidoscopic phantasmagoria."

Sylvester Weaver, president of the National Broadcasting Company, comment on inauguration of a radio variety program designed to last over an entire weekend, Time, *March 7, 1955.*

"For me problem-solving is the most interesting thing in life. To be handed something that's a complete mess and straighten it out. To organize where there is no organization. To give form to a medium that has no form."

Sylvester Weaver, quoted in a "profile" of him in Newsweek, July 18, 1955, when he was President of the National Broadcasting Company.

"Space, scope, sweep, mobility, bigness, stature, prestige—these are the qualities we want to get . . . a real grass-roots American feeling."

Sylvester Weaver, comment on plans for a new afternoon television program, news reports of November 1, 1955.

"He is forced to be literate about the illiterate, witty about the witless and coherent about the incoherent."

John Crosby, television critic for the New York Herald Tribune, comment on the role of a television critic in 1955; news summaries of March 20, 1955.

"We've allowed our shows to become unbearably dull, repetitious, predictable, wild, and sloppy. We've ignored a public that's sick and tired of watching, story in and story out, about Bringing the Boss Home to Dinner; and Forgetting the Wife's Birthday; and Getting Into This Disguise So's Husband Won't Recognize Me; and Is My Wife Killing Me For My Insurance Policy?; and Did He Forget My Anniversary?; and The Old Boy Friend; and The Old Girl Friend; and Let's Make Him Think He's Going Crazy; and Bringing the Boss Home to Dinner. . . . Fellas, we've just about dug our own graves! . . . We've gotta think. You know what that rhymes with. Our stock situations do."

Lou Derman, comedy writer, reporting in Variety June 22, 1955, on the state of American television plays; reprinted by permission.

"Television is now so desperately hungry for material that they're scraping the top of the barrel."

Gore Vidal, novelist and television writer, news reports of July 20, 1955.

"Some television programs are so much chewing gum for the eyes."
John Mason Brown, quoting a friend of his small son, interview with James Simpson, July 28, 1955.

"I wanted to set up an event where people would be tremendously interested, would care what happened, and not know until it happened what was going to happen."
Louis Cowan, television producer, comment concerning inspiration for the television program, "The $64,000 Question," The New York Times Magazine, August 21, 1955.

"You tell them what you're going to tell them. Then you tell them. Then you tell them what you've told them."
Louis Cowan, recollection of one of the large precepts of his life, given to him by the late Bishop Waldorf. Ibid.

"It is only forty years since, with the temerity of youth, I sent my boss a memorandum recommending the manufacture and sale of what I called a 'Radio Music Box' that could bring entertainment, music, news, and information—freely—into any home. The idea seemed at that time pretty far-fetched, and I was told as much. Yet, in that short span of years this new medium has become a mighty force in our daily lives—almost the symbol of the American domestic scene."
David Sarnoff, chairman of the board, Radio Corporation of America, address at the Advertising Club of Washington, D.C., September 20, 1955; text reprinted by National Broadcasting Company.

"The fact is that we are in an enterprise where larger horizons are opened up every time we cross a horizon already in sight."
David Sarnoff. Ibid.

"After we telecast our first ballet, some persons who hadn't seen ballet before thought the men's costumes too revealing. But since ballet costumes have been like that for a century, we don't worry about such complaints."

Stockton Helfrich, Director of Continuity Acceptance for the National Broadcasting Company, news summaries of September 25, 1955.

"Not even the sky is the limit. The potentials of television are as big as the potentials of American society—and I do not feel like setting a limit on that."

Frank Stanton, president, Columbia Broadcasting System, Time, October 17, 1955.

"You should realize that the community with which you deal is not the one of Forty-Second and Broadway, or Hollywood and Vine. These are the crusts on the great American sandwich. The meat is in between."

The Most Rev. Fulton Sheen, best-known television personality of the Roman Catholic Church, advice to broadcasting executives on their audiences, news summaries of November 9, 1955.

"School children ask us to trap their teachers in undignified or compromising situations; ordinary citizens want us to catch policemen and other authority figures unawares; little businessmen plead with us to capture the off-the-record attitudes of their larger competitors."

Allen Funt, speaking of his radio and television program, "Candid Camera," New York Herald Tribune TV Magazine, November 13, 1955.

"If you force a man to talk to you through a brick wall, you can hardly complain if he raises his voice."

Harold Macmillan, British Foreign Secretary, comment on Russian claim that the British Broadcasting Corporation was using too many frequencies to beam its broadcasts to East Europe, news reports of November 15, 1955.

"A television drama is one of the most perishable items known to man. . . . Television is a strange medium limited by a thousand technical problems, hemmed in by taboos and advertising policies, cheapened by the innumerable untalented and officious people you will always find in a billion-dollar industry. Nevertheless, for the writers there is still area for deep and unprobed work."

Paddy Chayefsky, television playwright, news summaries of December 29, 1955.

"The impact of television on our culture is just indescribable. There's a certain sense in which it is nearly as important as the invention of printing."

Carl Sandburg, news summaries of December 30, 1955.

"A reporter is always concerned with tomorrow. There's nothing tangible of yesterday. All I can say I've done is agitate the air ten or fifteen minutes and then boom—it's gone."

Edward R. Murrow, news commentator, new summaries of December 31, 1955.

"Everyone is a prisoner of his own experiences. No one can eliminate prejudices—just recognize them."

Edward R. Murrow. Ibid.

RELIGION

"Gentlemen: I am giving your corporation as of this date securities having a present market value of approximately twenty million dollars. The purpose of the gift is to strengthen and develop Protestant theological education in this country."

John D. Rockefeller, Jr., a two-sentence letter to the Sealantic Fund, Inc., a philanthropic corporation, announcing the largest single grant ever made for purposes of religious training, news reports of January 12, 1955.

"Modern man has tried the suspense of believing nothing, and because suspense is soon unbearable, he has ended by believing almost anything."

Dr. George Arthur Buttrick, pastor, Madison Avenue Presbyterian Church, New York City, news reports of January 15, 1955.

"We pray that our Diocese as well as our Parishes and our individual selves may continue to march from strength to strength in ever increasing service to God in this troubled world. Arkansas isn't a very big segment of the world—but it is bigger than the area in which the Light that lighteneth the world first shone."

The Rev. Carleton Lathrop, rector emeritus St. John's Episcopal Church, Fort Smith, Arkansas, writing in church bulletin, January 23, 1955.

". . . If the typewriter was abolished tomorrow a mass of vapid thought that goes on between human beings would be vastly reduced and the danger of a war would be vastly decreased."

The archbishop of Canterbury, Dr. Geoffrey Fisher, at the inauguration of new headquarters of the British Council of Churches, London, news reports, March 15, 1955.

"I say to you Baptists, 'Go on being good Baptists, thinking that you are more right than anybody else.' Unless you think it I have no use for you at all. The Church of England does precisely the same itself."

The archbishop of Canterbury, Dr. Geoffrey Fisher, address in London to the golden jubilee congress of the Baptist World Alliance, news reports of July 17, 1955.

"We need America to keep us moving, eager and young for our years and still adventurous. America needs us to keep her patient, sensitive and aware that if its size often shows on a great scale the splendors of God, His deepest secrets are to be found in the small, the simple and the domestic. And the world for its preservation desperately needs what whole-hearted trust and cooperation between us can bring to it."

The archbishop of Canterbury, Dr. Geoffrey Fisher, Reader's Digest, October 1955.

"Until you know that life is interesting—and find it so—you haven't found your soul. . . . What matters is that we do our best for the Kingdom of God. If we say we're not doing too badly, we're sunk. But if we say, things are frightful and we'll do our best, we're okay."

The archbishop of Canterbury, Dr. Geoffrey Fisher. Ibid.

"I do trust that there will not be a show made of this thing. . . . Members in this room want to be alone with their God."

Representative Sam Rayburn, Speaker of the House, comment on a prayer and meditation room opened in the U. S. Capitol Building, news reports, March 20, 1955.

"I don't think the time will ever come when just honest, straight-forward, simple giving of food and shelter to people who need it irrespective of whether they are enemy or friend, will be outmoded. That, I suppose, will always be one of the calls on decent human beings."

Clarence Pickett, veteran head of the American Friends Service Committee (Quakers) and co-winner of Nobel Peace Prize; comment in interview with Edward R. Murrow, "Person to Person," CBS-TV, April 1, 1955.

"The modern world has looked at the priest with eyes inflamed with hostile sarcasm and blinded by a utilitarian approach. The heir of the long-dead Middle Ages, the ally of selfish conservatism, the high priest of a silenced litany, the stranger in life: This is the priest. The clergy . . . has felt the repelling aversion of society in the midst of the new needs of the century. The clergy started its self-examination. . . . What is necessary is that the priest be able to hear the factory sirens, to understand the temples of technology where the modern world lives and throbs. It is up to him to become a missionary anew if he wants Christianity to endure. . . . A true, a good, a human, a saintly priesthood would save the world. The mission of the spirit cannot be contested. Even atheism has its own agitators, ideally devoted to its cause. . . . The capacity of expressing the ineffable truths that surround us, of approaching, without profanation, the mystery that envelops the universe, of giving a meaning to material things, an interior language to the spirit, and a resounding voice to man's labor, to his sorrow, to his love—this capacity is nothing but prayer, a prayer that must be true as light, a prayer that, like light, is poetry and reality as well. All this is priesthood. And this capacity is still alive in the heart of the twentieth century."

Cardinal Montini, archbishop of Milan, quoted in Newsweek, *June 13, 1955.*

> "Fear knocked at the door.
> Faith answered.
> No one was there."

Margaret Blair Johnstone, writer and Congregational pastor, quotation of ancient inscription on mantel of Hinds' Head Hotel, Bray, England, Better Homes and Gardens, *June 1955, and later reprinted in* Reader's Digest.

"*The New York Times,* in a review of books published in 1954, points out that from a glance at the sales charts it would seem that the average American wants most of all to (1) get religion, (2) reduce, (3) refinish an antique Chippendale highboy. Song writers are finding it to their advantage to feature religious themes—'I Believe,' 'Are You Friends With the King of Friends?' are samples. Film producers are more than ever aware of the box-office appeal of religious drama."

Dr. Robert McCracken, minister, Riverside Church of New York, comment on the popular appeal of religion in the mid-1950s, McCalls, *June 1955.*

"I sing what is in my heart. My only thought now is to sing as I have never sung before."

Mrs. Betty Robbins, Long Island housewife and mother of four, comment on becoming the first woman cantor in Jewish history, news summaries of August 15, 1955.

"I have taken this step because I want the discipline, the fire and the authority of the church. I am hopelessly unworthy of it, but I hope to become worthy."

Dame Edith Sitwell, statement on being received into the Roman Catholic Church at the age of sixty-seven, news summaries of August 15, 1955.

"If we sing hymns to practically every beat except the tango and the mambo, it's because it doesn't matter how you honor the Lord, just so you honor Him. The Lord doesn't want His children going around with long faces. He wants 'em to be happy."

Wally Fowler, of Possum Trot, Georgia, founder of the "All-Nite Gospel and Spiritual Sing Concerts," popular in the deep South, notable for his efforts to convert old-fashioned gospel singing into big-time show business; Collier's, *August 19, 1955.*

"It is true that Divine Providence has invested me, although unworthily, in this position as head of the Church, but as a man I am nothing . . . nothing . . . nothing."

Pope Pius XII, verbal reply to expression of loyalty given him by Fulton Sheen, American bishop, Look, *August 22, 1955.*

"I shall be able to rest one minute after I die."

Pope Pius XII, reply to doctors who asked him to curtail his work. Ibid.

"Labor is not merely the fatigue of body without sense or value; nor is it merely a humiliating servitude. It is a service of God, a gift of God, the vigor and fullness of human life, the gage of eternal rest."

Pope Pius XII, message for Labor Day, Guideposts, *September 1955.*

"No one who has had a unique experience with prayer has a right to withhold it from others."

Madame Chiang Kai-shek, "The Power of Prayer," Reader's Digest, *August 1955.*

"I felt there's a wealth in Jewish tradition, a great inheritance. I'd be a jerk not to take advantage of it."

Herman Wouk, explanation for his return to the Jewish Orthodox faith, Time, *September 5, 1955.*

"Anyone closely connected with the affairs of the Church recognizes the thoughtful, creative, and conscientious contribution being made by the women. They are ready and able to share in the responsibility, the difficulties, and the satisfactions of toiling to make straight in the desert a highway for our God."

> *Horace Donegan, Protestant Episcopal bishop of New York, address to the 1955 Diocesan Convention; the conclave later rejected the bishop's plea that women be allowed to serve on parish vestries and serve as convention delegates, news reports of September 8, 1955.*

"Modern man may not wish his temple to reach to Heaven, which was the sky to the man of the Middle Ages; he may wish, rather, that it be human in scale, appropriate to the inward search and responsive to . . . the needs of a complex age."

> *Pietro Belluschi, American architect, comment on religious construction during the nineteen-fifties, Time, September 19, 1955.*

"When thee gets back to thy kennel, I hope thy mother bites thee."

> *The Rev. Richard Key, Yuma, Arizona, minister, quotation of a Quaker woman motorist who squelched a blaspheming truck driver, Time, September 19, 1955.*

"Religion, in some quarters, is being identified with the cult of success, and prayer as but a means to promotion to the presidency of the company. This is not a worthy approach to the Eternal."

> *G. Bromley Oxnam, Methodist bishop, news reports of October 31, 1955.*

"I just want to lobby for God."

> *Billy Graham, evangelist, comment on establishing his national headquarters in Washington, D.C., news summaries of December 12, 1955.*

"I propose that God should be openly and audibly invoked at the United Nations in accordance with any one of the religious faiths which are represented here. I do so in the conviction that we cannot make the United Nations into a successful instrument of God's peace without God's help—and that with His help we cannot fail. To this end I propose that we ask for that help. . . ."

Henry Cabot Lodge, Jr., chief U. S. delegate to the UN, letter sent to each member state of the UN, news reports of December 30, 1955.

"I asked God for strength, that I might achieve,
I was made weak, that I might learn humbly to obey. . . .
I asked for health, that I might do greater things,
I was given infirmity, that I might do better things. . . .
I asked for riches, that I might be happy,
I was given poverty that I might be wise. . . .
I asked for power, that I might have the praise of men,
I was given weakness, that I might feel the need of God. . . .
I asked for all things, that I might enjoy life,
I was given life, that I might enjoy all things. . . .
I got nothing that I asked for—but everything I had hoped for,
Almost despite myself, my unspoken prayers were answered.
I am among all men, mostly richly blessed."

Prayer of an unknown Confederate soldier, reprinted on the greeting cards of Democratic presidential candidate Adlai Stevenson, Christmas 1955, Time, *January 2, 1956.*

"Do not our prayers for help mean: Help me to be better than I know myself to be. Help me to do this thing that I am doing better than my own limited capacities would permit without help. Help me to restrain my passions about to flare. Help me to discipline my tired mind. Help me to open my heart and imagination. Help me toward that wisdom which is more than knowledge. Help me to kindle and rekindle the divine spark of love. Help me to find the fortitude by which I may endure this sorrow, frustration, injustice, or disappointment. God help me to know, love, and trust in God and to perform his particular will for me?"

Dorothy Thompson, author and columnist, How Prayer Helps Me, *edited by Samuel Duff McCoy, The Dial Press, New York, 1955; reprinted by permission of the publisher.*

"Nine of the Ten Commandments are negative. If throughout life you abstain from murder, theft, fornication, perjury, blasphemy, and disrespect toward your parents, your Church, and your King, you are conventionally held to deserve moral admiration even if you have never done a single kind or generous or useful action. This very inadequate notion of virtue is an outcome of taboo morality, and has done untold harm."

> *Bertrand Russell,* Human Society in Ethics and Politics, *Simon and Schuster, Inc., 1955; reprinted by permission.*

"Ethics and moral codes are necessary to man because of the conflict between intelligence and impulse. Given intelligence only, or impulse only, there would be no place for ethics."

> *Bertrand Russell. Ibid.*

"My years in Carmel have taught me one thing: when God asks us to sacrifice the normal joys of living, it is only that He may give us a higher and holier joy. Living with God alone in the solitude of Carmel has proved sweeter far to me than all the pleasure and fickle applause of the world."

> *Mother Catherine Thomas,* My Beloved: The Story of a Carmelite Nun, *McGraw-Hill Book Company, Inc., copyright 1955 by Mother Catherine Thomas; reprinted by permission.*

"I explained to my sister that she could not understand my call to Carmel since she did not experience it. She could not know the love of God that was drawing me to the cloister. Did she not recall what Our Lord said about leaving mother and father and family and everything one had for His sake and how He would give such a one a hundredfold reward, even here on earth? Couldn't she see that I was not running away from life, that I wanted to get even more out of life? That was why I was asked to make a bigger sacrifice, just as when a person wishes to get a better car he has to pay a higher price."

> *Ibid.*

"For the religious it is her pleasure no longer to do her own will. It is her pleasure and joy to do the will of her Beloved. It is, or can be, that simple."

Ibid.

"We exchange the voice of a human suitor for the heavenly call of Christ, the Eternal Bridegroom; the earth, the here and the now, we exchange for the timelessness of the cloister; the tinsel treasures and the passing pleasures of the world we exchange for the priceless spiritual riches and the incomparable joy of living for others with Christ in poverty and penance. In exchange for running after shadows, we receive the privilege of touching reality. In exchange for the possibility of success in the world, we receive the certainty of the failure of Calvary; in exchange for social position and prestige, we accept the humility and hiddenness of Carmel. In exchange for the variable affections of the world, we receive the steadfast charity of Carmel; in exchange for radios and newspapers, we have the silence of Carmel; in exchange for mad jazz and concert music, we have the Gregorian chant whose only audience is God. . . ."

Ibid.

"A Carmelite nun should be, by the very nature of her vocation, a specialist in prayer. Or, to give it a more modern twist, she is a career woman in the field of prayer and contemplation."

Ibid.

ROYALTY

"Our child will not be raised in tissue paper! You quite understand, do you not, Miss Feith? Dogs are difficult to raise in a palace, ah yes, but children much more so! While she is still small she is to be called Trix. By everyone, even the servants. We don't want her to even hear the word princess."

Princess Juliana, on meeting Sophia Feith, nurse for Juliana's first child, Princess Beatrix, in March 1938, quoted in "Born to Be Queen," by Betty Hoffman, Ladies' Home Journal, March 1955, reprinted by permission.

"Trix says my job is running the country and my hobby is raising four daughters, but Irene, bless her heart, thinks it's quite the other way round!"

Queen Juliana, comment before ascending the throne. Ibid.

"I have been called to a task so heavy that no one who has the least notion of it would desire it. At the same time, this task is so splendid that I can only say, 'Who am I to be allowed to perform it?'"

Queen Juliana, coronation address. Ibid.

"This is not the feeling of the debtor toward the creditor; it is not the feeling of the small toward the great; but the feeling of friendship of the free for the free."

Queen Juliana, address to Congress during state visit to U.S. Ibid.

"I was just a good wife and tried to help him realize the best within himself."

Queen Mother Elizabeth of Britain, reply when praised for her aid to King George VI, news reports of April 15, 1955.

"I am commanded by the Queen to say that Her Majesty and the Duke of Edinburgh have decided that their son has reached the stage when he should take part in more grown-up educational pursuits with other children. In consequence, a certain amount of the Duke of Cornwall's instruction will take place outside his home; for example, he will attend classes and will visit museums and other places of interest. The Queen trusts, therefore, that His Royal Highness will be able to enjoy this in the same way as other children can without the embarrassment of constant publicity. In this respect, Her Majesty feels that it is equally important that those in charge of, or sharing in, the instruction should be spared undue publicity which can so seriously interrupt their normal lives. I would be grateful if you will communicate the above to your members and seek their cooperation in this matter, informing them at the same time that they are at liberty to publish this letter if they so wish."

Statement printed in London newspapers May 11, 1955; released by Commander R. Colville, press secretary to Queen Elizabeth II, through British Information Services, New York.

". . . I fully appreciate the problems which arise under the heading 'The Royal Family and the Press.' Some will be solved in time, while others will always remain a headache. But there are three points which I would like to bring to your attention. In the first place, Members of The Family are slightly different from other public figures in that they are public figures for life, except of course in certain circumstances. Presidents, film stars, politicians, even TV personalities, have their periods of obscurity especially while they are growing up. In many cases it is also very much in their interests to get into and remain in the public eye. The second point is that with ordinary people, which *we* are, unlike Presidents and Prime Ministers who are usually rather special people, the more one is quoted and reported the less one is inclined to leave to chance both what one says and what one does in public, and the more jealous one becomes of one's private life. The result, of course, is very dull for newspapermen and makes us appear to be rather unenterprising; but remember that our mistakes, instead of ending up in obscurity, are never forgotten, although of course they may be forgiven. . . . I am always aware that newspapermen who report our tours are inclined to become a little bored sometimes by the way each visit follows almost exactly the same pattern as the last. When that happens I think it is worth remembering that we are most unlikely to visit the same place more often than about once in five years and usually at much longer intervals."

The Duke of Edinburgh, Prince Philip, address at Newspaper Fund Dinner, London; full text supplied by British Information Services, New York.

"Yes, thank you. It was lovely."
Prince Charles of England, reply to questions about his first flight in an airplane, news reports of June 10, 1955.

"They seem to forget I'm a woman. Do you know they've allowed me the same time to get my hair done as they did my father?"
Queen Elizabeth II, comment in interview with biographer Geoffrey Bocca, news summaries of June 27, 1955.

"I can write. I can sew. I can bathe myself."
Princess Anne of England, comment on her fifth birthday, news reports of August 16, 1955.

"You are a member of the British Royal Family. We are never tired and we all love hospitals."

Queen Mary, wife of George V of England, comment recalled on occasion of Princess Margaret's birthday, news reports of August 21, 1955.

"The disintegration of Europe's royal houses since World War I has let loose on the world a flood of self-styled counts, marquesses, barons and others whose claim to their dignities has no more reality than the figures in a Ruritanian romance."

L. G. Pine, editor, Burke's Peerage, definitive record book of the British nobility, address at Third International Congress on Genealogy, Heraldry and Orders of Chivalry, Madrid, Spain; New York Herald Tribune, October 9, 1955.

"I would like it to be known that I have decided not to marry Group Captain Peter Townsend. I have been aware that subject to my renouncing my rights of succession it might have been possible for me to contract a civil marriage. But mindful of the Church's teaching that Christian marriage is indissoluble, and conscious of my duty to the Commonwealth, I have resolved to put these considerations before any others. I have reached this decision entirely alone and in doing so I have been strengthened by the unfailing support and devotion of Group Captain Townsend. I am deeply grateful for the concern of all those who have constantly prayed for my happiness."

Princess Margaret of England, statement issued marking the end of the most talked-about royal romance in many years, news reports of November 1, 1955.

"The real name is Prince Louis Ferdinand Viktor Eduard Adalbert Michael Hubertus of Prussia, head of the House of Hohenzollern. But ever since I was in America, working at the Ford plant in Detroit, I feel too close to Americans for such formality. . . . By them, I like to be called Louie."

Crown Prince Louis of Germany, grandson of Kaiser Wilhelm II, quoted by Phyllis Battelle, "Assignment: America," New York Journal-American, November 10, 1955.

SPORTS

"In a way an umpire is like a woman. He makes quick decisions, never reverses them and doesn't think you're safe when you're out."
Larry Goetz, baseball umpire; news summaries of April 17, 1955.

"It's necessary to relax your muscles when you can. Relaxing your brain is fatal."
Stirling Moss, comment on his reportedly relaxed appearance as a champion British racing-car driver, Newsweek, *May 16, 1955.*

"We are expecting our champions to be stadium automatons, the human equivalent of the balls in a super pinball machine. . . . We're watching for the numbers to light up and forgetting the play."
Maureen Connolly, tennis star retired at twenty-one, begins her first sports column for the San Diego Union, Time, *May 23, 1955.*

"I remember a moment when I stood barefoot on firm dry sand by the sea. The air had a special quality as if it had a life of its own. The sound of breakers on the shore shut out all others. I looked up at the great clouds, like white-sailed galleons, chasing proudly inland. I looked down at the regular ripples on the sand, and could not absorb so much beauty. I was taken aback—each of the myriad particles of sand was as perfect in its way. I looked more closely, hoping perhaps that my eyes might detect some flaw. But for once there was nothing to detract from all this beauty. In this supreme moment I leapt in sheer joy. I was startled and frightened by the tremendous excitement that so few steps could create. I glanced round uneasily to see if anyone was watching. A few more steps—more self-consciously and now firmly gripping the original excitement. The earth seemed almost to move with me. I was almost running now, and a fresh rhythm entered my body. No longer conscious of my movement, I discovered a new unity with nature. I had found a new source of power and beauty, a source I never dreamt existed. From intense moments like this, love of running can grow. . . ."
Roger Bannister, "The Joy of Running," Sports Illustrated, *June 20, 1955, reprinted by permission of Dodd, Mead & Company from* The Four Minute Mile, *copyright 1955 by Roger Bannister.*

"Anyone who can be a Dodger, in the first place, is quite a man. Anyone who can be a Dodger for fifteen years, and rise to be captain of the team, deserves to be a sports immortal. . . . Here's to you, Pee Wee Reese, long may you wave—that bat!"

Richard Nixon, U. S. Vice-President, letter marking Reese's thirty-sixth birthday, July 23, 1955.

"I could see the lake smooth as glass ahead of me and I put my foot down."

Donald Campbell, after establishing new record for speed on water (202.32 miles an hour) in his jet-powered Bluebird VII on Lake Ullswater, England; news reports of July 24, 1955.

"The last chapter of today's book is just the first paragraph of the new edition."

Ford Frick, baseball commissioner, remark to Joe DiMaggio as DiMaggio accepted membership in the Baseball Hall of Fame, news reports of July 25, 1955.

"His legs are buckled into clumsy shin guards; his face is hidden by the metal grille of a heavy mask. Behind him, vague and impersonal, rises the roar of the crowd. His chest is covered with a corrugated protective pad, and his big mitt is thrust out as if to fend off destruction. Exactly sixty feet, six inches straight ahead of him, the pitcher looms preternaturally large on his mound of earth. As he crouches close to the ground, his field of vision gives him his own special view of the vast ballpark. The white foul lines stretch to the distant fences; the outfielders seem to be men without legs. Between him and the flycatchers, from the far outfield grass to the brown base paths, the rest of the time twitches nervously in place. In a sense, the game belongs to him. He is the catcher."

Time, essay on place of the catcher in baseball, "profile" article on Roy Campanella of the Dodgers, August 8, 1955, copyright 1955 Time, Inc.; reprinted by permission.

"The art of running the mile consists, in essence, of reaching the threshold of unconsciousness at the instant of breasting the tape."

Paul O'Neil, "The Art of the Mile," Sports Illustrated, August 16, 1955; reprinted by permission.

"I have always adhered to two principles. The first one is to train hard and get into the best possible physical condition. The second is to forget all about the other fellow until you face him in the ring and the bell sounds for the fight."

Rocky Marciano, world heavyweight boxing champion, comment on his thirty-first birthday, news reports of September 2, 1955.

"BROOKLYN GOES WILD—BUMS AIN'T BUMS ANY MORE!"

New York Daily Mirror, October 5, 1955, front-page headline reporting Brooklyn Dodgers' victory in the 1955 World Series.

"Gentlemen, Start Your Engines. . . ."

Title of the autobiography of speed driver Wilbur Shaw, published by Henry Holt & Company; traditional command that starts the Indianapolis Speedway races.

"I started in training for the Olympics. . . . There were hedges in the yards all the way down our street. All but one of them were about the right height for hurdles. I went to the people in that one house and explained to them what I was trying to do. They cut their hedge down to the same size as the others for me."

"Babe" Didrikson Zaharias, Olympic champion and golf star, telling of her girlhood in Beaumont, Texas, This Life I've Led, copyright 1955 by A. S. Barnes and Company, Inc., New York.

"The years will take care of any girl who is a tomboy. When you get to a certain age, and you start growing in places where you weren't developed before, then nothing can stop you from changing. You've just got to go with it."

"Babe" Didrikson Zaharias. Ibid.

THEATER

". . . I was at a party feeling very shy because there were a lot of celebrities around, and I was sitting in a corner alone and a very beautiful young man came up to me and offered me some salted peanuts and he said, 'I wish they were emeralds' as he handed me the peanuts and that was the end of my heart. I never got it back."

Helen Hayes, recollection of first meeting her husband, Charles MacArthur, comment in interview with Edward R. Murrow, "Person to Person," CBS-TV, January 14, 1955.

"An actress's life is so transitory—suddenly you're a building!"

Helen Hayes, comment on being told that a Broadway theatre was being named in her honor, news reports of November 9, 1955.

"Dahling Congressman Boykin: Ten A.M. is an unprecedented time for a child of the grease paint to cope with the sandman."

Tallulah Bankhead, note to a congressman who asked her to speak at a campaign meeting for a civic auditorium for Washington; she gave her blessings to the project, but needed her sleep, news summaries of January 15, 1955.

"You must learn day by day, year by year, to broaden your horizon. The more things you love, the more you are interested in, the more you enjoy, the more you are indignant about—the more you have left when anything happens."

Ethel Barrymore, quoted in Walter Winchell's column, New York Daily Mirror, May 6, 1955.

"For an actress to be a success she must have the face of Venus, the brains of Minerva, the grace of Terpsichore, the memory of Macaulay, the figure of Juno, and the hide of a rhinoceros."

Ethel Barrymore. Ibid.

"This is not precisely the same treatment as the one filmed by my brother John some years ago. However, I think you'll dig it nonetheless."

Ethel Barrymore, introduction to television presentation, Svengali and the Blonde, *NBC-TV, July 30, 1955, quoted in reviews.*

"On opening night I had for the first time the terrible sense of responsibility which, ever since, has made every first night a kind of little dying. I would have been glad of an earthquake or some other great calamity that would stop people from coming in or me from going on. Years and years afterward on the first night of *The Corn Is Green*, although I knew it was a wonderful, beautiful play and that I was all right in it, I was still hoping for an earthquake."

Ethel Barrymore, recalling her first opening night of Captain Jinks of the Horse Marines, Memories, *Harper & Brothers, copyright, 1955; reprinted by permission.*

" 'I know some funny stories, but I think the American public likes to think of their President as being a sort of solemn ass and I think I'll just go on being a solemn ass.' "

Ethel Barrymore, recalling a remark made to her by President Coolidge. Ibid.

"It is more than I deserve, but please believe me, it is not more than I can take to my heart."

Ethel Barrymore, reply to greetings received on her seventieth birthday. Ibid.

"Has anybody ever seen a dramatic critic in the daytime? Of course not. They come out after dark, up to no good."

P. G. Wodehouse, London Punch, *quoted by Walter Winchell, May 27, 1955.*

"Predictions of greatness in the world of show business are usually, to borrow a few similes from the world of plant life, as sweet as the pomegranate and as impassioned as the orchid; as perishable as the crocus, as sticky as the fly trap and as common as the dandelion. Now and then the predictions are fulfilled, thereby endowing the forecaster with the reputation of a seer."

Gilbert Millstein, staff member of The New York Times Maga-*zine, writing in* Collier's, *July 22, 1955; reprinted by permission.*

"Everything in life is theatre."

Margo Jones, Broadway producer and founder of theatre-in-the-round movement in Dallas, reply to an interviewer who observed that "most persons consider the theatre a minor part of living"; comment recalled in obituaries reporting death of Miss Jones, news reports of July 25, 1955.

"The theatre has given me a chance not only to live my own life but a million others. In every play there is a chance for one great moment, experience, or understanding."

Margo Jones. Ibid.

"I thought I wanted to be an artist, but the pencil wouldn't go where I wanted it to. Then I thought I wanted to be a musician, but when I couldn't learn a concerto in the first lesson, I gave up. But when I spoke my few lines in that Sunday-school play with such fervor that someone in the audience cried, I decided to act."

Geraldine Page, on deciding on a career, Mademoiselle, *September 1955.*

"I got all the schooling any actress needs. That is, I learned to write well enough to sign contracts."

Hermione Gingold, British comedienne, Look, *October 4, 1955.*

". . . The bird that I hope to catch in the net of this play is not the solution of one man's psychological problem. I'm trying to catch the true quality of experience in a group of people, that cloudy, flickering, evanescent—fiercely charged!—interplay of live human beings in the thundercloud of a common crisis. Some mystery should be left in the revelation of character in a play, just as a great deal of mystery is always left in the revelation of character in life, even in one's own character to himself. This does not absolve the playwright of his duty to observe and probe as clearly and as deeply as he legitimately can; but it should steer him away from 'pat' conclusions, facile definitions which make a play just a play, not a snare for the truth of human experience."

Tennessee Williams, stage directions for the enactment of Cat on a Hot Tin Roof, *copyright 1955 by Tennessee Williams; reprinted by permission of the publisher, New Directions.*

"I look upon life as a party: One arrives long after it's started, and one's going to leave long before it's over, and it's as well, perhaps, not to try and be the life and soul of it, and not to try and take too much responsibility for it."

Robert Morley, British actor, news summaries of December 31, 1955.

"If you achieve success, you will get applause, and if you get applause, you will hear it. My advice to you concerning applause is this: Enjoy it but never quite believe it."

Robert Montgomery, comment to his daughter as she began an acting career, Woman's Home Companion, *December 1955.*

"To hold your place on the New York stage takes skill and foresight as well as talent. It is easy enough to be a successful ingénue. You have really to know nothing. You have only to be charming and young, and since New York is the most voluptuous city in the world, there are great rewards for charm and youth. But to hold your place in turn against the constantly rising tide of competing youth you must have something more lasting. Consider the superannuated ingénue. Is there anything more tragic? New York is not a city of fixed and settled theatregoers like London and Paris. There a favorite grows old among people who see her so often, and are so faithful to her that they are scarcely aware of the ravages that time is making on her. But New York is a place of shifting crowds, the majority of its theatregoers are irreverent strangers. And the man from Colorado seeing the smile and hair and eyes of the famous beauty for the first time, is unabashed and merely says, 'Oh, is that she? Why, she is older than I thought.' "

Laurette Taylor, Laurette, The Intimate Biography of Laurette Taylor, *by her daughter, Marguerite Courtney, copyright 1955 by Marguerite Courtney; reprinted by permission of Rinehart & Company, Inc.*

UNITED NATIONS

"It has been well said that a hungry man is more interested in four sandwiches than four freedoms."

Henry Cabot Lodge, Jr., American ambassador to the United Nations, appealing to the Senate Appropriations Committee for renewed support of the UN technical assistance program; news reports of March 29, 1955.

". . . As I look back over that ten years, I am convinced more than ever that our conference here in 1945 did much more than draft an international agreement among fifty nations. I believe our conference in 1945 set down on paper the only principles which will enable civilized human life to continue to survive on this globe."

Harry Truman, speaking at the tenth anniversary conference of the United Nations, San Francisco, news reports of June 25, 1955.

"The UN is not just a product of do-gooders. It is harshly real. The day will come when men will see the UN and what it means clearly. Everything will be all right—you know when? When people, just people, stop thinking of the United Nations as a weird Picasso abstraction, and see it as a drawing they made themselves."

Dag Hammarskjold, Secretary-General of the United Nations, Time, *June 27, 1955.*

"We have only begun to make use of the real possibilities of the United Nations as the most representative instrument for the relaxation of tensions, for the lessening of distrust and misunderstanding, and for the discovery and delineation of new areas of common ground and interest."

Dag Hammarskjold, introduction to tenth annual report of Secretary-General of the United Nations, news reports of August 8, 1955.

"It certainly is very important [but] frankly I have so many things in my lap already that I would be scared to get this one, which seems to be a youngster of rather violent temper."

Dag Hammarskjold, reply when asked if time had arrived for UN to rule on ownership of Antarctic islands, news reports of August 13, 1955.

"Whatever political system you have, it must be based upon respect for the individual. On the one hand, the individual should have the largest possible liberty to form his own life according to his own way of thinking, but on the other hand, we must demand justice and equality for all."

Dag Hammarskjold, statement of position as a political independent, This Week Magazine, October 2, 1955; copyright 1955, United Newspapers Magazine Corporation.

"So, let us strive together to bring these things to pass, so that when this Assembly meets at its twentieth session a decade from now, it will look back and call it the healing decade of true peace."

John Foster Dulles, address to UN in its tenth anniversary year, news reports of September 23, 1955.

"The United Nations can't guarantee peace any more than a doctor can guarantee health. But would that be a good reason for doing away with doctors?"

André Maurois, French novelist, Look, October 4, 1955.

"This accumulation, this torrent of receptions—sometimes three or four in a day—where you have to drink the same Scotch or the same Manhattan and eat the self-same shrimps, and where you have to talk to exactly the same people, are somewhat tiring. . . . That is why I would be in favor of the idea of holding longer receptions, so that people can have time not only to eat a little and drink a little, but to talk a little, and receptions to which fewer people would be invited."

José Maza, of Chile, comment on retiring as president of the 1955 General Assembly of the United Nations, news reports of December 21, 1955.

1956

THE ARMED FORCES

"Birdman's Slang" reported from the new U. S. Air Force Academy at Denver, Colorado:

"Scramble, Mister"—cut-in signal on the dance floor.

"Let's blast off"—invitation to a girl to take a walk.

"You really shoot me down"—the supreme cadet compliment.

Quoted in Life, *January 9, 1956.*

"The profusion of skills and learning we have in the Army is astonishing. If I need a shortstop who plays the violin, I can find him some place!"

General Maxwell Taylor, Army Chief of Staff, Time, *March 26, 1956.*

"If our air forces are never used, they have achieved their finest goal."

General Nathan Twining, Air Force Chief of Staff, "What Noted People Are Saying," International News Service, *March 1956.*

"The University of Iowa Dead"

"Some left an office, cornfield, factory,
But these men left the study of mankind,
Glory and gloom of mortal history,
The wonder, madness, logic of the mind,
The live cell, atoms cunningly combined.
They closed their books, death closed
Their eyes, so we,

The lucky Iowa living, still could find
A future in our human liberty."
*Paul Engle, poem on war memorial tablet at the University of
Iowa, used by permission of the University, copyright 1956 by
Paul Engle; quoted in* Life, *May 28, 1956.*

"The Navy is about to abandon the twentieth century zipper and sail
back with tradition to the medieval gusset and the thirteen-button 'broad-
fall front' in its bell-bottomed trousers."
*The New York Times, first paragraph of Washington dispatch
reporting navy men favor the traditional uniform over zippers
adopted in 1948, "The Navy Will Scuttle the Zipper," page 1,
June 12, 1956.*

"When we know as much about people as hog specialists know about
hogs, we'll be better off."
*Major General Lewis Hershey, Selective Service director, speak-
ing to a National 4-H Club assembly in Washington, quoted in
news dispatches of June 18, 1956.*

"It was only by the unanticipated timing of fate that any use was
made of my experience."
*Fleet Admiral Ernest King, World War II Chief of Naval Opera-
tions, comment on the fact that the U.S. entered the war less than
one year before he was scheduled to retire, statement recalled
in obituaries reporting his death, June 25, 1956.*

"We are the most fortunate of men. There was a time when a professional
soldier had to wait twenty-five years or so before he ever got into a war.
We only had to wait five years for this one. For all that time we have
been sitting on our fat behinds drawing our pay. Now we are going to
work at our trade. We have chosen to live by the sword. If necessary,
we will die by the sword."
*Lieutenant General Lewis Burwell Puller, United States Marine
Corps, address to his troops before the 1950 Inchon landing in
Korea. Quotation recalled in dispatch reporting the retired of-*

ficer's reappearance in the news to testify at the Parris Island, South Carolina, McKeon court-martial, The New York Times, August 3, 1956.

"I have only one request to make of you, perhaps the last request I will ever make of Marines. Do your duty. If you do that, no one, in a thousand years, will ever destroy the Marine Corps."

Lieutenant General Lewis Burwell Puller, comment to an assembly of three hundred Marines during the McKeon court-martial inquiry into the drowning of six recruits during a training march, news reports of August 3, 1956.

"I should have known better than to have tried to cross-examine a legend."

Major Charles Sevier, comment in failing to draw desired testimony from General Puller. Ibid.

"The colonel handed me the end of a rope and said: 'When I yell you stand on your toes, open your mouth wide, give a yell yourself and pull the rope.' I yanked the lanyard and the cannon went off and scared me half to death."

Albert Woolson, last surviving member of the Civil War's Union Army, recollection of cannon practice recalled in obituaries reporting his death in Duluth, Minnesota, at the age of one hundred and nine; news reports of August 3, 1956.

"The Yankees may have outfought us, but we're going to outlive them."

John Salling, at 110, one of three remaining Confederate veterans, on hearing of the death of Albert Woolson, 109, last remaining Union veteran; news summaries of August 20, 1956.

". . . Smiling faces have not been mistaken for friendly acts, or good words taken as a substitute for good deeds, for we are well aware of the build-up—not decrease—of military capabilities while the smiles have widened."

General Louis Norstad, U. S. Army, Supreme Commander of Allied Powers in Europe (SHAPE), Réalités, September, 1956.

"No nation is going to press that button if it means national suicide. That is just what it would mean."

>*General Alfred Gruenther, on the possibility of Russia launching guided missiles against the West; statement was made at Gruenther's final news conference before retiring as commander of the North Atlantic Treaty Organization (NATO), news reports of November 14, 1956.*

"If United States citizens are in danger, protect them. Take no guff from anyone."

>*Admiral Arleigh Burke, Chief of Naval Operations, message from Washington to Commander of U. S. Sixth Fleet in Mediterranean, news reports of November 15, 1956.*

"To the weeping mothers of its dead, I can only say that the sacrifice and halo of Jesus of Nazareth has descended upon their sons, and that God will take them unto Himself."

>*General MacArthur, tribute to the troops of Bataan, April 9, 1942, quoted in* MacArthur: His Rendezvous with History, *by Major General Courtney Whitney. Reprinted by permission of Alfred A. Knopf, Inc., 1956; copyright 1955 by Time, Inc.*

"Corregidor needs no comment from me. It has sounded its own story at the mouth of its guns. It has scrolled its own epitaph on enemy tablets. But through the bloody haze of its last, reverberating shot, I shall always seem to see a vision of grim, gaunt, ghastly men, still unafraid."

>*General MacArthur, comment on surrender of Corregidor, May 6, 1942. Ibid.*

"We can outguess, outmaneuver and out-think the enemy; we can put a finger right on his heart and paralyze him with surprise."

>*General MacArthur, comment on the Allied counterattack on New Guinea, a turning point of World War II in the Pacific. Ibid.*

"Expect only five per cent of an intelligence report to be accurate. The trick of a good commander is to isolate the five per cent."
General MacArthur. Ibid.

"By profession I am a soldier and take pride in that fact. But I am prouder—infinitely prouder—to be a father. A soldier destroys in order to build; the father only builds, never destroys. The one has the potentiality of death; the other embodies creation and life. And while the hordes of death are mighty, the battalions of life are mightier still. It is my hope that my son, when I am gone, will remember me not from the battle but in the home repeating with him our simple daily prayer, 'Our Father Who Art in Heaven.'"
General MacArthur, comment on being named Father of the Year in 1942. Ibid.

"We three drink of the same cup."
Mrs. Douglas MacArthur, comment turning aside chance to flee Corregidor with her young son when the Japanese were closing in. Ibid.

"Strike at every favorable opportunity. For your homes and hearths, strike! For future generations of your sons and daughters, strike! In the name of your sacred dead, strike! Let no heart be faint. Let every arm be steeled. The guidance of Divine God points the way. Follow in His name to the Holy Grail of righteous victory!"
General MacArthur, radio speech from the invasion beach on returning to the Philippines, October 20, 1944. Ibid.

"In war, when a commander becomes so bereft of reason and perspective that he fails to understand the dependence of arms on Divine guidance, he no longer deserves victory."
General MacArthur. Ibid.

"Today the guns are silent. A great tragedy has ended. A great victory has been won. The skies no longer rain death—the seas bear only commerce—men everywhere walk upright in the sunlight. The entire world is quietly at peace. The holy mission has been completed. And in reporting this to you, the people, I speak for the thousands of silent lips, forever stilled among the jungles and the beaches and in the deep waters of the Pacific which marked the way. I speak for the unnamed brave millions homeward bound to take up the challenge of that future which they did so much to salvage from the brink of disaster."

General MacArthur, address to the American people on accepting surrender of Japan, September 2, 1945. Ibid.

". . . Have our country's flag unfurled, and in Tokyo's sun let it wave in its full glory as a symbol of hope for the oppressed and as a harbinger of victory for the right."

General MacArthur, orders issued on establishing his occupation headquarters in the Japanese capital city, September 8, 1945. Ibid.

"There is no security on this earth; there is only opportunity."

General MacArthur. Ibid.

"I am closing my fifty-two years of military service. When I joined the Army, even before the turn of the century, it was the fulfillment of all my boyish hopes and dreams. The world has turned over many times since I took the oath on the Plain at West Point, and the hopes and dreams have all since vanished, but I still remember the refrain of one of the most popular barracks ballads of that day, which proclaimed most proudly that old soldiers never die; they just fade away. And like the old soldier of that ballad, I now close my military career and just fade away, an old soldier who tried to do his duty as God gave him the light to see that duty. Good-by."

General MacArthur, closing remarks in address to Congress, April 19, 1951, after being relieved of his command in the Far East. Ibid.

"Build me a son, O Lord, who will be strong enough to know when he is weak, and brave enough to face himself when he is afraid, one who will be proud and unbending in honest defeat, and humble and gentle in victory.

"Build me a son whose wishes will not take the place of deeds; a son who will know Thee—and that to know himself is the foundation stone of knowledge.

"Lead him, I pray, not in the path of ease and comfort, but under the stress and spur of difficulties and challenge. Here let him learn to stand up in the storm; here let him learn compassion for those who fail.

"Build me a son whose heart will be clear, whose goal will be high; a son who will master himself before he seeks to master other men; one who will reach into the future, yet never forget the past.

"And after all these things are his, add, I pray, enough of a sense of humor, so that he may always be serious, yet never take himself too seriously. Give him humility, so that he may always remember the simplicity of true greatness, the open mind of true wisdom, and the meekness of true strength.

"Then, I, his father, will dare to whisper, 'I have not lived in vain.'"
  General MacArthur, "A Father's Prayer," written by the general in the early days of World War II in the Pacific. Ibid.

ART

"When one starts from a portrait and seeks by successive eliminations to find pure form . . . one inevitably ends up with an egg. Similarly, by starting from an egg and following the opposite course, one can arrive at a portrait."
  Pablo Picasso, Look, *June 6, 1956.*

"If only we could pull out our brain and use only our eyes."
  Pablo Picasso, on painting objectively, "An Afternoon with Picasso," interview by James Thrall Soby, The Saturday Review, *September 1, 1956.*

"It's true. Matisse is dead now, and I must paint for both of us."
  Pablo Picasso. Ibid.

"The French look exactly like French, the faces of Dutchmen are Dutch. Danes look like Danes and Egyptians look very Canalish. Americans have a sad countenance. They probably look like this because they developed catarrh when they landed on Plymouth Rock."

Sir Alfred Richardson, President, Royal Academy of Art, news reports of September 17, 1956.

"Why should I paint dead fish, onions and beer glasses? Girls are so much prettier."

Marie Laurencin, noted French modernist painter, comment quoted in obituaries reporting her death, June 8, 1956. She was famous, as Time *put it, "for her wispy, pastel-toned portraits of doe-eyed young girls in diaphanous gowns . . . described as the only considerable figure who painted like a woman."*

"I believe that thinking is necessary in art as everywhere else and that a clear head is never in the way of genuine feelings."

Josef Albers, chairman, Design Department of Yale University, quoted in Time, *June 18, 1956, in article reporting on his work as "one of the nation's most influential art teachers."*

"There is only one difference between a madman and me. I am not mad."

Salvador Dali, "Dali Is a Dilly," by Henry La Cossitt, The American, July 1956.

"Always design a thing by considering it in its next larger context—a chair in a room, a room in a house, a house in an environment, environment in a city plan."

Eero Saarinen, leading U. S. architect, quoting valued advice given by his father, the Finnish-born architect Eliel Saarinen, Time, July 2, 1956.

"I feel my work is not an abstraction apart from life, but rather its clearest essence, distilled, as in all art, in terms of the materials and spirit of our time."

Richard Lippold, modern sculptor who created a series of noteworthy constructions including "Full Moon" (Museum of Modern Art) and "Variation Within a Sphere, No. 10: The Sun" (Metropolitan Museum of Art), Christian Science Monitor, *August 4, 1956.*

"I love it, its delicacy, its tentativeness, its allowing for transparency and probing of inner tensions."
Richard Lippold, on the use of wire in art forms, such as "The Sun," in which nearly two miles of fine gold wire was used, with 14,000 hand-welded joints. Ibid.

AUTHORS

"A bad book is as much of a labor to write as a good one, it comes as sincerely from the author's soul."
Aldous Huxley, Newsweek, January 2, 1956.

"I write at high speed because boredom is bad for my health. It upsets my stomach more than anything else. I also avoid green vegetables. They're grossly overrated."
Noel Coward, Tempo, January 15, 1956.

"I've sometimes thought of marrying—and then I've thought again."
Noel Coward, quoted in " 'Dear Noel' on Love and Marriage," by Ward Morehouse, Theatre Arts, November, 1956.

"To be out of jail. To eat and sleep regular. To get what I write printed in a free country for free people. To have a little love in the home and esteem outside the home."
Carl Sandburg, "personal happiness prescription," comment on his seventy-eighth birthday, Newsweek, January 16, 1956.

"If, after I depart this vale, you ever remember me and have thought to please my ghost, forgive some sinner and wink your eye at some homely girl."
H. L. Mencken, epitaph for himself, recalled in obituaries reporting his death, January 29, 1956.

"I set up my pitch in life on a busy and interesting street. I did a good business and I have no regrets."
H. L. Mencken. Ibid.

"I am by nature a vulgar fellow. . . . I delight in beef stews, limericks, burlesque shows, New York City, and the music of Haydn, that beery, delightful old rascal! I swear in the presence of old ladies and arch-deacons. When the mercury is above ninety-five, I dine in my shirt sleeves and write poetry naked."
H. L. Mencken, description of himself. Ibid.

"I've made it a rule never to drink by daylight and never to refuse a drink after dark."
H. L. Mencken. Ibid.

"To be in love is merely to be in a state of perpetual anesthesia."
H. L. Mencken. Ibid.

"No normal man ever fell in love after thirty when the kidneys begin to disintegrate."
H. L. Mencken. Ibid.

"Those tragic comedians, the Chamber of Commerce red hunters, the Women's Christian Temperance Union smellers, the censors of books, the Klan regulators, the Methodist prowlers, the Baptist guardians of sacred vessels—we have the national mentality of a police lieutenant."
H. L. Mencken, typical of the remarks that caused the New York Herald Tribune *to call him "a specialist in sentences that could lacerate millions at a time." Ibid.*

"I am an amused spectator of the world."
H. L. Mencken. Ibid.

"All I know is, it is better to tell the truth than to lie, better to be free than a slave, better to have knowledge than be ignorant."
H. L. Mencken. Ibid.

"The townspeople are morons, yokels, peasants and genus homo boobiensis . . . surrounded by gaping primates from the upland valleys."
H. L. Mencken, comment after covering the Scopes evolution trial at Dayton, Tennessee. Ibid.

"War will never cease until babies begin to come into the world with larger cerebrums and smaller adrenal glands."
H. L. Mencken, Minority Report: H. L. Mencken's Notebooks, copyright 1956 by Alfred A. Knopf, Inc., reprinted by permission.

"I'd just as soon play tennis with the net down."
Robert Frost, comment on the writing of "free" verse, Newsweek, January 30, 1956.

". . . Wherever they go, and whatever happens to them on the way, in that enchanted place on the top of the Forest, a little boy and his Bear will always be playing."
A. A. Milne, closing line in the last of the famed series of children's books which Milne wrote on "Winnie-the-Pooh." Written in 1928, it was recalled in obituaries reporting Milne's death, January 31, 1956.

"On the whole, I haven't found men unduly loath to say, 'I love you.' The real trick is to get them to say, 'Will you marry me?'"
Ilka Chase, This Week Magazine, February 5, 1956; copyright 1956, United Newspapers Magazine Corporation.

"I always start writing with a clean piece of paper and a dirty mind."
Edward Everett Tanner who, as Patrick Dennis, wrote Auntie Mame and other best-selling novels of the 1950s, Vogue, February 15, 1956.

"It began as a diary . . . little by little it began to turn itself into a story, by that mysterious process which I cannot explain, but which I recognize when it begins, and I go along with it out of a kind of curiosity, as if my mind which knows the facts is watching to see what my story-telling mind will finally make of them."

Katherine Anne Porter, comment on the writing of a novel,
The Atlantic, *March 1956.*

"We cannot get grace from gadgets. In the bakelite house of the future, the dishes may not break, but the heart can. Even a man with ten shower baths may find life flat, stale and unprofitable."

J. B. Priestley, British novelist, news summaries of April 1, 1956.

"Our illustrious and most high-hearted friend is dead but the legend of Charles MacArthur will begin to grow now around his fine name. His gaiety, his wildness, his kindness, his love for his bride, Helen, and his two children and his sturdy clan of brothers and sisters, his wit and his adventures will stay alive a long, long while."

Ben Hecht, eulogy at the funeral of Charles MacArthur, his long-time friend and collaborator, quoted in news reports of April 24, 1956.

"I wish to write and write well. If it weren't so, I would have become a businessman or an engineer long ago, and I might have been more successful at that."

Ernest Hemingway, comment on his love for his profession,
McCall's Magazine, *May 1956.*

"This is the security I am leaving behind for my family and my publishers won't have to worry either."

Ernest Hemingway, comment on four completed novels to be published when the tax rate is lower, possibly after his death. Ibid.

"No classic resembles any previous classic, so do not be discouraged."
Ernest Hemingway, advice to young people who would be writers. Ibid.

"I am very happy for any writer who deserves it to get the prize. I am sorry about any writer who deserves it and doesn't get it. This makes me very humble in accepting it. One shouldn't win the Nobel Prize, then rewrite the Bible and become a bore—I accepted the Bible in its original version."

Ernest Hemingway, reply when asked his opinion of the Nobel Prize for literature. Ibid.

"I specialize in murders of quiet, domestic interest. Give me a nice deadly phial to play with and I am happy."

Agatha Christie, Life, May 14, 1956.

"It is ridiculous to set a detective story in New York City. New York City is itself a detective story."

Agatha Christie. Ibid.

"My gifts are small. I've used them very well and discreetly, never straining them, and the result is that I have made a charming little reputation."

Sir Max Beerbohm, speaking of his work as an essayist, critic, and caricaturist; comment recalled in obituaries reporting his death at Rapallo, Italy, May 20, 1956.

"All poetry is an ordered voice, one which tries to tell you about a vision in the unvisionary language of farm, city and love. Writing is like this —you dredge for the poem's meaning the way police dredge for a body. They think it is down there under the black water, they work the grappling hooks back and forth. But maybe it's up in the hills under the leaves or in a ditch somewhere. Maybe it's never found. But what you find, whatever you find, is always only part of the missing, and writing is the way the poet finds out what it is he found."

Paul Engle, author of The Word of Love, West of Midnight, American Song, American Child, *and other books, Life, May 28, 1956.*

"Journalism allows its readers to witness history. Fiction gives its readers an opportunity to live it."

John Hersey, Pulitzer Prize novelist, Saturday Review, June 6, 1956.

"The good writer never applies to a foundation. He's too busy writing something. . . . I have no time to wonder who is reading me. . . . I am not a literary man but only a writer. . . . The only environment the artist needs is whatever peace, whatever solitude, and whatever pleasure he can get at not too high a cost."

William Faulkner, quoted in a Life *editorial, "Advice from and to Writers,"* Life, *June 11, 1956.*

"A television play follows a simpler line; it's like writing around a circle. With a novel, you plant a seed and you can't tell how it is going to grow. To a prose writer, dramatic writing is a separate department. A talent for drama is not a talent for writing, but is an ability to articulate human relationships."

Gore Vidal, novelist and television writer, "What Makes a Television Writer," The New York Times, *June 17, 1956.*

"To me it is utter nonsense to assume that an imaginative piece of poetry is lacking in reality. An imaginative experience is not only as real but far realer than an unimaginative one."

Walter de la Mare, internationally known British poet, comment recalled in obituaries reporting his death, June 22, 1956.

"Any man should be happy who is allowed the patience of his wife, the tolerance of his children and the affection of waiters."

Michael Arlen, author of The Green Hat *and other novels, advice to a friend, comment recalled in obituaries reporting his death, June 24, 1956.*

"I enjoyed it very much, although I didn't do much of anything. I think I wrote one-seventh of one seventh-rate picture while I was there."

Michael Arlen, on his experiences in Hollywood. Ibid.

"Listen carefully to first criticisms made of your work. Note just what it is about your work that the critics don't like—then cultivate it. That's the only part of your work that's individual and worth keeping."

Jean Cocteau, advice to a group of young artists, Leonard Lyons' column, New York Post, *June 27, 1956.*

"Never play cards with a man called Doc. Never eat at a place called Mom's. Never sleep with a woman whose troubles are worse than your own."

Nelson Algren, quoting a criminal's advice, which he also recommends to young writers, Newsweek, July 2, 1956.

"The world no heart may find untaught,
No mortal eyes unpurged may view
It is with beauty so enwrought:
The world the old magicians sought,
And long ago the wise men knew."

Ella Young, Irish poet and college lecturer, poetic summary of the mysticism which characterized her work, quoted in obituaries reporting her death at Oceana, California, July 24, 1956.

". . . Really, in the end, the only thing that can make you a writer is the person that you are, the intensity of your feeling, the honesty of your vision, the unsentimental acknowledgment of the endless interest of the life around you and within you. Virtually nobody can help you deliberately—many people will help you unintentionally."

Santha Rama Rau, "Letter to a Young Writer," Harper's Bazaar, August 1956.

"Isn't it strange that the author's idea for what has been called the world's greatest novel should have come from falling off a horse? . . . That was 1863. My father was thirty-five. He spent the next seven years on *War and Peace*."

Countess Alexandra Tolstoy, recollection of her father, Count Leo Tolstoy, who was stunned for several minutes after falling from a horse and on resuming consciousness heard himself saying, "I shall write a great book about war and peace and it will describe Napoleon's disastrous invasion of Russia." Countess Tolstoy, now seventy-three, was interviewed in New York a few weeks before the opening of the American film, War and Peace; New York World-Telegram & Sun, August 3, 1956.

"One man was so mad at me that he ended his letter: 'Beware. You will never get out of this world alive.'"

> John Steinbeck, *"The Mail I've Seen,"* Saturday Review, *August 3, 1956.*

"There is small chance in our fickle air for the hope of a durable fame that has always been thought a legitimate spur of writers, for we throw away our [literary] riches like a drunken sailor."

> Van Wyck Brooks, *author and critic, quoted in* The Saturday Review, *August 18, 1956.*

"Any writer worth the name is always getting into one thing or getting out of another thing."

> Fannie Hurst, *quoted by Sidney Fields,* New York Daily Mirror, *August 28, 1956.*

". . . writing is the loneliest job in the world. There's always that frustrating chasm to bridge between the concept and the writing of it. We're a harassed tribe, we writers."

> Fannie Hurst. *Ibid.*

"I just sit at a typewriter and curse a bit."

> P. G. Wodehouse, *on his technique as a writer,* Collier's, *August 31, 1956.*

"The hallway of everyman's life is paced with pictures; pictures gay and pictures gloomy, all useful for, if we be wise, we can learn from them a richer and braver way to live."

> Sean O'Casey, *writing about his autobiographical play,* Pictures in the Hallway, The New York Times, *September 16, 1956.*

"Between the writing of plays, in the vast middle of the night, when our children and their mother slept, I sat alone, and my thoughts drifted back in time, murmuring the remembrance of things past into the listening ear of silence; fashioning thoughts to unspoken words, and setting them down upon the sensitive tablets of the mind."

> Sean O'Casey. *Ibid.*

"I wrote the scenes . . . by using the same apprehensive imagination that occurs in the morning before an afternoon's appointment with my dentist."

John P. Marquand, "My Early Struggles," The Atlantic, September, 1956.

"The years between fifty and seventy are the hardest. You are always being asked to do things, and yet you are not decrepit enough to turn them down."

T. S. Eliot, quoted in The American Mercury, September, 1956.

". . . I have a stern, perhaps Puritan, feeling that—wonderful as it is to receive awards for one's work—somehow one ought not to be dwelling on one's past efforts, or patting oneself on the back for them, or allowing others to do so; but that one should rather resolutely leave them behind and go ahead, devoting one's present thoughts and energies to new work. . . ."

Anne Morrow Lindbergh, letter declining an invitation to receive an award for her best-selling book, Gift From the Sea; quoted in "Anne Morrow Lindbergh—Her Life Story in Pictures," McCall's, October, 1956.

"I shall live bad if I do not write and I shall write bad if I do not live."

Françoise Sagan, French novelist, comment during visit to U.S., The New York Times, *November 11, 1956.*

"Every book is like a purge; at the end of it one is empty . . . like a dry shell on the beach, waiting for the tide to come in again."

Daphne du Maurier, quoted in an article by Beverley Nichols, Ladies' Home Journal, *November, 1956.*

"Seeing is deceiving. It's eating that's believing."

James Thurber, Further Fables for Our Time, published by Simon and Schuster.

"Man wants a great deal here below, and Woman even more."

James Thurber. Ibid.

"The writer is a spiritual anarchist, as in the depth of his soul every man is. . . . He neither walks with the multitude nor cheers with them. The writer who is a writer is a rebel who never stops."

William Saroyan, preface to The Whole Voyald; *published by Little, Brown and Company, 1956.*

"There are no new plots, there are only new people, new treatment, new reactions, new locations, new times. . . . A professional writer will starve if he waits for inspiration; he must learn to combine spontaneity of emotion with sound technique to make the result read like inspiration."

Adela Rogers St. Johns, How to Write a Story and Sell It, *published by Doubleday & Company, 1956.*

"Even when a thing is difficult, if you are a writer you are never so happy as when you are writing."

Somerset Maugham, quoted in The Writer Observed, *by Harvey Breit, World Press, 1956.*

"I don't speak the idiom of today. Take the word 'integration.' I expect if I looked it up in the dictionary I'd find out what it meant. But I'll never use it."

Somerset Maugham, comment during a U. S. visit, news summaries of October 29, 1956.

"I have learned in my thirty-odd years of serious writing only one sure lesson: stories, like whiskey, must be allowed to mature in the cask."

Seán O'Faoláin, one of Ireland's best-known short-story writers, "Looking Back at Writing," The Atlantic, *December 1956.*

"Scores of books a day, thousands in a year, many of them good and all of them dressed up in brightly colored jackets. And all of them free. Could a booklover imagine a better version of the earthly paradise?"

Orville Prescott, on being a book reviewer, "These I've Liked and These I'd Give," The New York Times, *December 2, 1956.*

BUSINESS

"Thanks a thousand."
Nelson Rockefeller, a favorite "conservative" expression as opposed to the familiar "thanks a million"; news summaries of January 2, 1956.

"American Express is already planning the jet age week end in Europe."
Ralph Thomas Reed, president of American Express, Time, April 9, 1956.

"Mas Tiempo para el Amor." (Translation: "More Time for Love.")
Advertising slogan credited with swift sale of washing machines in Spain, news reports of April 29, 1956.

". . . Prosperity would seem more soundly shored if, by a saving grace, more of us had the grace to save."
Life *editorial, "Is Thrift Un-American?"* Life, *May 7, 1956.*

"Always do one thing less than you think you can do."
Bernard Baruch, advice to businessmen on how to maintain good health, Newsweek, May 28, 1956.

"The instability of the economy is equaled only by the instability of economists."
John H. Williams, Harvard University professor, quoted in book review in The New York Times, *June 2, 1956.*

"Unless we put an end to the current program of helping the big get bigger while the small get squeezed out, capitalism, as we know it, will disappear."
Senator Stuart Symington, comment in address at Mexico, Missouri, June 7, 1956.

"When I am doing this job, I am international. As a business corporation, we are not plagued by the multitude of difficult questions that can arise when one sovereign nation treats with another. We cannot be charged with invading national sovereignty, with economic exploitation, or with political discrimination. The World Bank has no interest except to help its members."

Eugene Robert Black, president of the World Bank, quoted in "profile" article in Time, *June 25, 1956.*

"I've had diarrhea in forty nations."

Eugene Robert Black, comment on his world travels. Ibid.

"Don't spend too much time studying the science of salesmanship. Spend more time practicing the art of selling. Never copy anybody—be yourself."

Thomas J. Watson, chairman of IBM (International Business Machines), comment on selling, statement recalled in obituaries reporting his death, June 19, 1956.

"Increased use of mechanical appliances does not result in decreased employment on the whole."

Thomas J. Watson. Ibid.

"The United States should benefit more through improvement in world living standards than any other country, because our industries are more mechanized and capable of expansion."

Thomas J. Watson. Ibid.

"The American Government has carried the idea of do-goodness so far that we have become the laughingstock of many thinking people in the rest of the world."

Merwin Hart, president, National Economic Council, Quote, July 29, 1956.

"This has not been a class struggle. We are just partners who tried to arrive at an understanding."

Dave McDonald, president of the Steelworkers Union, comment in joining John Stephens, U. S. Steel vice president, in ending a twenty-seven-day steel strike, news summaries of August 6, 1956.

"You can never tell what ships are worth. Why someday I may even have to sell the whole fleet for scrap iron."

Stavros Spyros Niarchos, reportedly the world's biggest independent shipowner, quoted in Time *"cover story" on him, August 6, 1956.*

"Next to the dog, the wastebasket is man's best friend."

A San Francisco executive, commenting on the vast amount of reading required of businessmen, "The Flood That Drowns the Boss," Business Week, *August 18, 1956.*

"The consumer is not a moron. She is your wife."

David Ogilvy, advice to advertising copywriters, New York Herald Tribune, *August 29, 1956.*

"In the tiny space of twenty years, we have bred a whole generation of working Americans who take it for granted that they will never be out of a job or go a single year without a salary increase."

K. K. DuVall, President, Chicago Merchandise National Bank, Time, *September 10, 1956.*

"I was born into it and there was nothing I could do about it. It was there, like air or food or any other element. . . . The only question with wealth is what you do with it."

John D. Rockefeller, Jr., quoted in profile article in Time, *September 24, 1956.*

"Giving is the secret of a healthy life. Not necessarily money, but whatever a man has of encouragement and sympathy and understanding."

John D. Rockefeller, Jr. Ibid.

"Once upon a time there was a little girl who *always* said 'Thank you' at birthday parties; who called friends of the family 'Aunt' Helen and 'Uncle' Jim; and who passed out free cookies *the day* her lemonade stand opened. When this little girl grew up she didn't go to heaven. She went into public relations. And learned that what to her had always been unconscious art is now classified as a science—'the engineering of consent'—worth a hundred a week to her and millions in good will to her clients."

> Mary Ann Guitar, "The Million-Dollar Science," Mademoiselle, September, 1956, reprinted by permission of the author.

"Doing business without advertising is like winking at a girl in the dark. You know what you are doing, but nobody else does."

> Steuart Henderson Britt, advertising consultant, New York Herald Tribune, October 30, 1956.

"I happen to have been left a great deal of money. I don't know what is going to happen to it and I don't give a damn. If I can't make myself worthy of three square meals a day, then I don't deserve them."

> Marshall Field III, reference to his inheritance of more than 160 million dollars, statement recalled in reporting his death, November 9, 1956.

WINSTON CHURCHILL

"We must avoid violence by every means in our power. The only unity that would come from violence would be a unity of ashes and death."

> Sir Winston Churchill, speech on receiving the Charlemagne Prize at Aachen, Germany, in May 1956.

"Modern science is standing on tiptoe, ready to open the doors of a golden age."

> Sir Winston Churchill, quoted by David Sarnoff in The New York Times Magazine, September 30, 1956.

"I see no reason why you shouldn't young man—you look hale and hearty enough."

Sir Winston Churchill, reply on his eighty-second birthday to a photographer who said he hoped to take Sir Winston's one hundredth birthday picture, news reports of December 1, 1956.

CRIME

"Money! It's not just getting money that counts; it's making money useful."

Minnie Mangum, comment to loan applicant at Norfolk, Virginia, bank, a few months before she was convicted of embezzling nearly three million dollars over a long period; "Miss Minnie's Stolen Millions," by Rowland Moriarty, The Saturday Evening Post, September 1, 1956.

"A policeman's gun is his cross, and he carries it always."

Stephen Patrick Kennedy, Police Commissioner of New York City, "New York's Toughest Cop," by Don Murray, The Saturday Evening Post, September 8, 1956.

"Juvenile delinquency starts in the high chair and ends in the death chair."

James D. C. Murray, veteran defense lawyer, quoted in interview with William Longgood, New York World-Telegram and The Sun, September 8, 1956.

"A woman will almost never tell you the truth, while most men defendants will. Women have a furtive, concealing nature, and to some extent they're pathological liars who can conceive of situations that never existed."

James D. C. Murray. Ibid.

"I am not here to defend O'Keefe. Maybe this is the first—and the last —good thing O'Keefe has ever done: to take from society these potential murderers, who were so cheap they wanted to keep all the money, even that which could identify them, and who in their desire destroyed themselves. So, men of Massachusetts, you take it from here, and decide whether or not you are to be a barrier against the onward rush of these thugs who would demolish the purity and decency of this Commonwealth."

Garrett Byrne, District Attorney for Boston, statement to the jury at close of the Brink's trial stemming from "the biggest robbery in history." Byrne referred to Specs O'Keefe of Springfield, Massachusetts, who broke the case by talking to FBI agents just six days before the sixth anniversary of the robbery, news reports of October 6, 1956.

"Crime is a logical extension of the sort of behavior that is often considered perfectly respectable in legitimate business."

Robert Rice, The Business of Crime, Farrar, Straus and Cudahy, 1956.

DEFINITIONS

"Anger is a warmth which lights itself."

African saying, reported by a Methodist missionary, the Rev. Walter Williams, quoted in news reports of February 5, 1956.

"Advertising is the foot on the accelerator, the hand on the throttle, the spur on the flank that keeps our economy surging forward."

Robert W. Sarnoff, "Advertising Challenge in 1956," Chicago address, February 23, 1956.

"Experience is not what happens to you; it is what you do with what happens to you."

Aldous Huxley, Reader's Digest, March 1956.

"Summer is a sailor in a rowboat and ice-cream on your dress when you're four years old. Summer is a man with his coat off, wet sand between your toes, the smell of a garden an hour before moonrise. Oh, summer is silk itself, a giant geranium and music from a flute far away!"
Michael Brown, excerpt from script for 1956 March of Dimes Fashion Show, New York, reprinted by permission of author.

"Humor is the other side of tragedy. Humor is a serious thing. I like to think of it as one of our greatest and earliest national resources which must be preserved at all costs. It came over on the *Mayflower* and we should have it, all of it."
James Thurber, "Omnibus," CBS-TV, March 4, 1956.

"Youth is so sure the rules have changed. Age is sure they haven't. Youth feels it knows how far it can go. Age is deeply aware of the danger. Youth feels it can always apply the brakes in time to save itself. Age knows it isn't always so."
Richard L. Evans, radio broadcast from Salt Lake City Tabernacle, March 4, 1956.

"Zest is the secret of all beauty. There is no beauty that is attractive without zest."
Christian Dior, Ladies' Home Journal, April 1956.

"Charm is that extra quality that defies description."
Alfred Lunt, Ladies' Home Journal, April 1956.

"Free speech is like garlic. If you are perfectly sure of yourself, you enjoy it and your friends tolerate it."
Lynn White, Jr., president of Mills College, Look, April 17, 1956.

"It's some sort of make-believe that's got some sort of truth in it—a little bit that's so fascinating you can't get rid of it."
Robert Frost, definition of poetry, broadcast on WQED, Pittsburgh, quoted in Collier's, April 27, 1956.

nastiest things in the nicest way."

itic, news reports of April 29, 1956.

are animal rather than vegetable,

peness. Tawny, buff, ocher, umber,

ay, chestnut, roan, palomino: the

d, dry, aromatic, warm; the color

ils, of sage, of ocean and desert

ght like a mirror. And this light itself

in Utah and New Mexico on fiercer

e, of sunup and sundown."

A Place to Hang Your Dreams,"

May 1956; copyright 1956, The

mpany; reprinted by permission.

pictures that it calls to the mind are end-

and bewildering—the stone fences of New England, New Haven's out-of-town theatre openings, day lilies in June, cities taller and more fabulous than Troy. It is whaling museums and subways and institutes of higher learning and some of the world's best restaurants. It is Maine's wildernesses and New York's Greenwich Village, clambakes and brownstone houses, dogwood and First Nights. It is old and it is young, very green in summer, very white in winter, gregarious, withdrawn, and at once both sophisticated and provincial."

Phyllis McGinley, "The East Is Home," Woman's Home Companion, July 1956 issue; copyright, 1956, The Crowell-Collier Publishing Company, reprinted by permission of publisher and author.

"Age seventeen is the point in the journey when the parents retire to the observation car; it is the time when you stop being critical of your eldest son and he starts being critical of you."

Sally and James Reston, authors of a Saturday Evening Post article, "So We Sent Our Son to College," May 5, 1956.

"Taste . . . is a matter of ignorance. You taste, and you like the taste, and you taste again because it pleases you, but you taste because you don't know. If you knew you wouldn't have to taste. . . ."
> *Frank Lloyd Wright, "The Architect Preaches a Sermon," Church of the Divine Paternity, New York, June 3, 1956.*

"The common man is a man who believes in only what he sees and he sees only what he can put his hand on. . . . He is on speaking terms with progress, and progress must be in spite of him, although for him."
> *Frank Lloyd Wright. Ibid.*

"Architecture presents man, literature tells you about him, painting will picture him to you. You can listen and hear him, but if you want to realize him and experience him go into his buildings, and that's where you'll find him as he is. He can't hide there from you and he can't hide from himself."
> *Frank Lloyd Wright. Ibid.*

"Art is not an escape; it is not a subterfuge; it is the expression of a whole man's noblest instinct. . . . Art is the measure of a man's response to life. Mind you, I say 'response' and not 'reaction.' A work of art collates experience, and distills it. Strictly speaking, nothing is left out, for a man's art is the sum of the man."
> *Dimitri Mitropoulos, conductor of the New York Philharmonic Symphony, "What I Believe," Hi-Fi Music at Home, May-June 1956.*

"Position is only what you are yourself and what you give to those around you."
> *Elsa Maxwell, comment on social position, "Paris Report," New York Journal-American, August 4, 1956.*

"Anita Ekberg is a young matron who could not be more awesome, architecturally, if put together by Frank Lloyd Wright."
> *Phyllis Battelle, writing of the Swedish actress Anita Ekberg, "Assignment: America," New York Journal-American, August 6, 1956.*

"(It is) a lightning-quick epidemic which forces different and antagonistic persons all to obey the same mysterious order, to submit themselves to new habits which overturn their old ways of life, up to the moment when a new order arrives and obliges them to turn their coat once more."

Jean Cocteau, description of fashion, Paris Arts, *August 1956.*

"Wit has truth in it; wisecracking is simply calisthenics with words."

Dorothy Parker, in interview with Marion Capron, The Paris Review, *Summer, 1956.*

"Culture is not an affair of academies or authorities. It is each man expanding to his full growth, becoming all he is capable of. It's what he brings home by himself, to himself, every day of his life."

Definition in "Culture Begins at Home," by the staff of House Beautiful, *September, 1956.*

"The adjective is the banana peel of the parts of speech."

Clifton Fadiman, "Beware the Awful Adjective," The Reader's Digest, *September, 1956.*

"Cooking is like love. It should be entered into with abandon or not at all."

Harriet Van Horne, Vogue, *October 15, 1956.*

"Charm is a glow within a woman that casts a most becoming light on others."

John Mason Brown, Vogue, *November 15, 1956.*

"Like a resplendent chandelier, Paris in winter is made up of many parts. It is a classic Degasesque ballet dancer rehearsing in the Opéra, the Champs-Élysées in the rain, the academic seriousness of study at the Beaux-Arts, the Bohemian bonhomie of all of St.-Germain-des-Prés, the light eating and deep conversation of Les Deux Magots, a formal concert by the visiting Viennese, the ever-changing patterns of the river Seine by night, the smile of service and master music, youth and a dog, fresh flowers and wet pavements in the Étoile, the Gare des Invalides and its magnificent clock, the illuminated night tracery of leafless plane trees, the mysterious solace of the bridges, the glistening, triumphant majesty of the nighttime vistas . . . the heart-lifting silhouette of the Eiffel Tower, a businesslike bus and a proud set of arches. . . . It is Notre Dame . . . it is Paris . . . Fairest Lady of Europe."

> *W. A. Powers, "Paris In Wintertime,"* Town & Country, *December 1956, reprinted by permission.*

"Time is a dressmaker specializing in alterations."

> *Faith Baldwin,* Face Toward the Spring, *Rinehart and Company, Inc., 1956.*

"Metaphysics is almost always an attempt to prove the incredible by an appeal to the unintelligible."

> *H. L. Mencken,* Minority Report: H. L. Mencken's Notebooks, *copyright 1956 by Alfred A. Knopf, Inc., reprinted by permission.*

"There are some people who read too much: the bibliobibuli. I know some who are constantly drunk on books, as other men are drunk on whiskey or religion. They wander through this most diverting and stimulating of worlds in a haze, seeing nothing and hearing nothing."

> *H. L. Mencken. Ibid.*

"An alcoholic is someone who drinks too much—and you don't like anyway."

> *Variously attributed, a popular saying of 1956.*

"What Is a Boy?" by Alan Beck, reprinted by permission of New England Life Insurance Company of Boston.

"Between the innocence of babyhood and the dignity of manhood we find a delightful creature called a boy. Boys come in assorted sizes, weights, and colors, but all boys have the same creed: To enjoy every second of every minute of every hour of every day and to protest with noise (their only weapon) when their last minute is finished and the adult males pack them off to bed at night.

"Boys are found everywhere—on top of, underneath, inside of, climbing on, swinging from, running around, or jumping to. Mothers love them, little girls hate them, older sisters and brothers tolerate them, adults ignore them, and Heaven protects them. A boy is Truth with dirt on its face, Beauty with a cut on its finger, Wisdom with bubble gum in its hair, and the Hope of the future with a frog in its pocket.

"When you are busy a boy is an inconsiderate, bothersome, intruding jangle of noise. When you want him to make a good impression his brain turns to jelly or else he becomes a savage, sadistic, jungle creature bent on destroying the world and himself with it.

"A boy is a composite—he has the appetite of a horse, the digestion of a sword swallower, the energy of a pocket-size atomic bomb, the curiosity of a cat, the lungs of a dictator, the imagination of a Paul Bunyan, the shyness of a violet, the audacity of a steel trap, the enthusiasm of a firecracker, and when he makes something he has five thumbs on each hand.

"He likes ice cream, knives, saws, Christmas, comic books, the boy across the street, woods, water (in its natural habitat), large animals, Dad, trains, Saturday mornings, and fire engines. He is not much for Sunday school, company, schools, books without pictures, music lessons, neckties, barbers, girls, overcoats, adults, or bedtime.

"Nobody else is so early to rise, or so late to supper. Nobody else gets so much fun out of trees, dogs, and breezes. Nobody else can cram into one pocket a rusty knife, a half-eaten apple, three feet of string, an empty Bull Durham sack, two gum drops, six cents, a sling shot, a chunk of unknown substance, and a genuine supersonic code ring with a secret compartment.

"A boy is a magical creature—you can lock him out of your workshop, but you can't lock him out of your heart. You can get him out of your study, but you can't get him out of your mind. Might as well give up— he is your captor, your jailer, your boss, and your master—a freckled-faced, pint-sized, cat-chasing bundle of noise. But when you come home at night with only the shattered pieces of your hopes and dreams he can mend them like new with two magic words—'Hi, Dad!'"

"What Is a Girl?" by Alan Beck, reprinted by permission of New England Life Insurance Company of Boston:

"Little girls are the nicest things that happen to people. They are born with a little bit of angelshine about them and though it wears thin sometimes there is always enough left to lasso your heart—even when they are sitting in the mud, or crying temperamental tears, or parading up the street in mother's best clothes.

"A little girl can be sweeter (and badder) oftener than anyone else in the world. She can jitter around, and stomp, and make funny noises that frazzle your nerves, yet just when you open your mouth she stands there demure with that special look in her eyes. A girl is Innocence playing in the mud, Beauty standing on its head, and Motherhood dragging a doll by the foot.

"Girls are available in five colors—black, white, red, yellow, or brown, yet Mother Nature always manages to select your favorite color when you place your order. They disprove the law of supply and demand— there are millions of little girls, but each is as precious as rubies.

"God borrows from many creatures to make a little girl. He uses the song of a bird, the squeal of a pig, the stubbornness of a mule, the antics of a monkey, the spryness of a grasshopper, the curiosity of a cat, the speed of a gazelle, the slyness of a fox, the softness of a kitten, and to top it all off He adds the mysterious mind of a woman.

"A little girl likes new shoes, party dresses, small animals, first-grade noise makers, the girl next door, dolls, make-believe, dancing lessons, ice cream parlors, coloring books, make-up, cans of water, going visiting, boys in general, large dogs, hand-me-downs, straight chairs, vegetables, snow suits, or staying in the front yard. She is loudest when you are thinking, the prettiest when she has provoked you, the busiest at bed-time, the quietest when you want to show her off, and the most flirtatious when she absolutely must not get the best of you again.

"Who else can cause you more grief, joy, irritation, satisfaction, embarrassment, and genuine delight than this combination of Eve, Salome, and Florence Nightingale? She can muss up your home, your hair, and your dignity—spend your money, your time, and your temper—then just when your patience is ready to crack, her sunshine peeks through and you've lost again.

"Yes, she is a nerve-racking nuisance, just a noisy bundle of mischief. But when your dreams tumble down and the world is a mess—when it seems you are pretty much of a fool after all—she can make you a king when she climbs on your knee and whispers, 'I love you best of all!' "

EDUCATION

"I want to commend you for your courage and foresight in taking your place where you could accomplish so much toward making our country a better place for every citizen."

Mamie Eisenhower, comment in letter to Judy Genier, fourteen-year-old Moriah Center, N.Y., white girl who chose to attend a nonsegregated high school at Asheville, North Carolina, news reports of January 26, 1956.

"The man who reads only for improvement is beyond the hope of much improvement before he begins."

Jonathan Daniels, Three Presidents and Their Books, *University of Illinois Press, 1956.*

"People have got to think. Thinking isn't to agree or disagree. That's voting."

Robert Frost, poet, broadcast on WQED, Pittsburgh, quoted in Collier's, *April 27, 1956.*

"Helping your eldest son pick a college is one of the great educational experiences of life—for the parents. Next to trying to pick his bride, it's the best way to learn that your authority, if not entirely gone, is slipping fast."

Sally and James Reston, "So We Sent Our Son to College," The Saturday Evening Post, *May 5, 1956.*

"No greater nor more affectionate honor can be conferred on an American than to have a public school named after him."

Herbert Hoover, address at dedication of Herbert Hoover Junior High School, San Francisco, June 5, 1956; news reports of June 6, 1956.

"To the youngsters I, as an engineer, would suggest that there are no professions of greater satisfaction. The engineer has the fascination of watching a figment of imagination emerge into a plan on paper. Then it moves to realization in cement, in metal or energy. Then it brings new jobs and better homes. And I might add that on average it is the highest paid profession in the country—and there are today five bids to a job for every graduate."

Herbert Hoover. Ibid.

"America has need of thousands of leaders who will never be elected President or even a governor of a state or president of a professional society, but who, quietly and without ostentation, nevertheless will exert true leadership in their several walks of life."

Dr. Harold W. Dodds, president of Princeton University, baccalaureate address to the Class of 1956, June 10, 1956.

"Year after year these congregations hear the same exhortations, the same appeals to youth to sally forth, knight-errant, and slay the same old dragons in the same old sinful world. Yet these dragons, unlike their mortal cousins the dinosaurs, have managed to keep well ahead of the game. If Darwin himself had picked them as favorites in the cosmic sweepstakes, they could not have run a better race."

Whitney Griswold, president of Yale University, comment in 1956 baccalaureate address.

". . . At the height of our power we hesitate because we can see in a terrifying self-knowledge the necessity of putting reason before will, persuasion before assertiveness, asking before answering, concern before self-regard. . . ."

Nathan Pusey, president, Harvard University, speaking at Bryn Mawr College.

"Heu vatum ignarae mentes! quid vota repulsum, quid promissa iuvant? tua quid praesagia, Gallup?"
("The seers saw not defeat, poor souls,
Vain prayers, vain promises, vain Gallup poll!")

Oxford University's Latin citation awarding former President Harry Truman the honorary degree of Doctor of Civil Law, at

Oxford, England, June 20, 1956 ("to Harricum Truman, Doctoris in Iure Civili").

"Harricum! Harricum! Give 'em hell, Harricum!"
Oxford University student cheer for former President Truman.
Ibid.

"I venture to send you a few words because I think I may be able to hearten you in regard to the future of your little child, Michael.

"Out of the fullness of my experience, I can assure you that he has a good fighting chance and you can help him with an education just like any other child.

"Guided by the understanding and faith of those who study the blind and their problems, he can gain knowledge and grow up strong and able to find joy in living.

"He can gallantly overcome a disaster that threatens to destroy his spirit as well as his sight. Of course, you will share his restored interest and delight in life and be proud of the skills he acquires in a trade, a craft, or an industrial process, and you will be unexpectedly consoled, besides adding to his happiness.

"Tenderly I greet you, (signed) Helen Keller."
Letter sent to the Rev. and Mrs. James W. Sibole of Orlando, Florida, after their four-year-old son, already blind in one eye, had lost his other eye in surgery to stop cancer; letter released for publication by the American Foundation for the Blind, July 20, 1956, at Westport, Connecticut.

"Professional jargon is unpleasant. Translating it into English is a bore. I narrow-mindedly outlawed the word 'unique.' Practically every press release contains it. Practically nothing ever is."
Fred Hechinger, open letter to Sloan Wilson, succeeding Hechinger as education editor of the New York Herald Tribune, *August 5, 1956.*

"These fellows knocked out the playboy era of American colleges. They set a pace that is still with us—and it is here to stay."

John Monro, director of financial aid, Harvard University, comment as time ran out for the "GI Bill," government-supported program in which almost eight million World War II veterans received more than fourteen billion dollars' worth of educational benefits; Time, August 6, 1956.

"They had men's heads on men's shoulders."

Frank Bailey, acting president, Kenyon College. Ibid.

"Trying to answer students' questions, I soon learned there were great gaps in our scientific knowledge of sex—plenty of folktales, mythology and misunderstanding, of course, but little of the data we have on other phases of life. I resolved to try and fill in those gaps."

Dr. Alfred Kinsey, recollection of why, in 1938, he began interviewing for the now-famous Kinsey Reports, statement recalled in obituaries of August 26, 1956, reporting his death.

". . . We are recorders and reporters of the facts—not judges of the behavior we describe."

Dr. Alfred Kinsey, in defense of the Kinsey Reports. Ibid.

"Education is the established church of the United States. It is one of the religions that Americans believe in. It has its own orthodoxy, its pontiffs and its noble buildings."

Sir Michael Sadler, British educator, The New York Times, September 1, 1956.

"A student is not a professional athlete. . . . He is not a little politician or junior senator looking for angles . . . an amateur promoter, a glad-hander, embryo Rotarian, café-society leader, quiz kid, or man about town. A student is a person who is learning to fulfill his powers and to find ways of using them in the service of mankind."

Dr. Harold Taylor, President, Sarah Lawrence College, address to U. S. National Students Association Congress, news summaries of September 3, 1956.

"I'll bet that last night hundreds of young men were playing Dylan Thomas to hundreds of young girls in Greenwich Village."

Randall Jarrell, on the increasing popularity of poetry in America, comment on becoming poetry consultant to the Library of Congress, news summaries of September 17, 1956.

"Any sort of exclusiveness is not good."

Arthur Howe, Jr., Yale University Dean of Admissions, on the wisdom of admitting women students, New York Post, September 30, 1956.

"There is a danger of adding to our lexicon the term 'guilt by unassociation,' which might be defined as the practice of one zealot's suspecting another who is not as noisy as he is."

Henry Heald, President of the Ford Foundation, The New York Times Magazine, September 30, 1956.

"There are two ways to teach mathematics. One is to take real pains toward creating understanding—visual aids, that sort of thing. The other is the old British system of teaching until you're blue in the face."

James R. Newman, compiler of the 2,535-page The World of Mathematics, comment in interview with Lewis Nichols, The New York Times Magazine, September 30, 1956.

"If you choose to work, you will succeed; if you don't, you will fail.
If you neglect your work, you will dislike it; if you do it well, you will enjoy it.
If you join little cliques, you will be self-satisfied; if you make friends widely, you will be interesting.
If you gossip, you will be slandered; if you mind your own business, you will be liked.
If you act like a boor, you will be despised; if you act like a human being, you will be respected.
If you spurn wisdom, wise people will spurn you; if you seek wisdom, they will seek you.
If you adopt a pose of boredom, you will be a bore; if you show vitality, you will be alive.

If you spend your free time playing bridge, you will be a good bridge player; if you spend it in reading, discussing and thinking of things that matter, you will be an educated person."

Sidney Smith, President, University of Toronto, address to the student body, quoted in The Queen's Journal, *Kingston, Ontario, Canada, October 2, 1956.*

"The Forgotten Man works and votes and generally he prays—but his chief business in life is to pay. His name never gets into the newspapers except when he marries or dies. He may grumble sometimes to his wife, but he does not frequent the grocery and does not talk politics in a tavern. So he is forgotten. . . ."

Dr. Albert Galloway Keller, Yale University professor who introduced the "Forgotten Man" phrase used in Franklin Roosevelt's 1932 presidential campaign, paraphrase of William Graham Sumner recalled in obituaries reporting Dr. Keller's death, October 31, 1956.

"Each new generation of children brings its own problems—problems which require new approaches, new inventiveness, new countermeasures —and above all new knowledge and greater skill on the part of adults. All of these things are of the future—the children are the future."

Dr. Martha Eliot, chief of the Children's Bureau of the U. S. government, final paragraph in her forty-year history of the Bureau, statement quoted in reports of her retirement, November 9, 1956.

". . . A university where, at last, the Jews are hosts, and not guests as we have always been before."

Abram Sachar, President, Brandeis University, explanation of reason for Brandeis' founding in 1946, news summaries of November 19, 1956.

AMERICAN GOVERNMENT

"Balancing this budget is not simply a bookkeeping exercise or a businessman's fetish. It is the very keystone of financial responsibility."
Treasury Secretary George Humphrey, comment at news conference, January 14, 1956.

"You have to take chances for peace, just as you must take chances in war. Some say that we were brought to the verge of war (in Korea in June 1953; in Indo-China in April 1954; in the Formosa Straits in January 1955). Of course we were brought to the verge of war. The ability to get to the verge without getting into war is the necessary art. If you cannot master it, you inevitably get into war. If you try to run away from it, if you are scared to go to the brink, you are lost."
John Foster Dulles, widely discussed statement quoted in interview in Life, *January 16, 1955.*

"Now that Sir Winston Churchill is no longer active, you are the dean of the Western World."
John Foster Dulles, Washington dinner toast to German Chancellor Konrad Adenauer.

"It's great. It's wonderful per se."
Chief Justice Earl Warren, legalistic comment on learning of the birth of a grandson, Newsweek, *March 19, 1956.*

"First we just gave them these surpluses. Next we agreed to pay freight on transportation to ports. Then we agreed to mill the grain and package it. The next thing we'll be asked to cook and serve it."
Senator Allen Ellender, comment on complaints of relief and charitable agencies against food given them by U. S. Government, news reports of April 1, 1956.

"And now I'm back again as a junior Senator. I am willing to be a junior. I'm glad to sit on the back row. I would rather be a servant in the House of the Lord than to sit in the seats of the mighty."

Alben Barkley, final words before a fatal collapse while speaking at Lexington, Virginia, April 29, 1956. The former U. S. Vice-President was paraphrasing a Bible verse.

"This is not a day of triumph; it is a day of dedication. Here muster, not the forces of party, but the forces of humanity. Men's hearts wait upon us; men's lives hang in the balance. Who shall live up to the great trust? Who dares fail to try?"

President Woodrow Wilson, excerpt from first inaugural address, one of four quotations (others follow) chosen by the Wilson family to be engraved on the former President's tomb begun in the Washington National Cathedral in 1956; The New York Times, June 4, 1956.

"The right is more precious than peace, and we shall fight for the things which we have always carried nearest our hearts—for democracy, for the right of those who submit to authority to have a voice in their own government, for the rights and liberties of small nations, for a universal dominion of right by such a concert of free people as shall bring peace and safety to all nations and make the world itself at last free."

Woodrow Wilson, excerpt from his World War I message to Congress. Ibid.

"The stage is set, the destiny is closed. It has come about by no plan of our conceiving, but by the hand of God who led us into this way. We cannot turn back. We can only go forward, with lifted eyes and freshened spirit, to follow the vision. It was of this that we dreamed at our birth. America shall in truth show the way. The light streams upon the path ahead, and nowhere else."

Woodrow Wilson, excerpt from address submitting World War I peace treaty to the U. S. Senate. Ibid.

"The sum of the whole matter is this, that our civilization cannot survive materially unless it be redeemed spiritually. It can be saved only by

becoming permeated with the spirit of Christ and being made free and happy by the practices which spring out of that spirit."
Woodrow Wilson, selection from his last published words. Ibid.

"For why could it not be said that national security . . . requires not merely loyal and trustworthy employes but also those that are industrious and efficient? The relationship of the job to the national security being the same, its demonstrated inadequate performance because of inefficiency or incompetence would seem to present a surer threat to national security, in the sense of the general welfare, than a mere doubt as to the employe's loyalty."
U. S. Supreme Court majority opinion, delivered by Mr. Justice Harlan, calling for the reinstatement of a federal food and drug inspector dismissed from his job because of alleged association with Communists; Kendrick M. Cole, petitioner, v. Philip Young et al., Washington, June 11, 1956.

"We believe the court's order has stricken down the most effective weapon against subversive activity available to the Government. It is not realistic to say that the Government can be protected merely by applying the act to sensitive jobs. One never knows just which job is sensitive. The janitor might prove to be in as important spot security wise as the top employe in the building."
U. S. Supreme Court minority opinion, three justices dissenting, delivered by Mr. Justice Clark. Ibid.

"They get along pretty well with everything they really need, but not everything the kids would like to have."
Defense Secretary Charles E. Wilson, comparing the military budget to budget of the average family, news reports of May 9, 1956.

"The price of progress is trouble, and I must be making a lot of progress."
Charles E. Wilson, comment after being under fire for using the word "phony" in connection with efforts to hike the defense appropriation, news reports of July 1, 1956.

"The Navy is presently going through the most tremendous change it has ever undergone. It is passing from steam to nuclear power, from gunpowder to nuclear weapons, from guns to guided missiles, and in the air, from propeller-type planes to supersonic planes, all at the same time."

Charles Thomas, Navy Secretary, Time, *May 21, 1956.*

The Panama Declaration

(Text of the declaration of the Presidents of the American Republics, including President Eisenhower of the U.S.)

"We, the Presidents of the American Republics commemorating in the historic city of Panama the assembly of the plenipotentiaries of the American states of 1826, convoked by the Liberator Simón Bolívar, which constituted the first collective manifestation of Pan-Americanism, and recognizing the continuing validity of the ideals which inspired the precursors of continental solidarity, subscribe to the following declarations:

I

The destiny of America is to create a civilization that will give tangible meaning to the concept of human liberty, to the principle that the state is the servant of man and not his master, to the faith that man will reach even greater heights in his spiritual and material development and to the proposition that all nations can live together in peace and dignity.

II

The full realization of the destiny of America is inseparable from the economic and social development of its peoples and therefore makes necessary the intensification of national and inter-American cooperative efforts to seek the solution of economic problems and to raise the standards of living of the continent.

III

The accomplishments of the Organization of American States, and assurance of peace among the member states and of security for the Continent, demonstrate how much can be achieved in the various fields of international endeavor through a loyal cooperation among sovereign nations, and move us to strengthen the inter-American organizations and their activities.

IV

In a world in which the dignity of the individual, his fundamental rights and the spiritual values of mankind are seriously threatened by totalitarian forces, alien to the tradition of our peoples and their institutions, America holds steadfastly to its historic mission to be a bulwark of human liberty and national independence.

V

An America united, strong and benevolent, will not only promote the well-being of the Continent but contribute toward achieving for the whole world the benefits of a peace based on justice and freedom, in which all peoples, without distinction as to race or creed, can work with dignity and with confidence in the future."

Signed in the City of Panama this twenty-second day of July 1956.

"If the distinguished Senator will allow me I will try to extricate him from his thoughts."

Senator Eugene Millikin, comment interrupting a hopelessly wandering colleague; quotation, typical of the Millikin wit which had delighted the Senate since 1941, recalled in reports of Millikin's retirement from public life and decision not to seek another term, news reports of July 29, 1956.

"Under this reasoning, you start a navigable river every time a dog visits a fireplug."

Eugene Millikin, reply to a pork-barrel argument for classifying a small stream as navigable on the ground that it flowed into the Missouri. Ibid.

"I have . . . introduced a bill in Congress to establish a Department of Urbiculture. Its job would be to deal with the problems of the new forgotten man—the American who lives in the city or suburbs."

Representative Arthur Younger of California, "We Need a 'Department of Urbiculture,'" as told to James Poling, This Week Magazine, *August 5, 1956; copyright 1956 by United Newspapers Magazine Corporation.*

"We see the time not too far distant when we can have a four-day week. . . ."

Richard Nixon, comment in first major speech of campaign for re-election to the vice-presidency, news reports of September 23, 1956.

"Many people interpret the absence of a major war as peace. Armistice is a better word. And an armistice will be the only peace that we will ever know in our times."

Thomas Gates, Jr., Under Secretary of Navy, news summaries of November 4, 1956.

"In the past decade, hundreds of our Congressmen seeking information about America's role of leader in the free world have embassy-hopped around the globe. They themselves have picked up a considerable amount of useful information about their own and other nations' foreign problems at these 'operational fund' dinners, receptions, luncheons. I have even heard them pause in their investigations to say: 'You can make mine dry.'"

Clare Boothe Luce, address to annual dinner of the Advertising Council of New York a few days after resigning as Ambassador to Italy, news reports of November 29, 1956.

FOREIGN GOVERNMENTS

"Hitler was a madman, too. It's likely that, in another ten years, people will be admiring his castle without any one's pointing out, 'He was mad, you know.'"

Visitor to Neuschwanstein, castle of Ludwig the Mad of Bavaria, quoted by Rhea Talley in Toledo, Ohio, Blade of February 12, 1956.

"Very much less than a millionth part of one hydrogen bomb."

Prime Minister Anthony Eden, replying to question on cost of entertaining Soviet Prime Minister and Communist party chief during their visits to Great Britain, news reports of March 26, 1956.

"All my life I have been a man of peace, working for peace, striving for peace. And I am still the same. I couldn't be other."

Anthony Eden, Prime Minister of Great Britain, telecast address informing the British people that his government had felt it necessary to bomb targets in Egypt, news summaries of November 12, 1956.

"The Irish are a hard-headed people and realistic, and underneath it all they are essentially spiritual. They are certainly not sentimentalists."

John A. Costello, Prime Minister of Ireland, first to visit the U.S., news reports of March 30, 1956.

"He is forever poised between a cliché and an indiscretion."

Harold Macmillan, comment on the life of a British Foreign Secretary (one of his former posts), Newsweek, April 30, 1956.

"We will put our fingers around a glass together. We will put our hands in yours to shake in friendship. But we will not put our fingers on the ink pad."

Nikolai Bulganin, Soviet Premier, comment on fingerprinting of applicants for American visas, news reports of May 28, 1956.

"Everyone wants my blood, but no one wants my job."

Premier Guy Mollet of France, comment a few hours before winning a vote of confidence, 279-51, from the French National Assembly; the vote took place during debate on the Arabian uprising in French Algeria, news summaries, June 10, 1956.

"Each year humanity takes a step towards Communism. Maybe not you, but at all events your grandson will surely be a Communist."
Nikita Khrushchev, Soviet party chief, comment to British Ambassador Sir William Hayter, news summaries of June 19, 1956.

"It is a magnificent gesture that in Catholic Ireland it is possible to elect to this important office a man of a different faith, particularly my own, which proves that in this Catholic Ireland tolerance exists. I hope it will go forth from this chamber to the world that in a free Catholic Ireland there would be no intolerance."
Robert Briscoe, statement on being elected the first Jewish Lord Mayor of Dublin, a city ninety percent Roman Catholic, news reports of June 28, 1956.

"The Lash," a collection of quotations from South Africa's segregationists cited in "African Showdown," special international report in *Newsweek*, July 2, 1956 (reprinted by permission):

"The Negro does not need a home. He can sleep under a tree."
Daniel F. Malan, ex-Prime Minister.

"Our view is that in every sphere the European must retain the right to rule . . . and keep it a white man's country."
Johannes G. Strijdom, Premier.

"There is no place for the native in European society above the level of certain forms of labor."
Hendrik Frensch Verwoerd, Minister of Native Affairs.

"Negroes can do skilled labor if trained for it; that is why we must never [train] them."
Barend Jacobus Schoeman, Minister of Transport.

"Once we give [Negroes] political rights, the time will come when we will be ruled by numbers. Therefore we cannot afford to give them political rights."
Theophilus Ebenezer Donges, Minister of Interior.

"What are five lashes between friends?"
Charles Robert Swart, Minister of Justice, rejecting a proposal to limit floggings to ten rather than fifteen lashes with the cat-o'-nine-tails.

"It has no real value; it is just a showboat."
Soviet Rear Admiral V. F. Kotov, comment to Rotterdam newsmen that aircraft carriers such as his Sverdlov *are too vulnerable for modern warfare, news summaries of July 23, 1956.*

"I say to those behind the uproar, 'May your hate choke you to death.'"
Gamal Abdel Nasser, President of Egypt, comment on withdrawal of American financial offer, news summaries of July 29, 1956.

"Egypt will not submit to the dollar or to force."
Gamal Abdel Nasser. Ibid.

"We shall fight a bitter battle. We shall fight from village to village, from house to house, because each one of you, my fellow countrymen, is a soldier in the armed forces, to defend our honor and to defend our dignity and to defend our freedom."
Gamal Abdel Nasser, Cairo Radio broadcast vowing warfare against Britain and France for the Suez Canal, news reports of November 2, 1956.

"When people ask me why I am so pleased with myself, I tell them: because I have always done exactly what I wanted to regardless of consequences."
Jawaharlal Nehru, Prime Minister of India, comment during visit to Hamburg, Germany, to receive two honorary degrees, Time, *July 30, 1956.*

"Standing on my head increases my good humor."
Jawaharlal Nehru, explanation of his habit of standing on his head for twenty minutes each day at 6:15 A.M. Ibid.

"You are a people of cow-dung mentality, living in a cow-dung world."
Jawaharlal Nehru, remark to a group of Indians. Ibid.

"Communism has nothing to do with love. Communism is an excellent hammer which we use to destroy our enemy."
Mao Tse-tung, Premier of Red China, Réalités, August, 1956.

"A room should be swept, otherwise it will be covered with dust. This also applies to our ideology."
Mao Tse-tung. Ibid.

"With singular agility,
And technical facility
We seek convertibility,
Which means (I'll have you know)
A quid for every quo."
Robert Gordon Menzies, Prime Minister of Australia, notation on a memo pad during London conference on stabilization of the pound sterling, Time, September 10, 1956.

"My only task is to be silent. I must feel my way back in the world."
Grand Admiral Karl Doenitz, Adolf Hitler's successor, on being released after serving a ten-year sentence for war crimes, news reports of October 1, 1956.

"In Israel, in order to be a realist you must believe in miracles."
Ben-Gurion, Prime Minister of Israel. Comment in interview with Edward R. Murrow, "Person to Person," CBS-TV, October 5, 1956.

"A minister of finance is a legally authorized pickpocket."
Paul Ramadier, French Minister of Finance, translation in Quote, October 7, 1956.

"Democracy down here is like a baby—and nobody gives a baby everything to eat right away. I'm giving 'em liberty, but in my style."
Anastasio Somoza, President of Nicaragua, quotation recalled in obituary reporting his assassination, Life, October 8, 1956.

"I secreted my frame in every corner and have baffled them all. . . ."
Benjamin Disraeli, Victorian era Prime Minister of Britain, writ-
ing to his wife of his purchase of the Suez Canal, letter from the
Donald Crisp collection made public by Hy Gardner, New York
Herald Tribune, *October 31, 1956.*

"You do what you have to do in life, when you form a philosophy that
you can't talk yourself out of. . . . People who decide they came to
earth to work, who make work their personal philosophy, are kept very
busy."
Constantine Karamanlis, Prime Minister of Greece, comment to
columnist Phyllis Battelle during visit to U.S., news reports of
November 14, 1956.

"It is bad to be a chore boy of the United States. It is equally bad to
be a colonial chore boy running around shouting 'ready, aye, ready.' "
Lester Pearson, Canadian Secretary of State for External Af-
fairs, defense of Canadian policy in Middle Eastern crisis, news
reports of November 28, 1956.

HOLLYWOOD

"We didn't worry about dialogue too much. If we ran out of it, we
simply said things like 'Now, really, 78, 45, 32, 89, 91' and so on, anything that came into our heads."
Leatrice Joy, recollection of her days as a star of silent films,
news summaries of March 19, 1956.

"I want to thank my mother for giving me the idea of going into this
wonderful business, my pop for being steadfast, and my lovely wife
for helping me."
Ernest Borgnine, accepting an Oscar for best performance by
an actor in films produced in 1955, news reports of March 22,
1956.

"If you are joking me, I will get up immediately and kill you wherever you are."
> *Anna Magnani, on learning from a reporter's phone call that she had been awarded an Oscar for best performance by an actress in films produced in 1955. Ibid.*

"It was so cold I almost got married."
> *Shelley Winters, various sources, including* The New York Times, *April 29, 1956.*

". . . Fundamentally I feel that there is as much difference between the stage and the films as between a piano and a violin. Normally you can't become a virtuoso in both."
> *Ethel Barrymore, comment in newspaper interview at her Pacific Palisades home,* New York Post, *June 7, 1956.*

"I am a typed director. If I made *Cinderella,* the audience would immediately be looking for a body in the coach."
> *Alfred Hitchcock, quoted in "profile" article in* Newsweek, *June 11, 1956.*

"It is self-evident that the poloist, the steeplechaser, the speedboat racer, and the fox hunter ride for the thrill that comes only from danger . . . and for every person who seeks fear in the real or personal sense, millions seek it vicariously, in the theatre and in the cinema."
> *Alfred Hitchcock. Ibid.*

" 'Playing our parts.' Yes, we all have to do that and from childhood on I have found that my own character has been much harder to play worthily and far harder at times to comprehend than any of the roles I have portrayed on stage and screen."
> *Bette Davis, "A New Day Is Coming,"* This Week Magazine, *July 22, 1956.*

"Creation is a drug I can't do without."
> *Cecil B. de Mille, comment in interview on his seventy-fifth birthday,* The New York Times Magazine, *August 12, 1956.*

"Hollywood money isn't money. It's congealed snow. . . ."
   Dorothy Parker, on Hollywood as provider for the artist, in interview with Marion Capron, The Paris Review, Summer, 1956.

"If you're going to write, don't pretend to write down. It's going to be the best you can do, and it's the fact that it's the best you can do that kills you. . . ."
   Dorothy Parker. Ibid.

"A wide screen just makes a bad film twice as bad."
   Samuel Goldwyn, Quote, September 9, 1956.

"I class myself with Rin-Tin-Tin. At the end of the Depression, people were perhaps looking for something to cheer them up. They fell in love with a dog, and with a little girl. . . . I think it won't happen again."
   Shirley Temple, on her success as a child star, "Out Of the Past," New York Post, September 13, 1956.

"If I look like this, I need the trip!"
   Gloria Swanson, comment on her passport photograph, quoted by Hy Gardner, New York Herald Tribune, September 17, 1956.

"Honestly, I think I've stretched a talent which is so thin that it's almost opaque over a quite unbelievable term of years—thirty of them actually."
   Bing Crosby, comment in letter to London Daily Express, quoted by Time, October 15, 1956.

"He would have to talk, and to talk he would have to step off his pedestal, the pedestal of the silent film. The Orientals have gods, but they never take them out of their shrines."
   Charlie Chaplin, declaring that he will never do his famed tramp impersonation in talking pictures, The New York Times, October 28, 1956.

"Speed is good when wisdom leads the way."
   Edward R. Murrow, prologue for the film, Eighty Days Around the World, produced by Michael Todd, 1956.

MEDICINE

"I feel that the greatest reward for doing is the opportunity to do more."

Dr. Jonas E. Salk, comment on receiving a gold medal from President Eisenhower for developing a vaccine against polio, quoted in news reports of January 27, 1956.

"My good health is due to a soup made of white doves. It is simply wonderful as a tonic."

Madame Chiang Kai-shek, comment on gaining relief from a prolonged skin rash, Time, February 27, 1956.

"Psychoanalysis has changed American psychiatry from a diagnostic to a therapeutic science, not because so many patients are cured by the psychoanalytic technique, but because of the new understanding of psychiatric patients it has given us and the new and different concept of illness and health."

Dr. Karl Menninger, Menninger Clinic, Topeka, Kansas, comment on Freud and American psychiatry, American Psychoanalytic Association annual meeting, Chicago, news reports of April 29, 1956.

"It was his optimism that Freud bequeathed to America and it was the optimism of our youthfulness, our freedom from the sterner, sadder tradition of Europe which enabled us to seize his gift."

Dr. Karl Menninger. Ibid.

"What is new is not always true, and what is true is not always new."

Dr. William Sargent of St. Thomas's Hospital, London, writing in The British Medical Journal on new tranquilizing drugs, Newsweek, May 21, 1956.

". . . [There] is the concept that modern medical care must be looked upon as a matter of teamwork. . . . In this view, no particular type of physician—whether he be a general practitioner, a surgeon, or a medical specialist—should be considered the 'golden boy,' the all-American, entitled to the lion's share of prestige and reward."

Dwight Murray, M.D., "The Personal Touch in Medicine," inaugural address given as 1956–57 president of the American Medical Association, Chicago, news reports of June 13, 1956.

"Our mutual task—both physicians and the public—is to regain our individuality. To do so, we must humanize and personalize the practice of modern medicine. Such action is imperative, in my opinion, because the public wants it, we doctors want it, and medical care is not complete without it."

Dwight Murray, M.D. Ibid.

"No matter how complex or specialized medicine may become in the decades ahead . . . there always will have to be the equivalent of the family doctor."

Dwight Murray, M.D. Ibid.

". . . Several matters of profound importance have already become clear: bacteria or fruit fly, mouse or man, the chemical nature of the hereditary material is universally the same; the main pattern of hereditary transmission of traits is the same for all forms of life reproducing sexually; and the nature of the effects of high-energy radiations upon the genetic material is likewise universally the same in principle."

"Biological Effects of Atomic Radiation," comment in report released at Washington by the Genetics Committee of the National Academy of Sciences, news reports of June 16, 1956.

"We may find it desirable or even almost obligatory that we spend a certain amount on atomic power plants. But we must watch and guard all our expenditures. From the point of view of genetics, they are all bad."

"Biological Effects of Atomic Radiation," concluding sentences. Ibid.

"There are three basic types of doctors coming out of U. S. medical schools: the healer, the scientist, and the mechanic. We are looking for the healer and the scientist. Sometimes we get both in our package, and that is fine, but we are content if we have one or the other."

Dr. Stafford Warren, dean, University of California School of Medicine at Los Angeles, Time, July 2, 1956.

"To add life to years, not just years to life."

Unofficial motto of U. S. specialists in medicine for the aging and aged, "The Problem of Old Age," Time, July 23, 1956.

"We sit at breakfast, we sit on the train on the way to work, we sit at work, we sit at lunch, we sit all afternoon . . . a hodgepodge of sagging livers, sinking gall bladders, drooping stomachs, compressed intestines, and squashed pelvic organs."

Dr. John Button, Jr., East Orange, New Jersey, address to a meeting of the American Osteopathic Association in New York on theory that frequent, erect standing would help avoid "indigestion, neurasthenia, chronic grouch, and a thousand and one similar ailments"; news reports of July 19, 1956, and Newsweek, August 6, 1956.

". . . Middle-aged rabbits don't have a paunch, do have their own teeth and haven't lost their romantic appeal."

Dr. Aurelia Poter, endocrinologist, explaining that "rabbit food" may be as good for business executives as it is for rabbits, The New York Times, September 22, 1956.

". . . Certainly no aspect of human biology in our current civilization stands in more need of scientific knowledge . . . than that of sex."

Dr. Alan Gregg, veteran official of the Rockefeller Foundation, on his initial financial sponsorship of the Kinsey reports, "℞ for Medicine," by Leonard Engel, The New York Times Magazine, November 4, 1956.

"The human race has had long experience and a fine tradition in surviving adversity. But we now face a task for which we have little experience, the task of surviving prosperity."

Dr. Alan Gregg. Ibid.

MUSIC

"I accept life unconditionally. . . . Most people ask for happiness on condition. Happiness can only be felt if you don't set any condition."

Artur Rubinstein, concert pianist, comment in interview on the fiftieth anniversary of his American debut, news reports of February 5, 1956.

". . . When I was young I used to go into the practice room and lock the door behind me. I'd put a beautiful novel in with my sheet music and a box of cherries on the right-hand side of the piano and a box of chocolates on the left and play runs with my left hand and eat cherries with my right and all the time be reading my book."

Artur Rubinstein. Ibid.

"I live with music like a monk who prays every moment, including the night when he gets up to say 'Ave Maria.' It is no more or no less. Simply utter devotion. The utmost devotion."

Dimitri Mitropoulos, conductor of the New York Philharmonic Symphony, comment on eve of his sixtieth birthday, news reports of February 19, 1956.

"Success can corrupt; usefulness can only exalt."

Dimitri Mitropoulos, "What I Believe," Hi-Fi Music at Home, May–June 1956.

"Regard your voice as capital in the bank. When you go to sing, do not draw on your bank account. Sing on your interest and your voice will last."

Lauritz Melchior, news reports of April 1, 1956.

"Most of them sound like they live on seaweed."

Sir Thomas Beecham, comment on sopranos, Newsweek, *April 30, 1956.*

"The cats sound the same and they dig the same. It's like that all over the world."

Louis "Satchmo" Armstrong, comment after a London perform-ance, news summaries of May 14, 1956.

"If I was a good trumpet player I wouldn't be here. I got desperate. I hadda look for a job. I went in the union business."

James C. Petrillo, president, American Federation of Musicians, quoted in a "profile" article in The New York Times, *June 14, 1956.*

"My great virtue is that I have no vanity. People criticize me, but when they meet me nobody can help liking me."

Liberace, quoted by Dorothy Kilgallen, New York Journal-American, *June 19, 1956.*

"This hooby doopy, oop-shoop, ootie ootie, boom boom de-addy boom, scoobledy goobledy dump—is trash."

The Denver Post, *reporting a reader's comment on the syncopa-tions of "rock 'n' roll" music popular in the U.S. in the spring and summer of 1956.*

"It's a tiny isolated village with no singers around. I have singers all the year. I don't want any now."

Rudolf Bing, on the Italian village he picked for a vacation from managing the Metropolitan Opera, news summaries of July 21, 1956.

"We have the same problems today that we had when I came here six years ago, and no matter where we are, we'll probably have most of them six years from now. The problems of opera are eternal—that's part of its fascination."

Rudolf Bing, manager of the Metropolitan Opera, New York Herald Tribune, *October 28, 1956.*

"The new techniques of recording make it possible to get all sorts of new sounds. But some of them were not meant for human ears. They were meant for hounds. Sensitive hounds. I am old-fashioned enough to believe that the musical side of the performance is what counts."
Jascha Heifetz, Look, *August 7, 1956.*

"Music means more to me the longer I live. I cannot imagine what it will be like when I am one hundred."
Bruno Walter, conductor, comment on nearing his eightieth birthday, The New York Times Magazine, *September 9, 1956.*

"My best hours are in bed, and my best work too, with my dog cuddling beside me and my husband asleep."
Maria Callas, soprano, quoted on eve of her Metropolitan Opera debut, Time, *October 29, 1956.*

PERSONALITIES

"I never give them hell. I just tell the truth, and they think it is hell."
Harry Truman, on his campaign technique, Look, *April 3, 1956.*

"Indeed, he was anything but insane . . . he was a smart hombre."
Harry Truman, recollection of Russian Premier Joseph Stalin, news summaries of May 31, 1956.

"Totally unnecessary, and planned by some squirrel-headed general."
Harry Truman, comment attributed during a vacation visit to the Salerno, Italy, beachhead of World War II. Mr. Truman afterwards denied the remark but Fred Zusy of the Associated Press stood by his report, news summaries of June 4, 1956.

"Never, never in my life did I ever think I'd be a Yank at Oxford."
Harry Truman, remark in London a few days before receiving an honorary degree from Oxford University, news reports of June 19, 1956.

"I am a Democrat with a big D."

Harry Truman, address to Democratic National Convention, Chicago, news reports of August 17, 1956.

"A boy has two jobs. One is just being a boy. The other is growing up to be a man."

Herbert Hoover, address to fiftieth anniversary celebration of the Boys Clubs of America, news summaries of May 21, 1956.

"There is no joy to be had from retirement except by some kind of productive work. Otherwise, you degenerate into talking to everybody about your pains and pills and income tax. Any oldster who keeps at even part-time work has something worthwhile talking about. He has a zest for the morning paper and his three meals a day. The point of all this is not to retire from work or you will shrivel up into a nuisance to all mankind."

Herbert Hoover, on his eighty-second birthday, news reports of August 10, 1956.

"I have lived a long life. I have witnessed, and even taken part in, many great and threatening crises. With each time they have been surmounted, the American dream has become more real."

Herbert Hoover, address to Republican National Convention, San Francisco, news reports of August 22, 1956.

"I've run more risk eating my way across the country than in all my driving."

Duncan Hines, news summaries of May 27, 1956.

"They look at the moon and they expect to see people walking around on it. Or they look at Mars—gosh, I hate Mars! It's so overrated. Every one has heard about the canals on Mars, and they feel cheated when they don't see the canals. I try to explain that only one man ever saw those canals, one time over in Italy where the air is clear, not like here with bus fumes. I try to explain how wonderful it is to see the Moon and Mars, so many millions of miles closer than they appear to the naked eye. But still they complain that it's just a dirty old ball with markings on it. They expect such marvels."

Proprietor of telescope in Times Square, New York, quoted by Rhea Talley in Houston, Texas, Post of May 29, 1956.

"Money alone can't bring you happiness, but money alone has not brought me unhappiness. . . . I won't say my previous husbands thought only of my money, but it had a certain fascination for them."

Barbara Hutton, news summaries of June 4, 1956.

"Every time I tell them my name down here, they knock me down. They think I'm being sacrilegious or something."

Robert E. Lee, an Ohio-born man who complained to Tampa, Florida police of being forced into street fights with strangers, Time, June 25, 1956.

"I have completely changed my party tactics. I have become a dictator —not a hostess—and I think that is the reason why my party was tops. You see, I don't have to care if anyone speaks to me or not, or what they think of me, or what they may say or do, and bores are my clay pigeons to bring down when they fly too near."

Elsa Maxwell, comment on her "annual party," "Paris Report," New York Journal-American, August 4, 1956.

"We call upon the people of America for their own good, for your good, for our good, wedded as you are to the cause of social progress—dedicated to the cause of democracy—consecrated to the cause of honesty, decency and morality in government—to rise up as one and smite down these money-changers who have invaded and violated the people's temple of justice on Capitol Hill."

Governor Frank Clement of Tennessee, keynote speech at Democratic National Convention, Chicago, news reports of August 14, 1956.

". . . Every race, creed and color, let us go forward, singing in unison the inevitable victory hymn: 'Precious Lord, take our hand, lead us on!' "
Governor Frank Clement, conclusion of keynote address. Ibid.

"I am here tonight as a delegate to this convention because without prefix, without suffix and without apology, I am a Democrat."
Sam Rayburn, Speaker of the House of Representatives, address as Permanent Chairman of Democratic National Convention, Chicago, news reports of August 15, 1956.

"The Democratic party emphatically reaffirms its support of the historic principles that ours is a government of laws and not of men."
Democratic National Convention party platform, plank on civil rights, a carefully worded statement which observers felt "at last dealt with the issue of civil rights without splitting the party," news reports of August 16, 1956.

"History's headlong course has brought us, I devoutly believe, to the threshold of a new America—to the America of the great ideals and noble visions which are the stuff our future must be made of. I mean a new America where poverty is abolished and our abundance is used to enrich the lives of every family. I mean a new America where freedom is made real for all without regard to race or belief or economic condition. I mean a new America which everlastingly attacks the ancient idea that men can solve their differences by killing each other."
Adlai Stevenson, address accepting nomination for President of the United States, Democratic National Convention, Chicago, news reports of August 18, 1956.

"The idea that you can merchandise candidates for high office like breakfast cereal—that you can gather votes like box tops—is, I think, the ultimate indignity to the democratic process."
Adlai Stevenson. Ibid.

"In our hearts we know that the horizons of the new America are as endless, its promise as staggering in its richness as the unfolding miracle of human knowledge. America renews itself with every forward thrust of the human mind."

Adlai Stevenson. Ibid.

"We live at a time when automation is ushering in a second industrial revolution."

Adlai Stevenson. Ibid.

". . . There is a New America every morning when we wake up. It is upon us whether we will it or not. The New America is the sum of many small changes—a new subdivision here, a new school there, a new industry where there had been swampland—changes that add up to a broad transformation of our lives. Our task is to guide these changes. For, though change is inevitable, change for the better is a full-time job."

Adlai Stevenson, campaign address at Miami, Florida, news reports of September 26, 1956.

". . . You somehow feel that [when] you talk to masses of people everywhere and bespeak their support [it] is honest and worthwhile, because what you are doing is larger than you are or than any selfish interest."

Adlai Stevenson, on being a presidential candidate, campaign address at Oakland, California, news reports of October 12, 1956.

". . . We are being offered for campaign consumption a brand of Pollyanna politics labeled peace, prosperity and progress."

Adlai Stevenson, on Republican opposition. Ibid.

"Perish forbid."

Adlai Stevenson, reply to newsmen who asked if he would run a third time for the U. S. presidency, news reports of November 8, 1956.

"Take heart—there are things more precious than political victory; there is the right to political contest."
Adlai Stevenson, statement to Democratic gathering in Chicago a few hours after conceding defeat. Ibid.

". . . Our party's purpose in this campaign is not to 'give 'em hell,' but to give them leadership."
Governor Arthur Langlie of Washington, keynote address to Republican National Convention, San Francisco, news reports of August 21, 1956.

"The nerve center of our progress lies in the Congress of the United States."
Representative Joseph Martin of Massachusetts, address as Permanent Chairman of Republican National Convention, San Francisco, news reports of August 22, 1956.

"With utmost confidence in the future and with justifiable pride in our achievements, the Republican Party warmly greets the dawn of our second Century of service in the cause of unity and progress in the Nation."
Declaration of Dedication concluding platform written for Republican National Convention, San Francisco, news reports of August 22, 1956. The convention marked the party's centennial.

"Take your Joe Smith and get out of here."
Representative Joseph Martin, order ousting Terry Carpenter, Nebraska delegate, from the Republican Convention floor after Carpenter had placed a fictitious name in nomination for Vice President as a symbol of "an open convention." News summaries of August 25, 1956.

"If you're going to have centralization, why not have it!"
Frank Lloyd Wright, announcing plans for a 510-story office building for Chicago's Loop, news summaries of September 10, 1956.

"We seemed to be playing Russian roulette with an atomic pistol which would destroy ourselves and everyone else, too."

Dean Acheson, Secretary of State in the Truman administration, comment on Republican foreign policy, news reports of September 27, 1956.

"Nature gives you the face you have at twenty; it is up to you to merit the face you have at fifty."

Madame Chanel, quoted in Ladies' Home Journal, *September, 1956.*

"A woman concerned with her appearance does not need many dresses . . . [but] this selection requires great honesty with oneself. To be well dressed is, above all, to know oneself."

Christian Dior, quoted in Ladies' Home Journal, *September, 1956.*

"The wife in curlpapers is replaced by the wife who puts on lipstick before she wakens her husband."

Margaret Mead, on changes in American marriages, quoted in article entitled "The American Woman," Look, *October 16, 1956.*

"I told him to put the engines on stand by, blow the horn, call me and never get closer than one mile to another ship."

Captain Gunnar Nordenson of the liner Stockholm, *testimony during inquiry into collision of* Stockholm *and* Andrea Doria, *recollection of instructions to third mate; news summaries of October 25, 1956.*

"What I do is, I wiggle my shoulders and I shake my legs and I walk up and down the stage and I hop around on one foot. . . . I'd never do anything that was vulgar before an audience. My mother would never allow it."

Elvis Presley, description of the song-and-guitar act that gained him national fame in 1956, Sunday Mirror Magazine, *November 11, 1956.*

THE PRESIDENCY

"Our country is at peace. Our security posture commands respect. A spiritual vigor marks our national life. Our economy, approaching the 400-billion-dollar mark, is at an unparalleled level of prosperity. The national income is more widely and fairly distributed than ever before. The number of Americans at work has reached an all-time high. As a people, we are achieving ever higher standards of living—earning more, producing more, consuming more, building more and investing more than ever before."

President Eisenhower, State of the Union message presented to Congress, January 5, 1956.

"Our resources are too many, our principles too dynamic, our purposes too worthy, and the issues at stake too immense for us to entertain doubt or fear. But our responsibilities require that we approach this year's business with a sober humility."

President Eisenhower. Ibid.

"Our farm people are not sharing as they should in the general prosperity. They alone of all major groups have seen their incomes decline rather than rise."

President Eisenhower. Ibid.

"We are going to foster the march of science in helping expand our economy and increasing productivity. We are going to be certain about the security of the United States in this world of today. We are going to continue to seek a just peace. And we are going to devote single-minded attention to the common good of America—all its citizens."

President Eisenhower, informal comment to newsmen on the meaning of his State of the Union message.

"Every problem that you take up has inevitably a terrific meaning for many millions of people. . . ."

President Eisenhower, reply to question of whether the presidency was the most physically taxing job he ever held, news conference held at Key West, Florida, January 8, 1956.

"I certainly sincerely trust that all of my actions in respect to public duty over the past forty years have been inspired and directed by my own sense of duty. . . . But where does the sense of duty point, and who determines what the duty is? That is a very tricky question when you go into the problem."

President Eisenhower, reply to question of whether he would again seek the presidency out of a sense of duty. Ibid.

"It is a very critical thing to change governments in this country at a time that is unexpected. . . . It is a rather startling thing. They tell me that even some disturbance in the stock market at the time I got sick—I didn't know it till six weeks later—they told me there was."

President Eisenhower. Ibid.

"I believe that hard work is not only a very, very fine thing for most humans but keeps them healthy."

President Eisenhower. Ibid.

"In all our efforts for education—in providing adequate schools, research, and study—we must never lose sight of the very heart of education: good teaching itself. Good teachers do not just happen. They are the product of the highest personal motivation, encouraged and helped in their work by adequate salaries and the respect, support, good will of their neighbors. The quality of American teaching has never been better. But the rewards for too many teachers are not commensurate with their work and their role in American life. It is my earnest hope that along with progress in other aspects of education, the states and communities will give increasing attention to this tap-root of all education—good teachers, and hence good teaching."

President Eisenhower, Education Message to Congress, January 12, 1956.

"My own future role . . . remains undetermined. . . . I could devoutly wish that there were some method by which the American people could . . . point out the path of my true duty. But it appears that this is a question that first I alone must answer."

President Eisenhower, address on closed circuit television to "Salute-to-Eisenhower" dinners of Republicans in fifty-six cities, January 20, 1956, prior to announcement that he would seek re-election if nominated.

"Today, we believe as strongly in economic progress through free and competitive enterprise as our fathers did, and we resent as they did any unnecessary intrusion of government into private affairs. But we have also come to believe that progress need not proceed as irregularly as in the past, and that the federal government has the capacity to moderate economic fluctuations without becoming a dominant factor in our economy."

President Eisenhower, Economic Report to Congress, January 24, 1956.

". . . I have to guess as to the next five years, and the problem is what will be the effect on the presidency, not on me. . . ."

President Eisenhower, comment on the main factor in his consideration of seeking re-election, news conference of January 25, 1956.

". . . There are so many things that I have to do—I have piled up stacks of books I never had a chance to read, and I am trying to get through. I, as you know, daub with paints; I like the actual roaming around of a farm. I love animals. I like to go out and see them. I have got a thousand things to do in this world, so I don't think I would be bored, no matter what it was."

President Eisenhower, when asked if he missed "the bustle of the presidency" during time spent at his Gettysburg, Pennsylvania, farm home. Ibid.

". . . In the light of the human and economic toll still taken by disease, in the light of the great opportunities open before us, the nation still has not summoned the resources it properly and usefully could summon to the cause of better health."

President Eisenhower, Health Message to Congress, January 26, 1956.

"I have often said, and I now repeat, that there is nothing I would not do to promote peace with justice for the world. But we know that it is deeds and not words alone which count."

President Eisenhower, letter to Soviet Premier Nikolai Bulganin, January 28, 1956, rejecting treaty proposed by the Russians.

"While resolutely pursuing these aims, which are the products of our faith in God and in the peoples of the earth, we shall eagerly grasp any genuine opportunity to free mankind of the pall of fear and insecurity which now obscures what can and should be a glorious future."

President Eisenhower, conclusion of joint statement made with British Prime Minister Anthony Eden at end of three-day Washington conference, February 1, 1956.

"When you begin to talk about a corporation or organization, organizations and pressure group contributions, I think we have got a field that we should do some very earnest study on, and I do believe that we must continuously watch the whole proposition of putting in money into political campaigns from the standpoint of, is it absolutely disinterested money or is someone trying to get something for it. I think it is a field that we can never let up on."

President Eisenhower, comment during news conference of February 8, 1956, when asked what he thought of large campaign contributions and their relationships to influence on public actions of officials.

"I have my own ideas, as everyone else does, of what is a proper sphere of activity for the President of the United States. One of them . . . is

that he doesn't go out barnstorming for himself under any conditions. . . ."
President Eisenhower. Ibid.

"Seventy-five years this organization has been serving America; in a way it has been sort of the conscience of America, America doing here and abroad what we, as citizens, believe should be done. . . . Through this Red Cross we are enabled to discharge or to satisfy our real desire to be humans."
President Eisenhower, tribute on occasion of yearly campaign of Red Cross, news conference of February 29, 1956.

"I have reached a decision. But I have found, as I did so, that there were so many factors and considerations involved, that I saw the answer could not be expressed just in the simple terms of yes and no. Some full explanation to the American people is not only necessary, but I would never consent to go before them unless I were assured that they did understand these things, these influences, these possibilities."
President Eisenhower, announcement that he would seek re-election. Ibid.

"I have a record established before the American people; that is my campaign."
President Eisenhower. Ibid.

"And I assure you of this: My answer would not be affirmative unless I thought I could last out the five years."
President Eisenhower, concluding remark in initial announcement that he would run again. Ibid.

"I have decided that if the Republican party chooses to renominate me I shall accept that nomination. Thereafter, if the people of this country should elect me I shall continue to serve them in the office I now hold."
President Eisenhower, formal announcement that he would seek re-election, address to the American people, February 29, 1956.

". . . This decision was my own. Even the closest members of my family have declined to urge me to any specific course, merely saying that they would cheerfully abide by whatever I decided was best to do."
President Eisenhower. Ibid.

"From the moment that any man is first elected President of the United States there is continued public interest in the question as to whether or not he will seek re-election."
President Eisenhower. Ibid.

"Both in war and in peace, it has been my conviction that no man can isolate himself from the men and women he is attempting to serve and really sense what is in their hearts and minds."
President Eisenhower. Ibid.

". . . If a political party does not have its foundation in the determination to advance a cause that is right and that is moral, then it is not a political party, it is merely a conspiracy, which is to seize power."
President Eisenhower, speech for the fourth annual Republican women's national conference, Washington, March 6, 1956.

"If ever there was a time when we must be patient without being complacent, when we must be understanding of other people's deep emotions, as well as our own, this is it. Extremists on neither side are going to help this situation, and we can only believe that the good sense, the common sense, of Americans will bring this thing along. . . ."
President Eisenhower, comment on desegregation measures, news conference of March 14, 1956.

"As a matter of fact, I think this is a wonderful institution. . . . While I have seen all sorts of statements that presidents have considered it a bore and it is a necessary chore to go through, it does a lot of things for me personally. For one thing, at least once a week I have to take a half hour to review in my own mind what has happened during that

323

week, so that I don't make errors, just through complete inadvertence and failure to look them up."

President Eisenhower, comment on the forty-third anniversary of the presidential press conferences. Ibid.

"These trips, of course, are onerous burdens on an individual, but we have found them extremely worthwhile. The personal contact with leaders of other countries is something that we have tried to bring about and to sustain, and we find that through it we gain better understanding of common problems than we do merely by trusting to the normal diplomatic exchanges."

President Eisenhower, comment on a trip to the Far East by Secretary of State Dulles, news conference of March 21, 1956.

"Now, this is what I see in Billy Graham: A man who clearly understands that any advance in the world has got to be accompanied by a clear realization that man is, after all, a spiritual being. He teaches, he carries his religion to the far corners of the earth, trying to promote peace, trying to promote mediation instead of conflict, tolerance instead of prejudice. Now, he does that in this country, he does it abroad. Therefore, because of the very great crowds that he attracts to listen to him, I am very much interested in Billy Graham's activities, but for that reason only. I have never discussed with him any plan for mobilizing nations."

President Eisenhower. Ibid.

"There is nothing that takes place at home of any great importance— if it is a difficult problem, at least—that is not caused by or at least colored by some foreign consideration."

President Eisenhower, address to twelfth annual Washington Conference of the Advertising Council, April 3, 1956.

"The need in government is time to think, with the ability of people to do it."

President Eisenhower. Ibid.

". . . let us use our brains to make certain we sustain our position by helping everybody else to realize their own aspirations and legitimate ambitions, not necessarily in the exact pattern of this country. Of course not. Nobody starts from the same place and no other nation would possibly reach the same end."

President Eisenhower. Ibid.

"Government is nothing but individuals. Every one of the individuals in government belongs to you. He is your 'boy' in some form or other. You put him there directly or indirectly. So the job is still that of the American people, and I couldn't conceive of any job in this world being in better hands than that of the American people."

President Eisenhower, conclusion of address to Advertising Council. Ibid.

"It has proved itself a fine agency for bringing together the thinking, the greater unity of thought among the people of the Western world. I think that today we are in a better position because of its existence."

President Eisenhower, tribute to NATO (North Atlantic Treaty Organization) on its seventh anniversary, news conference of April 4, 1956.

"I have never been one to say, to believe, that you must hold up good things in order to attain perfection. You will recall the old German saying, 'The best is always the enemy of the good.' We have got to get something good, and in its over-all effect it must not be bad."

President Eisenhower, comment indicating that he might sign a farm bill containing some provisions objectionable to him. Ibid.

"I never attempt to go into other people's motives. They take certain decisions, they perform certain actions, and the results are there for all to see. So I wouldn't even attempt to interpret the motives of anybody that opposes me in anything that is political at all."

President Eisenhower, declining to join in charges by other Republicans that the Democratic leadership in Congress had been deliberately frustrating the Administration legislative program. Ibid.

"I am not going to do anything that will militate against the opportunity of the Executive Department to construct and to get before the Congress the kind of treaties that will serve our country's best interest. I am never going to agree to any diminution of that authority."

President Eisenhower. Ibid.

"Morale is the most important thing that a human being has, whether he is tackling a job or whether he is going to war or whether he is trying to gain a peace. It is the belief in the spirit, and when you know someone is with you, if the people sitting alongside you are ready to support what you say, what you do, you believe together, you have got a strength that is very hard to defeat. It is the strength of a democracy in war."

President Eisenhower. Ibid.

"I am always a little bit astonished when any American puts his cross behind my name for anything. Now, for whoever did it, I thank them for their vote of confidence, and the bigger the number, of course, the greater my thanks."

President Eisenhower, comment on the Wisconsin primary elections. Ibid.

"I would think in my strict capacity as commander in chief I ought to go and see one of these things, but I am trying to prove to the world that my chief interest in the nuclear science is peace. . . . I go to every demonstration that I can find of the peaceful uses of the atomic weapon, and I merely don't use the presidency to publicize the other, and, I admit, very necessary parts of it. But having talked it over with my people, I believe it is not an essential that I go, because the reports are very detailed. You know exactly what is going on."

President Eisenhower, reply to the question of why he had not witnessed the detonation of an atomic bomb or hydrogen bomb. Ibid.

"I get discouraged sometimes here. I have announced time and time and time again I will never be guilty of any kind of action that can be interpreted as war until the Congress, which has the constitutional authority, says so. Now, I have said this so often that it seems to me almost ridiculous to ask me the question. I am—look, how can a war be conducted? You have got to have troops, you have got to have draft laws, you have got to have money. How could you conduct a war without Congress. . . . Now, there are times when troops, to defend themselves, may have to, you might say, undertake local warlike acts, but that is not the declaration of war, and that is not going to war, and I am not going to order any troops into anything that can be interpreted as war, until Congress directs it."

President Eisenhower. Ibid.

"Only when we have created a career military service which can compete with the attractive opportunities available in civilian pursuits will we be able to stop the wasteful losses from our armed forces and attract individuals to those services. We cannot move too soon in our efforts to increase the number and quality of volunteers for long-term career military service in both enlisted and officer ranks."

President Eisenhower, letter to Vice-President Richard Nixon and House Speaker Sam Rayburn urging laws to combat heavy turnover in the Armed Forces, dated April 10, 1956.

"This bill represents what I believe in—treating a whole river valley as a unit, as a whole thing. It goes from top to bottom. It recognizes one thing that is also true—that water is getting to be our most valuable resource."

President Eisenhower, comment on signing the Upper Colorado River Bill, April 11, 1956.

"I have one yardstick by which I test every major problem—and that yardstick is: Is it good for America?"

President Eisenhower, national address on his farm bill veto, April 16, 1956.

". . . Any man who through 35 minutes or 30 minutes has been trying to hit the high spots of the world today, and America's position in the international situation, certainly feels that he has been jumping from jag to jag on the mountain tops."

President Eisenhower, extemporaneous remark after formal address to the American Society of Newspaper Editors, April 21, 1956.

"We must constantly keep 'up to snuff' because if we don't, we are bound to lose. We must be ahead of the problem. We must see its major parts. We must get its critical factors set up so that we understand them thoroughly in simple fashion, and then we must pursue a common course vigorously, persistently, and with readiness to make whatever sacrifices may be demanded."

President Eisenhower. Ibid.

"I have learned that a bill that comes out of Congress often bears little resemblance to the way it went in."

President Eisenhower, comment during news conference of April 25, 1956.

"I want to get results through thrashing out things on the anvil of logic and good sense, what is good for America, and that is my sole purpose."

President Eisenhower. Ibid.

"It is a little bit of a paradox to urge that we work just as hard as we know how on the guided missile and that we stop all research on the hydrogen bomb, because one without the other is rather useless."

President Eisenhower. Ibid.

"We go ahead with this hydrogen bomb, not to make a bigger bank, not to cause more destruction, [but] to find out ways and means in which you can limit it, make it useful in defensive purposes, of shooting against a fleet of airplanes that are coming over, to reduce fall-out, to make it more of a military weapon and less one just of mass destruction."

President Eisenhower. Ibid.

"I think research without test is perfectly useless, a waste of money."
President Eisenhower. Ibid.

"I know of nothing more important than the United States gain a constantly improving understanding of what are the main difficulties in the world, what are the principal ways of attacking those difficulties so we can achieve a program of peace."
President Eisenhower. Ibid.

"First, any individual coming anywhere in this government is first assured of courteous treatment. I will not stand for arrogance on the part of government officials. . . . My second thing has been this: If anyone ever comes to any part of this government and claiming some privilege for even to as low as an introduction to an official he wants to meet on the basis that he is part of my family or of my friends, that he has any connection with the White House, he is to be thrown out instantly."
President Eisenhower, comment on ethics in government, news conference of May 4, 1956.

"The interests of New England are a long ways from the interests of Southern California; the interests of the South are a long ways from the industrialized sections of Pennsylvania and Ohio and of the other sections of the East. So we must have a maximum of local government. . . ."
President Eisenhower. Ibid.

"I might delegate somebody, 'You take action but I will take the gaff,' you might say. But that I have to do, and I expect to do it, and I should do it."
President Eisenhower, on delegating responsibilities of the presidency. Ibid.

". . . At no time, I think, did it mean more to me than the morning of June 6 [1944, Allied invasion of Normandy]. Something along the order, I think, of about 2:30, the air troopers had taken in radios with them and some tiny little transmitter said, 'We are O.K., and the situation around Ste. Mère Eglise is in fine shape.' And since I had been told by experts that we would lose ninety percent of that command before it went, and I had to take it all on my own shoulders, it was a very great thing."

President Eisenhower, tribute to Radio Week, comment opening news conference of May 9, 1956.

"I think that we are raised in the tradition of no supermen and no indispensable men, and therefore if you do retain some of the humility and modesty with which you hope you were born, why, I believe that when another one comes along and says this, 'I believe that you are doing a pretty fair job as President of the United States,' you would be rather astonished."

President Eisenhower, explanation of why he had said he was amazed that people would take the trouble to vote for him. Ibid.

". . . The day that discipline disappears from our forces, we will have no forces, and we would be foolish to put a nickel into them."

President Eisenhower, comment during news conference of May 23, 1956.

". . . Communism is, in deepest sense, a gigantic failure. Even in the countries it dominates, hundreds of millions who dwell there still cling to their religious faith; still are moved by aspirations for justice and freedom that cannot be answered merely by more steel or by bigger bombers; still seek a reward that is beyond money or place or power; still dream of the day that they may walk fearlessly in the fullness of human freedom. The destiny of man is freedom and justice under his Creator. Any ideology that denies this universal faith will ultimately perish or be recast. This is the first great truth that must underlie all our thinking, all our striving in this struggling world."

President Eisenhower, comment during commencement address at Baylor University, Waco, Texas, May 25, 1956.

"Now much as we are dedicated to this expression of lofty sentiment, [referring to a national security directive] it will count for little unless every American—to the extent of his influence and capacity—daily breathes into it the life of his own practice. The test is the readiness of individuals to cleave to principle even at the cost of narrower, more immediate gains. For you graduates, and for all citizens, opportunities to strengthen our assault on injustice and bigotry will be as numerous as the tasks you undertake and the people that you meet each day."

President Eisenhower. Ibid.

"The responsibility for carrying forward America's part in helping improve international cooperation cannot be met through paper work in a governmental bureau. But it can be met through a combined effort by all of us, in and out of government, all trying to develop the necessary understanding that every international problem is in reality a human one."

President Eisenhower. Ibid.

"The difficulties and misfortunes of the weaker are met by help from the stronger. To be backward, or penny-wise, in our practice of this truth can lead only to greater risk and greater cost—far greater cost to ourselves."

President Eisenhower. Ibid.

". . . The whole free world would be stronger if there existed adequate institutions of modern techniques and sciences in areas of the world where the hunger for knowledge and the ability to use knowledge are unsatisfied because educational facilities are often not equal to the need. Do we not find here a worthy challenge to America's universities and to their graduates? I firmly believe that if some or all of our great universities, strongly supported by private foundations that exist in number throughout our land, sparked by the zeal and fire of educated Americans, would devote themselves to this task, the prospects for a peaceful and prosperous world would be mightily enhanced. I honestly believe that the opportunity here for each educated American is invaluable beyond the comprehension almost of any one of us."

President Eisenhower (principal recommendation in address).
Ibid.

"America never got discouraged in the war. Possibly that is because the objective was so clear: Defeat and destroy the enemy; make him stop fighting."

President Eisenhower, on twelfth anniversary of D-day invasion of World War II, a comment opening his news conference of June 6, 1956.

"As long as we are not shooting, we are not spending one-tenth as much as we would if we were shooting. . . . There is no destruction that you have seen that would even give a hint of what another war would bring."

President Eisenhower. Ibid.

"You have a long time on this earth, and if you will meet your problems as they come up and get the satisfaction of a job well done—play hard —have fun doing it—be true to your friends—stick with them—despise wickedness and dictatorship and the oppressors of humans, I think you will have a lot of fun every single day."

President Eisenhower, informal remarks to a group of young Republicans calling at the White House, June 6, 1956.

"What a bellyache!"

President Eisenhower, comment to an attending physician a few hours after undergoing an emergency operation for ileitis at Walter Reed Hospital, Washington, June 9, 1956.

"On behalf of the American people, I send their greetings to you on this solemn day of homage and rededication and I join with them in proud tribute to the men who rest forever at Cambridge, my comrades in arms in the crusade against tyranny."

President Eisenhower, message read by Major General William "Wild Bill" Donovan at Cambridge, England, at dedication of the first of six major European cemeteries and memorial chapels for the American dead and missing of World War II, July 16, 1956.

"We here pay tribute to the faith of our fathers, which was translated into new institutions and new works. But we cannot go on forever merely on the momentum of their faith. We, too, must have our faith and see that it is translated into works."

> *President Eisenhower, address to the presidents of the American Republics, Panama City, Panama, July 22, 1956.*

". . . If any man were nominated as Vice-President that the President felt he could not, in good conscience, run with, he would have just one recourse: to submit his own resignation."

> *President Eisenhower, comment during news conference of August 1, 1956.*

". . . I have told some of you people at times about the so-called Battle of the Bulge. I didn't get frightened until three weeks after it had begun when I began to read the American papers and found out how near we were to being whipped."

> *President Eisenhower, implying that he didn't know how sick he was during his June 1956, operation, until he read about it in the newspapers, a comment at his first news conference since that illness. Ibid.*

". . . I don't think it is too important to the individual how his end comes, and certainly he can't dictate the time."

> *President Eisenhower, on whether he should seek the presidency at the risk of his health, or retire. Ibid.*

"The path of human progress is not along the path of hatreds; it is not along the path of the extremes. It is along the path that represents the road where people of good will and real sensibilities can get together and say, 'Here is a way we can go together.'"

> *President Eisenhower, on the part of civil rights in southern primaries. Ibid.*

"The American people have lost the last personal link with the Union Army. His passing brings sorrow to the hearts of all of us who cherished the memory of the brave men on both sides of the War Between the States."

President Eisenhower, statement issued on the death of Albert Woolson, the last Union veteran of the Civil War, August 2, 1956.

"Today we are competing for men's hearts, and minds, and trust all over the world. In such a competition, what we are at home and what we do at home is even more important than what we say abroad."

President Eisenhower, comment in address accepting nomination for a second term, Republican National Convention, San Francisco, August 23, 1956.

"A Government worker, when he first arrived in Washington in 1953, was passing the National Archives Building in a taxi, where he saw this motto carved on one of its pedestals: 'What is past is prologue.' He had heard that Washington cab drivers were noted for their knowing all the Washington answers, so he asked the driver about the motto. 'Oh, that,' said the driver. 'That's just bureaucrat talk. What it really means is—"You ain't seen nothing yet."' "

President Eisenhower, story related in acceptance speech. Ibid.

"One American put it this way: 'Every tomorrow has two handles. We can take hold of it with the handle of anxiety or the handle of faith.' My friends, in firm faith, and in the conviction that the Republican purposes and principles are 'in league' with this kind of future, the nomination that you have tendered me for the Presidency of the United States I now—humbly but confidently—accept."

President Eisenhower, conclusion of acceptance speech. Ibid.

". . . The more that that work is done privately and behind the scenes rather than charging up on the platform and hammering desks, the better and more effective it will be."

President Eisenhower, on the writing of party platforms, news conference of August 31, 1956.

". . . We believe that things can become too centralized in our economic life in this country, and we go to great extent . . . to keep these things competitive, to keep them in smaller units and not to let them get so big that they have control over us."

President Eisenhower, on the place of the farmer and other groups in the American economy. Ibid.

". . . They have produced the strongest economy, an economy whose productivity is the envy of the world—and I am proud to say the terror of any who would be our enemies."

President Eisenhower, at White House ceremonies marking issuance of Labor Day commemorative stamps, news reports of September 2, 1956.

"Worry is a word that I don't allow myself to use."

President Eisenhower, news conference of September 12, 1956.

". . . This country will not go to war ever while I am occupying my present post unless the Congress is called into session, and Congress declares such a war; and the only exception that would be in the case of unexpected and unwarranted attack on this nation, where self-defense itself would dictate some quick response while you call Congress into action."

President Eisenhower, on the possibility of war in Egypt. Ibid.

"The force and impact of this one word—peace—reach all persons, all problems, in our land. Its meaning embraces past achievement, present problems, future hopes. It touches all things in our life and school, factory and farm, knowledge, from home and to the most distant points on earth—a frontier in Europe, an island in the Pacific, a canal in the Middle East. And this meaning ranges, too, from the highest kind of principle to the most personal kind of fact."

President Eisenhower, first of series of televised talks to the nation during 1956 campaign, September 19, 1956.

"We have insisted that, in the American design, each group in our nation may have special problems, but none has special rights. Each has peculiar needs, but none has peculiar privileges."

President Eisenhower. Ibid.

". . . I come today to pay my respects to the plow. Ever since I had the invitation to this meeting, I have been trying to think in my mind of some instrument invented by man that has meant more to him than the plow. I can think of none. In fact, the plow has become the symbol of peace. . . . I think, therefore, that no group of American citizens can feel closer to peace, feel closer to the need for peace, than does the great agricultural community."

President Eisenhower, address at Newton, Iowa, September 21, 1956.

". . . Farming looks mighty easy when your plow is a pencil, and you're a thousand miles from the corn field."

President Eisenhower, on "synthetic farmer" experts in Washington, address at Peoria, Illinois, on government farm program, September 25, 1956.

"I believe when you are in any contest you should work like there is— to the very last minute—a chance to lose it. This is battle, this is politics, this is anything."

President Eisenhower, on the 1956 presidential elections, comment during news conference of September 27, 1956.

". . . Most important of all in getting on with the job is our understanding of one general principle: The need always to encourage the full and free energies of labor and industry, of private organizations and individual citizens. These are the energies that make America prosper and grow."

President Eisenhower, campaign address at Lexington, Kentucky, October 1, 1956.

". . . By and large, the United States ought to be able to choose for its President, anybody that it wants, regardless of the number of terms he has served. . . . Now, some people have said, 'You let him get enough power and this will lead toward a one-party government.' That, I don't believe. I have got the utmost faith in the long-term common sense of the American people."

President Eisenhower, on amendment limiting a President to two terms, news conference of October 5, 1956.

". . . The truth before us is clear. Strong, we shall stay free; weak, we shall have only our good intentions to be written as our epitaph."

President Eisenhower, campaign address at Pittsburgh, October 9, 1956.

"The history of free men is never really written by chance but by choice —their choice."

President Eisenhower. Ibid.

"As I tried to explain . . . at Columbia, if I am sixty and they are twenty, they certainly own forty years more of the future than I do, and they ought to be vitally interested right now and begin to prepare themselves."

President Eisenhower, on the wisdom of lowering voting age, news conference of October 11, 1956.

". . . The sending of your note in the midst of a national election campaign of which you take cognizance, expressing your support of the opinions of 'certain prominent public figures in the United States' constitutes an interference by a foreign nation in our internal affairs of a kind which, if indulged in by an Ambassador, would lead to his being declared *persona non grata* in accordance with long-established custom."

President Eisenhower, reply to a letter from Soviet Premier Nikolai Bulganin, October 21, 1956.

". . . We develop weapons, not to wage war, but to prevent war. Only in the clear light of this greater truth can we properly examine the lesser matter of the testing of our nuclear weapons."

President Eisenhower, statement on hydrogen bomb tests, October 23, 1956.

"Eventually, as in the satellites today, the cost [of subjugation] proves greater to a once proud and independent people than the value of the monuments or factories—or prisons—that have been erected."

President Eisenhower, address to seventy-fifth anniversary dinner of the Brotherhood of Carpenters and Joiners, October 23, 1956.

"Above all, in the struggle between the cause of freedom and the cause of communism, you are the living proof that Marx was wrong."

President Eisenhower. Ibid.

"The real vision of the atomic future rests not in the material abundance which it should eventually bring for man's convenience and comfort in living. It lies in finding at last, through the common use of such abundance, a way to make the nations of the world friendly neighbors on the same street."

President Eisenhower, conclusion of message to conference on the statute of the International Atomic Energy Agency of the United Nations, news reports of October 27, 1956.

"There can be no peace without law. And there can be no law if we work to invoke one code of international conduct for those who oppose, and another for our friends."

President Eisenhower, address to the nation, October 31, 1956, on Mideast crisis and fighting in Egypt.

"We judge no man by his name or inheritance, but by what he does, and for what he stands. And so likewise do we judge other nations. There can be no second-class nations before the law of the world community."

President Eisenhower, campaign speech from Philadelphia, November 1, 1956.

"We value deeply and lastingly the bonds with those great nations, those great friends with whom we now so plainly disagree. And I, for one, am confident that those bonds will do more than survive. But this we know above all: there are some firm principles that cannot bend—they can only break. We shall not break ours."

President Eisenhower. Ibid.

"But let me say we hold firmly to a vital paradox and to a fixed purpose: We maintain strength only in order some day to yield it—in league with all other nations."

President Eisenhower. Ibid.

". . . I think that modern Republicanism has now proved itself. And America has approved of modern Republicanism."

President Eisenhower, remark in brief address at Election Night victory celebration in Washington, news reports of November 8, 1956.

"With whatever talents the good God has given me, with whatever strength there is within me, I will continue—and so will my associates —to do just one thing: to work for 168 million Americans here at home —and for peace in the world."

President Eisenhower, conclusion of remarks at Election Night victory celebration. Ibid.

". . . Leadership is a word and a concept that has been more argued than almost any other I know. I am not one of the desk-pounding type that likes to stick out his jaw and look like he is bossing the show. I would far rather get behind and recognizing the frailties and the requirements of human nature, I would rather try to persuade a man to go along, because once I have persuaded him he will stick. If I scare him, he will stay just as long as he is scared, and then he is gone."

President Eisenhower, comment on his personal leadership in working with members of Congress; news conference of November 15, 1956 (the first after his re-election to the presidency).

THE PRESS

"I would publish no book which would destroy a man's simple faith in God without providing an adequate substitute. I would publish no book which would destroy the institution of marriage without providing a substitute order of society which would be protective of the younger generation. All else I would cheerfully publish."

> *George Doran, prominent Canadian-American publisher, credo recalled in obituaries reporting his death, January 7, 1956.*

"No iron can stab the heart with such force as a period put just at the right place."

> *Isaac Babel, late Russian author quoted in news report by Joe Morgan of United Press,* Editor & Publisher, *February 4, 1956.*

Letter received by the *New York Daily Mirror,* quoted in Walter Winchell's column, March 30, 1956: "My husband has told me he doesn't love me any more and is going to leave me. I've been a good wife and cannot understand why all of a sudden he wants to get rid of me. Any day now I expect he won't come home at all and I'll never see him again. I need help in a hurry, but I do not know which of your advice columns can help me. Which of your many experts shall I appeal to for counsel and comfort? Alma Archer or Dear Abby or Dorothy Dix or Dr. Wiggam or Dr. Molner or Emily Post??? (signed) Desperate."

"From the American newspapers you'd think America was populated solely by naked women and cinema stars."

> *Lady Nancy Astor,* Editor & Publisher, *April 7, 1956.*

"I [have] eleven pieces of luggage . . . but there's just no way of covering a royal wedding without the proper equipment . . . a sapphire mink stole . . . an ermine wrap . . . a little chinchilla wrap . . . a white cashmere coat . . . a gold brocade evening raincoat. . . . Journalism is growing more complicated every day."

> *Dorothy Kilgallen,* New York Journal-American, *comment on reporting the wedding of Grace Kelly and Prince Rainier III of Monaco, news summaries of April 15, 1956.*

"The younger people, who grew up during the paper shortage, aren't used to filling the space. But that is journalism—an ability to meet the challenge of filling the space."

> Rebecca West, The New York Herald Tribune, *April 22, 1956.*

"The publisher and the editors have a heavy obligation—but I would argue that this is only half the story. The other half is just as important and not enough has been said about it: We need responsible readers just as much as we need responsible publishers."

> *Arthur Hays Sulzberger, president and publisher of* The New York Times, *commencement address at Knox College, Galesburg, Illinois, June 11, 1956.*

"You are to be the 'freedom editor.' It will be your job to stand up and shout whenever freedom is interfered with in any part of the world."

> *Arthur Hays Sulzberger, inviting Anne O'Hare McCormick to join the editorial board of* The New York Times, *comment recalled twenty-one years later in* The World at Home: Selections From the Writings of Anne O'Hare McCormick, *edited by Marion Turner Sheehan, published by Alfred A. Knopf, 1956.*

" 'A little touch of Harry in the night' worked wonders for British morale at Agincourt. The little touch of Harry S. Truman at his press conference yesterday was equally invigorating. It is no discourtesy to President Eisenhower to say that his former commander in chief, more than any other living American, embodies the sparkle and freshness, idealism and energy of the new world."

> London Daily Telegraph, *editorial comment on Harry Truman's stopover in England at the end of a seven-week European tour in June 1956.*

"Methuselah lived 969 years and all they said about him was that he died. But what was he doing for 969 years? What a story, and all the reporters missed it!"

> *Francis Albert "Bee" Behymer, since 1888 a reporter on the* St. Louis Post-Dispatch, *a favorite saying recalled in obituaries reporting his death, news summaries of July 30, 1956.*

"And he murmured soft endearments,
And she talked of Dostoevsky. . . .
As they landed at the airport
Braves in blue restrained the tribesfolk
Held at bay the howling pressmen. . . .
Some there were who liked her front view;
Some more partial to the back view.
Others strove to take her sideways
Thus to get the best of both worlds. . . .
And the grateful British public
Rose rejoicing from its breakfast."

Percy Cudlipp of the London News Chronicle, *"Highbrow-Arthur's Honeymoon," a parody of "Hiawatha" inspired by the arrival in England of the film star Marilyn Monroe and her new husband, playwright Arthur Miller, news summaries of July 30, 1956.*

"Hell, that's what the news is—an emergency. Why, we look at this as pretty much routine."

Turner Catledge, managing editor, The New York Times, *comment on the comprehensive, 5000-word coverage* The Times *gave the* Andrea Doria's *sinking in the newspaper's final edition issued seven hours after learning of the accident;* Time, *August 6, 1956.*

"After the skirmish, the sacramental feast."

The Manchester Guardian, *on the end of the Democratic National Convention and the beginning of the Republican Convention, news summaries of August 21, 1956.*

". . . While there are no pains to which a journalist should not go to cultivate a professional brain, he will be wise to preserve, if possible, an amateur's heart."

Carl Kesler, editor, The Quill: A Magazine for Journalists, *conclusion of editorial appearing in October 1951, issue, reprinted in August 1956 issue reporting Mr. Kesler's death.*

"Covering the Supreme Court is an exacting assignment. It is a rewarding one to the reporter interested in telling the story of a great American institution, dealing vitally with the life of the nation. I would not trade it for a ride on the first rocket to the moon."

> *Luther Huston, veteran Washington reporter for* The New York Times, *"Why Is the Supreme Court Ignored as a Source of Top National News?"* The Quill: A Magazine for Journalists, *August 1956.*

"He is the man who taught beavers to be eager."

> *James Reston, Washington correspondent of* The New York Times, *tribute to his colleague, Anthony Leviero, recalled in obituaries of September 4, 1956, reporting Leviero's death.*

"Listen, world—I'm not licked yet."

> *Elsie Robinson, by-words of her "Listen, World" column which reached millions, quotation recalled in obituaries reporting her death, September 8, 1956.*

"An unnerving squeal went up, like forty thousand Persian cats having their tails trodden on simultaneously."

> The Manchester Guardian, *on Liberace's appearance in the Royal Festival Hall, London, before a capacity audience which was ninety per cent female, news summaries of October 3, 1956.*

"I was part of that strange race of people, aptly described as spending their lives doing things they detest to make money they don't want to buy things they don't need to impress people they dislike."

> *Emile Henry Gauvreau, editor noted for sensationalism in New York journalism, statement recalled in obituary reporting his death,* Time, *October 29, 1956.*

"I prefer to be loved rather than disliked. But I don't think you can really write the news in Washington and be loved."

> *Drew Pearson, "Confessions of 'an S.O.B.,'"* The Saturday Evening Post, *November 3, 1956.*

"It can't be allowed that people attack tanks with their bare hands."
Szabad Nep, Budapest newspaper, teletype message to The Associated Press bureau in Vienna appealing for aid in the wake of Russian attack, news reports of November 5, 1956.

"I wanted to be a sports writer, but it took me too long to turn out my stuff. I found I could become Vice President faster than I could become a newspaper man."
Richard Nixon, Vice President of the U. S., reminiscing with Chicago newsmen on his early newspaper experiences, Quote, November 25, 1956.

"I live for tomorrow. I can scarcely wait until it comes."
Louis Seltzer, editor of The Cleveland Press, opening words of his autobiography, The Years Were Good, published by the World Publishing Company, 1956.

"Motives in government propaganda news may be obscure. But they can be and always ought to be suspected. Reasonable suspicion is the only insurance against being imposed upon by his government which the reader can confer upon himself."
Kent Cooper, former general manager of the Associated Press, comment in his book, The Right to Know, published by Farrar, Straus & Cudahy, Inc., 1956.

"The more I observed Washington, the more frequently I visited it, and the more people I interviewed there, the more I understood how prophetic L'Enfant was when he laid it out as a city that goes around in circles."
John Mason Brown, on political reporting, preface to Through These Men, Harper & Brothers, 1956.

RADIO AND TELEVISION

"I wish my 'children' wouldn't speak and show such long commercials. I hear we will have two billion dollars' worth of cartoons and beer ads this year. God help us!"

> *Lee DeForest, pioneer in development of radio and television, Time, March 19, 1956.*

"People in TV pay too much attention to money. Though I'm devoted to it myself."

> *Noel Coward, on being interviewed about American television, New York Journal-American, April 4, 1956.*

"The American public's taste is impeccable. They like me."

> *Noel Coward. Ibid.*

"He had an extraordinary ability to put public issues into simple language. . . . Today, I still meet people who tell me they miss his voice in their living rooms."

> *Eleanor Roosevelt, comment on eleventh anniversary of the death of her husband, Franklin D. Roosevelt, Look, April 17, 1956.*

"It has occurred to me that an actor's security and the eye of a hurricane have a great deal in common."

> *Jackie Gleason, quoted in Simon & Schuster publicity release, April 30, 1956.*

"There will always be a need and a desire to read about news events. The eye is more accurate than the ear."

> *H. V. Kaltenborn, on the durability of newspapers as opposed to radio and television news reporting, interview with James Simpson, May 5, 1956.*

"I believe that a certain upper mental level group is listening to radio now rather than to television."

> *Clifton Fadiman, comment during an NBC program, quoted by columnist Jack O'Brien, June 8, 1956, New York Journal-American.*

"They were more interesting, I find, than admirable."

> *Mary Margaret McBride, comment on the hundreds of persons she has interviewed on radio programs. Ibid.*

"When I was a young man, I had an uncle who frequently took me out to dinner. He always accompanied these dinners with minutely detailed stories about himself. But I listened—because he was paying for the dinner. I don't know why I am reminded of this but we are about to have one of our commercials."

> *Alfred Hitchcock, introduction to a television commercial,* News-week, *June 11, 1956.*

"A network . . . is built like a triangle. The base of this triangle is service to the public. The other two sides are service to affiliated stations and service to advertisers. These three aspects of network service are as inseparable as the three sides of a triangle. Only as the network serves the public well will it be able to develop the circulation to give good service to the advertisers and stations."

> *Robert Sarnoff, president, National Broadcasting Company, comment in statement made before the U. S. Senate Committee on Interstate and Foreign Commerce, June 14, 1956 (text privately distributed by NBC).*

"The advertiser is really not in a position to decide what the American people should see. His interest cannot lie in 'editorial' judgment of what types of programs should be on the air. . . . That should be the job of someone in the position of the periodical editor, who, to be sure, must have his magazine make a profit, but at the same time recognizes his responsibility to provide a balance of all that makes a good, constructive, and always-improving publication. When network and station executives realize this necessity and assume this responsibility to the public, television will grow up."

Fairfax Cone, chairman of the board of the advertising agency, Foote, Cone, & Belding, quoted by Robert Sarnoff. Ibid.

"You can absolutely feel the axes being ground or the laurel leaves being gathered before the show."

Gore Vidal, television writer, comment on the critics, "What Makes a Television Play?" The New York Times, June 17, 1956.

"Television is not a vending machine for higher learning. The coaxial cable alone will not pump culture into anyone's veins."

Dr. Frank Baxter, television personality and Professor of English at University of Southern California, quoted by Frances Rummell in Television Age, August, 1956.

"Day people love red tape, switchboards, lists, offices, routine of a busy, active life. Night people aren't eggheads, but they wouldn't mind spending a year in Maine doing nothing."

Jean Shepherd, postmidnight disk jockey on WOR, New York, viewing his listening audience, news summaries of September 3, 1956.

"The joint is full of cameras, lights, and googly-eyed gear. Loudspeakers and mikes hang like bats from our belfry. Millie and I are trussed with special built-in transmitters. My microphone is in my navel. Disaster impends."

Bob Considine, report on remote telecast from his home, New York Journal-American, September 24, 1956.

"All they wanted of me were head shots. That certainly seemed strange. Nobody's ever paid attention to my face before."

Gypsy Rose Lee, on her television debut as an actress, quoted by Marie Torre, New York Herald Tribune, September 24, 1956.

". . . They offered me the part of Chrystal, the gal who takes that bubble bath. I said absolutely not. If I'm going to take a bath in public, I'll do it in a night club where not too many people would see me."

Gypsy Rose Lee, on turning down a television appearance in The Women. *Ibid.*

". . . I hate television. I hate it as much as peanuts. But I can't stop eating peanuts."

Orson Welles, quoted by Marie Torre, New York Herald Tribune, October 12, 1956.

"Spiritually, radio and television are beautiful examples of the inspired wisdom of the ages. Radio is like the Old Testament, inasmuch as it is hearing of wisdom without seeing; television is like the New Testament because in it the wisdom becomes flesh and dwells among us. What was heard is now seen."

Bishop Fulton Sheen, writing as guest columnist for critic John Crosby, New York Herald Tribune, November 9, 1956.

RELIGION

"Notwithstanding the splendor and national significance of this occasion, the service in the abbey is in all essentials exactly the same as it would be for any cottager who might be married this afternoon in some small country church in a remote village in the dales."

The archbishop of York, Dr. Cyril Forster Garbett, comment in address delivered at the marriage of the then Princess Elizabeth and the Duke of Edinburgh in Westminster Abbey in 1947, recalled in obituaries reporting his death, news reports of January 1, 1956.

"If the new technique spares her the sufferings of childbirth, the mother can accept it without any scruple of conscience; but she is not obliged to do so. In the case of partial success or failure, she knows that suffering can be a source of good, if she bears it with God and in obedience to His will."

Pope Pius XII, comment in address on the science and morality of painless childbirth, January 8, 1956.

"The life and sufferings of our Saviour, the pains which so many great men have born and even sought and through which they have matured and risen to the summits of Christian heroism, the daily examples we see of acceptance of the cross with resignation: all this reveals the meaning of suffering, of the patient acceptance of pain in the present plan of salvation, for the duration of this earthly life."

Pope Pius XII. Ibid.

". . . This year's celebration of Easter should be primarily a recall to faith in Christ, addressed to people who, through no fault of their own, are still unaware of the saving work of the Redeemer; to those who, on the contrary, would wish to have His name wiped out of the minds and hearts of nations; and finally, in a special manner, to those souls of little faith who, seduced by deceptive enticements, are on the point of exchanging the priceless Christian values for those of a false earthly progress."

Pope Pius XII, Easter address to throngs in St. Peter's Square, Rome, April 1, 1956.

"The enemy of peace exerts pressure to sow confusion in the mind . . . here discussing, there blaming, today exalting his myths, tomorrow deriding them; today harshly withdrawing, tomorrow making an approach; today announcing a new system, to return tomorrow to the old."

Pope Pius XII, comment in the wake of the Moscow Communist party congress' explosion of the Stalin myth. Ibid.

"Bodily pain affects man as a whole down to the deepest layers of his moral being. It forces him to face again the fundamental questions of his fate, of his attitude toward God and fellow men, of his individual and collective responsibility and of the sense of his pilgrimage on earth."

Pope Pius XII, comment to a group of international heart specialists received in audience at the Vatican, news summaries of September 1, 1956.

"The Church continues to fight, not in the field of politics and economics as she has often been falsely accused of doing, but with weapons that are proper to her: the perseverance of her faithful, prayer, truth and love."

Pope Pius XII, address from Rome to thousands of Catholics attending seventy-seventh Catholic Day at Cologne, Germany, news reports of September 3, 1956.

"Ireland is a land that combines the smile and the tear. Also, alas, what a flood of tears, drowning out the joy and laughter of home and hearth, has poured through when the dike of temperance has been shattered."

Pope Pius XII, to a group of visiting Irish policemen who belonged to a total-abstinence association, news reports of September 16, 1956.

"God has no intention of setting a limit to the efforts of man to conquer space."

Pope Pius XII, on interplanetary explorations, news reports of September 21, 1956.

"The economy must be organized to fulfill ever better its ultimate aim, which is to satisfy the needs of man."

Pope Pius XII, on the need for private ownerships in business, news reports of September 22, 1956.

"The concept of the woman of the shipyards, of the mines, of heavy labor as it is exalted and practiced by some countries that would want to inspire progress is anything but a modern concept. It is, on the contrary, a sad return toward epochs that Christian civilization buried long ago."

Pope Pius XII, address to several thousand members of an Italian feminist group, news reports of October 15, 1956.

". . . They doubtlessly must be inclined to choose the road of justice and not to venture down the steep slope of violence, if they consider the great dangers of a war which, starting from a small spark, can develop into an enormous blaze."

Pope Pius XII, encyclical calling for prayer to end fighting in Middle East, news reports of November 3, 1956.

"In the name of religion, of civilization and of the right human sentiment, let there be an end of illegal and brutal repressions, to plans of war, to political preponderance among powers—all of which are things that can change the earthly life into an abyss of anxiety and terror, deaden the spirit and nullify the fruits of work and progress."

Pope Pius XII, radio address to the people of the world to unite for peace, reported by the Vatican to be the first appeal of this kind made by the Pope since the one he uttered more than seventeen years ago on the eve of World War II, news reports of November 11, 1956.

"We have been pleased to recall the harmony of relations between Christian principles and sporting activities. . . . Make manifest in your acts how, without losing any of its technical value, sport, being a school of energy and of self mastery, must be ordained towards the intellectual and moral perfecting of the soul."

Pope Pius XII, message to the Olympic Games at Melbourne, Australia, news reports of November 28, 1956.

"Silence should fall around me. I must not always talk about myself to the world. Let me be simple and modest. . . . I would not be true to myself should I address myself again and again to the world."

Dr. Albert Schweitzer, medical missionary, terse reply to newsmen who sought a statement on Dr. Schweitzer's eighty-first birthday, Time, January 23, 1956.

"Day by day we should weigh what we have granted to the spirit of the world against what we have denied to the spirit of Jesus, in thought and especially in deed."

Dr. Albert Schweitzer, Guideposts, March 1956.

"The course of human history consists of a series of encounters between individual human beings and God in which each man or woman or child, in turn, is challenged by God to make his free choice between doing God's will and refusing to do it. When Man refuses, he is free to make his refusal and to take the consequences. When Man accepts, his reward for willing what is the will of God is that he finds himself taken by God into partnership in the doing of God's creative work. When Man is thus cooperating with God, Man's freedom is at its maximum, because Man is then realizing the potentialities for which God has created him. God has created Man to be God's free partner in the work of creation."

Arnold Toynbee, historian, Collier's, *March 30, 1956.*

"Into this world of flimsy, false, and dying hopes, comes the one hope that can endure. Christian hope faces all facts, and is trained by Christ to face them at their worst possible, where no room is left for easy excuse of self-deception."

The archbishop of Canterbury, Dr. Geoffrey Fisher, comment in Easter message for 1956, Episcopal Church News, *April 1, 1956.*

"I don't care a rap if people call me a matchmaker. . . . Matchmaking is part of my priestly ministry."

The Rev. Francis Tucker, chaplain to Prince Rainier of Monaco, comment on eve of the prince's marriage to actress Grace Kelly, news summaries of April 9, 1956.

"Ultimately, this is what you go before God for: You've had bad luck and good luck and all you really want in the end is mercy."

Robert Frost, poet, broadcast on WQED, Pittsburgh, quoted in Collier's, *April 27, 1956.*

"I feel very happy that my son has found a faith and the satisfaction of his faith. I have three children, all of whom, I'm happy to say, are very devout and religious. They have each in their own way found a communion with God and for that I'm very happy."

John Foster Dulles, U. S. Secretary of State and a life elder in the Presbyterian Church, comment after attending the ordina-

tion of his son, Avery, as a Roman Catholic priest in the So-
ciety of Jesus, Fordham University, New York City, news reports
of June 17, 1956.

"I say, when there are spats, kiss and make up before the day is done and
live to fight another day."
The Rev. Randolph Ray, D.D., rector of New York's "Little
Church Around the Corner," favorite advice to brides and bride-
grooms, quoted by Gay Pauley in United Press story, New
York World-Telegram & Sun, *June 30, 1956.*

"You can boil it down to the really basic things. This man or woman
whom I don't especially like, with whom I have nothing in common but
a passion for oysters or ballet or mystery novels, is flesh and bone and
blood; so am I. Stab him and he'll bleed; I will too. This man has been
born as I have been, thru a channel of physical suffering; he has in his
lifetime known joy, sorrow, and fear, and has in his own way worshiped
God. Therefore, however alien we may appear on the surface one to the
other we are brothers, in human experience, in common mortality and
in the immortality of the spirit."
Faith Baldwin, on brotherhood, "Just Thinking Aloud," Chris-
tian Herald, July 1956, copyright 1956 by Christian Herald and
used by special permission.

"America to us is a dream in the constant process of realization, a vision
constantly being fulfilled. A dream and a vision, as old as the ancient
Hebrew prophets, as new as the yearning in the hearts of men today."
Rabbi Judah Nadich, invocation at Republican National Con-
vention, news reports of August 22, 1956.

"There is something distinctive that I always look for in men of serious
purpose. Those who so live and work are, I find, believing men. Many
are praying men. Again, many seem to do their praying not in words,
but in the best work they can perform."
J. C. Penney, noted merchandising executive, "Something to
Lean On," The Rotarian, August 1956.

"A human life is like a single letter in the alphabet. It can be meaning-less. Or it can be part of a great meaning."

Opening sentences of an essay, "Who Takes Delight in Life?" printed on full pages purchased in The New York Times *and* New York Herald Tribune *by the National Planning Committee of the Jewish Theological Seminary of America, on Rosh Hashana, September 5, 1956.*

"The first duty of the Christian in relation to peace and war is to under-stand and help to remove the underlying causes of war."

Cardinal point of public "message" adopted by Ninth World Methodist Conference, Lake Junaluska, North Carolina, news reports of September 13, 1956.

". . . Still more today is the demand laid upon Christians, not only to think and work in their service of the present age, but most of all to be constant in prayer; the conference therefore invites the people called Methodists to claim by faith and prayer that transformation of personal and social life which is offered by the full Gospel of Christ, Our Lord."

World Methodist Conference. Ibid.

"These Jews are men, these Jewesses are women, these aliens are men and women. All is not permissible against them, against these fathers and mothers. They belong to mankind. They are our brethren as are so many others. No Christian can forget that."

Jules Cardinal Saliège, Archbishop of Toulouse, France, known as the "Prelate of the Resistance" because he was the first ec-clesiastic to protest publicly against deportation of Jews during German occupation of France in World War II; statement re-called in news reports of his death, November 6, 1956.

"And how beautiful the look of her face. . . . And how fine is the hair of her head, how fair indeed are her eyes and how pleasing her nose and all the radiance of her face. . . . How beautiful her breast and how lovely all her whiteness. Her arms goodly to look upon, and her hands how perfect . . . all the appearance of her hands. How fair her palms and how long and fine all the fingers of her hands. Her legs how beautiful and without blemish her thighs. And all maidens and all brides that go beneath the wedding canopy are not more fair than she. And above all women she is lovely and higher is her beauty than that of them all, and with all her beauty there is much wisdom in her. And the tip of her hands is comely."

Dead Sea scroll, one of seven found in the Qumran cave in the Judean desert in 1947, translation released November 8, 1956, describing Abraham's sojourn in Egypt and the great beauty of Sarah, his wife.

"Far quicker and more effective steps are needed. A man who is drowning needs no messages. What we need is that the Secretary General [of the United Nations] come to Budapest today and not tomorrow. There has been much too much voting and oratory. What we need is action now."

Josef Cardinal Mindszenty, on Hungarian uprising against the Russians, news reports of November 12, 1956.

"I suffered torture bodily and in my soul. It's God's miracle that I am here and that I am as I am."

Josef Cardinal Mindszenty, on his eight years of confinement by Russian occupation troops. Ibid.

ROYALTY

"Even as April's footsteps that unseen
Touch upon March's earth and make it green,
So be the Africk visit of our Queen.
May it so speed, that spirits may attempt
The new, the bright, upon a base swept clean
To gladden destiny in ways undreamt."

John Masefield, poet laureate of Britain, poem to mark the departure of Queen Elizabeth II and the Duke of Edinburgh on their three-week tour of Nigeria, The New York Times, January 27, 1956.

"I believe that you'll make just as big a mess of things as we have. In fact, you are absolutely bound to. . . . The only thing I hope is that you will not make the same mistakes we did. But I expect even that is asking for too much."

The Duke of Edinburgh, to pupils at school dedication at Ipswich, England, Newsweek, May 14, 1956.

"It's no good shutting your eyes and saying 'British is best' three times a day after meals and expecting it to be so. We've got to work for it by constantly criticizing and improving."

The Duke of Edinburgh, comment on national complacency, "The Queen's Controversial Husband," Look, August 7, 1956.

". . . If people like doing nothing, I have no objection . . . [but they] should not be forced to do nothing because there is no opportunity for them to do something. . . ."

The Duke of Edinburgh, in support of a vast project for bringing sporting facilities to ordinary people everywhere in the British Isles. Ibid.

"Some nations remain friends with or without formal alliances. Others are held together with difficulty even by the most carefully devised treaties. In our case I venture to suggest it is the well-founded friendship, developing generation by generation, through the mutual confidence of honest trade, a generous understanding of each other's problems, and the shared traditions of the sea, which has kept our relations free from any sort of conflict or hard feelings for three hundred years."

Queen Elizabeth II, response to state banquet toast by King Gustaf Adolf of Sweden during state visit to Stockholm, Sweden, news reports of June 9, 1956.

"Elizabeth knows that, bar Philip's occasional jets of temper and impatience, he is as good a Cinderella as any Princess Charming could fairly expect to find. Philip knows that, bar an occasional pinch from his glass shoe, it is probably as comfortable and certainly as resplendent as any in the land. And if there is any one point of agreement in this

wrangling world, it is surely the hope that they both will live happily
ever after."

*J. Bryan III, "The Duke of Edinburgh," concluding paragraph
in a series of articles first published in Holiday, July 1956; copyright 1956 by the Curtis Publishing Company, reprinted by permission.*

"It is for the princess and myself a great joy to share with you this happy
news. I would like to accent the profound significance of this news
that is a guaranty of the continuation of our dynasty and represents
the continuation of the privileges and advantages of the Monagasques.
This must reinforce our hope in the future."

*Prince Rainier III, ruler of Monaco, broadcast announcing the
expected birth of a royal heir to his wife, former actress Grace
Kelly, an event of extreme importance to Monacans since they
would be subject to French taxes and the French military draft
if Rainier died without a child; news reports of August 3, 1956.*

"I believe absolutely in the existence of small countries, lying like cush-
ions, as it were, between the greater powers."

*Prince Rainier of Monaco, comment during visit to U.S., The
New York Times, September 14, 1956.*

"I'm sure that people all over the world got awfully tired of reading
about us. I know I did."

*Princess Grace of Monaco, formerly Grace Kelly of Philadelphia
and Hollywood, commenting on press coverage of her marriage
in April to Prince Rainier, news summaries of September 12,
1956.*

"We both feel that there is no more wasteful or foolish or frustrating
exercise than trying to penetrate the fiction of what might have been.
But I do know what has been in the twenty years since we were married. They have been rewarding years, years of great happiness, years

of no regrets, and years when we have preferred to look to the future. . . ."

Duke of Windsor, reflection on his decision to abdicate the British throne to wed Wallis Warfield Simpson, comment to Edward R. Murrow, CBS-TV, September 28, 1956, quoted in news summaries of October 8, 1956.

"Edward, Duke of Kent—seventh in line of succession, soldier, jazz fan, playboy, unlucky car smasher—who becomes a man this morning."

London Daily Mirror, editorial salute to the Duke of Kent on his twenty-first birthday, October 9, 1956.

"We never discuss the heir's hair."

Brief announcement by Trumper's, a London barbershop which services Buckingham Palace, when a national controversy raged on why Prince Charles's hair was allowed to cover his forehead; news reports of October 11, 1956.

"I never wanted to be a Queen. Ever since I was a child I dreaded the thought of it. . . . I hated the hypocrisy, the superficiality and the false admiration shown to me because I happened to be born to a position of royalty."

Elizabeth of Rumania, Queen of Greece with King George II of the Hellenes from 1923 to 1935, comment recalled in obituaries of November 16, 1956, reporting her death in exile at Cannes, France.

SPORTS

"There is a need to feel our bodies have a skill and energy of their own, apart from the man-made machines they may drive. There is the desire to find in sport a companionship with kindred people. I have found all these."

Roger Bannister, English track star, news summaries of January 8, 1956.

"No trainer can put anything into a horse that the good Lord hasn't put there already. . . . All a good trainer can do is bring out what's in a horse, that's all. The bad trainers can spoil what's in a horse, though."

James Fitzsimmons, "Mr. Fitz," eighty-one-year-old trainer of Nashua and other famed race horses, Collier's, *March 30, 1956.*

"I look upon this job as the protection and fostering of a great American institution. It may be true that horse racing draws more money, but you cannot measure comparative interest in the two sports by dollars. Baseball is not only organized baseball; it's much broader than that. And it is, emphatically, the American national pastime."

Ford Frick, commissioner of baseball, The New York Times, *April 15, 1956.*

"Boxing has been my world; it's been everything to me. I want to do everything I can to help boxing. I want to try to tell youngsters how good it can be."

Rocky Marciano, comment in announcement of his retirement as heavyweight boxing champion of the world, news reports of April 28, 1956.

"When I made my move at the turn, it seemed as if the horses just spread out and he went through them."

Jockey Dave Erb, on riding Needles to victory in the 1956 Kentucky Derby, news reports of May 6, 1956.

"I just belittle things. I belittle the shot I'm making, the hole I'm playing, the tournament, everything. 'Hell,' I tell myself, 'it's warm and sunny and the country is green and, man, you're lucky to be living in the middle of all this.' . . . It used to be I couldn't get in the right frame of mind at the right time. That was before I knew about belittling."

Jack Burke, Jr., ace golfer and 1956 winner of the National PGA championship, comment on learning to avoid pressure, Newsweek, *August 6, 1956.*

". . . Sport is [also] working its changes on them and the atmosphere in which they live. A banker rounding a buoy, a stenographer on horseback, a mechanic in a duck blind can all savor—even in the age of the desk, the lathe, the tractor and the split-level-with-mortgage—that expansiveness of spirit, that sense of uniqueness, which have always been the hallmarks of a full and satisfying life."

Paul O'Neil, "Nobody Falls Asleep on Sunday Afternoon,"
Sports Illustrated, August 20, 1956.

"I think of that day every time I go into the water."

Gertrude Ederle, comment thirty years after becoming the first woman to swim the English Channel, quoted in interview with Jim Cook, New York Post, September 5, 1956.

"To me, the sea is like a person—like a child that I've known a long time. It sounds crazy, I know, but when I swim in the sea I talk to it. I never feel alone when I'm out there."

Gertrude Ederle. Ibid.

"George, I ain't going to die."

Mildred "Babe" Didrikson Zaharias, last words to her husband before dying of cancer at the age of forty-two, news reports of September 28, 1956.

"Man, I can't help myself. I've got to go out there and cut loose with everything I've got."

Mildred "Babe" Didrikson Zaharias, on hitting a 250-yard drive the first time she ever played golf, statement described as "her philosophy of life" in obituary in New York Daily News, September 28, 1956.

"I'm not what you call a real praying man but once out there, in the eighth or ninth, I think it was, I said to myself, 'Help me out, somebody.'"

Don Larsen, New York Yankees pitcher who made World Series history by hurling a perfect game, news summaries of October 9, 1956.

"Catching a fly ball is a pleasure but knowing what do with it after you catch it is a business."

Tommy Henrich of the New York Yankees, quoted by Arthur Daley in The New York Times, *November 5, 1956.*

THEATER

"Every actor in his heart believes everything bad that's printed about him."

Orson Welles, comment during impromptu performance at New York City Center, news reports of January 13, 1956.

". . . The first of our senses which we should take care never to let rust through disuse is that sixth sense, the imagination. . . . I mean the wide-open eye which leads us always to see truth more vividly, to apprehend more broadly, to concern ourselves more deeply, to be, all our life long, sensitive and awake to the powers and responsibilities given to us as human beings."

Christopher Fry, "On Keeping the Sense of Wonder," article appearing in Vogue, *January 1956; reprinted by permission. (Originally written and orally presented by Christopher Fry to the boys of his alma mater in England, the Bedford Modern School.)*

"When somebody says they're writing something with you in mind, that's the end. I want them to write with Katharine Cornell or Helen Hayes in mind and then let me have a go at it."

Beatrice Lillie, Theatre Arts, *March 1956.*

"Sex is very big this year. I'm glad that I am, too. If I didn't have a large bosom, people would talk about my small one. So what's the difference. I'm glad I have a big one."

Jayne Mansfield, star of the Broadway play, Will Success Spoil Rock Hunter?, *New York World-Telegram & Sun, March 22, 1956.*

". . . A lot of life is sitting and an evening dress should sit prettily. Entrances and exits are a matter of minutes, but sitting goes on for hours."

> *Gladys Cooper, comment on the ideal evening dress,* Vogue, *April 1, 1956.*

"Every night of that time I could feel every breath, every stir from those people out there. How can you grow stale when you sense every move, feel every flicker of an eyelash? Every night a different audience. What a marvelous stimulation!"

> *Ethel Barrymore, recollection of her four-year runs in* Declassee, The Constant Wife, *and* The Corn Is Green, *comment during newspaper interview at her Pacific Palisades home,* New York Post, *June 7, 1956.*

"I never let them cough. They wouldn't dare."

> *Ethel Barrymore, comment on control of audience coughing during tense moments in a play. Ibid.*

"Every now and then, when you're on stage, you hear the best sound a player can hear. It's a sound you can't get in movies or in television. It is the sound of a wonderful, deep silence that means you've hit them where they live."

> *Shelley Winters, "That Wonderful Deep Silence,"* Theatre Arts, *June 1956, an article appearing as she neared the end of a successful season as a star of the Broadway play,* A Hatful of Rain.

"Many plays—certainly mine—are like blank checks. The actors and directors put their own signatures on them."

> *Thornton Wilder, quoted by Walter Winchell,* New York Daily Mirror, *July 13, 1956.*

". . . In learning what I know of love, I have learned a great deal about myself, that I have a personality and I can develop it. I have a mind and I can feed that. I have a temper and I can control it. I have a heart and I can open that to love. With all these things I know that at any age I shall be an attractive woman. I know in my heart, as well as in my brain, that I have what is really essential in life."

Deborah Kerr as told to Barbara L. Goldsmith, "What I Know of Love," Woman's Home Companion, July 1956; copyright 1956, The Crowell-Collier Publishing Company, reprinted by permission.

"America is not playwright-conscious. There are still hordes of theatre-goers who say in all innocence, 'I love to go see Lynn Fontanne. She always says such witty things.' . . . For those who are aware that such creatures as playwrights exist, he is usually thought of as a slightly benighted child of nature who somehow or other did it all on a ouija board."

Robert Anderson, on the playwright in the modern theatre, New York Herald Tribune, August 5, 1956.

"The clamoring for novelty in the method of telling a story is as though we were suddenly to say, 'I'm tired of faces with two eyes and a nose and a mouth.' What we want, I think, is not faces with three eyes, but more beautiful, strong, truthful, wise, humorous faces with the usual complement of eyes, noses, and mouths."

Robert Anderson. Ibid.

"The work of a writer, his continuing work, depends, for breath of life, on a certain privacy of heart—and how is he to maintain it with that wreath on his head and that crowd at his heels?"

Tennessee Williams, "On Meeting a Young Writer," Harper's Bazaar, August 1956.

"Good plays drive bad playgoers crazy."

Brooks Atkinson, Theatre Arts, August, 1956.

"If you do climb upon his knee, do it with love and remember he is a great human person. Make him happy that the children in this great city of New York want to hold his hand, touch his head and sit on his lap. For here we are today, all these 150 years later, still loving his stories. I think it's pretty wonderful. . . ."

Eva Le Gallienne, on conducting a story hour at the new Hans Christian Andersen statue in Central Park, New York Herald Tribune, *September 23, 1956.*

"I am just a nice, clean-cut, Mongolian boy."

Yul Brynner, self-description, "The Story of Yul Brynner," by Fern Marja, New York Post, *September 24, 1956.*

"When I am dead and buried, on my tombstone I would like to have it written, 'I have arrived.' Because when you feel that you have arrived, you are dead."

Yul Brynner. Ibid., September 30, 1956.

"An artist carries on throughout his life a mysterious, uninterrupted conversation with his public."

Maurice Chevalier, on the theatrical profession, quoted in article on Beatrice Lillie, "The Lady Is a Clown," by Kenneth Tynan, Holiday, *September, 1956.*

"Go on writing plays, my boy. One of these days one of these London producers will go into his office and say to his secretary, 'Is there a play from Shaw this morning?' and when she says 'No,' he will say, 'Well, then, we'll have to start on the rubbish.' And that's your chance, my boy."

George Bernard Shaw, advice quoted by William Douglas Home, author of The Reluctant Debutante *and other plays,* The New York Times, *October 7, 1956.*

"No, Virginia, there is no Auntie Mame. Although I've known a great many eccentric people like Mame, she is a distillation and a moonbeam and nothing more. . . . Auntie Mame, as I see her, isn't made of meat and bones and rules and conventions like the rest of us. She's a froth of whipped cream and champagne and daydreams and Nuit de Noël perfume. She's not mortal at all."

Patrick Dennis, comment on his book, Auntie Mame, *on the eve of its debut as a Broadway play,* The New York Times, *October 28, 1956.*

"A playwright must be his own audience. A novelist may lose his readers for a few pages; a playwright never dares lose his audience for a minute. In point of fact, I have to please myself, constantly."

Terence Rattigan, quoted by John McClain, New York Journal-American, *October 29, 1956.*

"It's the way to get over a deep inferiority complex, being onstage; you become another person and shed your own frightened personality."

Shirley Booth, New York Journal-American, *October 30, 1956.*

"We tore them up, bit by bit, together. . . . It was awful, it was like tearing up children."

Mrs. Eugene O'Neill, on how she helped her husband destroy all of his unfinished plays before his death, quoted by Seymour Peck on the eve of the New York opening of O'Neill's auto-biographical Long Day's Journey Into Night; The New York Times, *November 4, 1956.*

"Sweden did this for O'Neill, not America. America was not a damn bit interested, excuse my language."

Mrs. Eugene O'Neill, on revival of interest in O'Neill's works. Ibid.

"Women like silent men. They think they're listening."

Marcel Achard, French playwright, Quote, *November 4, 1956.*

"In the theatre, I was brought up in the tradition of service. The audience pays its money and you are expected to give your best performance—both on and off the stage."

Helen Hayes, New York Daily Mirror, *November 9, 1956.*

"The play is about nothing. All is nothing. All comes to nothing. All is nothing from the beginning. Life is nothing. Death is nothing. Everything is nothing."

> *William Saroyan, excerpt from introduction to Columbia Records' recording of the Broadway play,* Waiting for Godot.

UNITED NATIONS

"Constant attention by a good nurse may be just as important as a major operation by a surgeon."

> *Dag Hammarskjold, Secretary-General of the United Nations, comment on the UN's role in keeping peace in the Middle East, news summaries of March 18, 1956.*

"I have never seen difficulties that prevented leading politicians of great maturity and strong personalities from getting together when they felt it made sense."

> *Dag Hammarskjold. Ibid.*

"'Freedom from fear' could be said to sum up the whole philosophy of human rights."

> *Dag Hammarskjold, address at the 180th anniversary of the Virginia Declaration of Rights, news summaries of May 20, 1956.*

"I never discuss discussions."

> *Dag Hammarskjold, concealing the topic of his talks with Russian leaders, Look, September 18, 1956.*

"I have no use for women who want the world to be run by women. I could not think of anything more ghastly."

> *Madame Vijaya Lakshmi Pandit, Indian delegate to the UN, Look, April 3, 1956.*

"We have done something here that makes it more likely that we and our children will live out our lives in peace . . . [possibly] a turning point in history. . . ."

James Wadsworth, Chief of U. S. delegation to the United Nations Atoms for Peace Conference, news summaries of October 28, 1956.

"My delegation cannot refrain from speaking on this question. We have had such an intimate knowledge of boxcars and of deportations to unknown destinations that we cannot be silent."

Mrs. Golda Meir, Foreign Minister of Israel and head of that nation's delegation to the United Nations, address in UN General Assembly on Soviet action in Hungary, news reports of November 21, 1956.

"I'll put it this way—Now the prodigal has returned home after squandering a fortune. The prodigal has reformed."

Toshikazu Kase, Japan's first permanent delegate to the United Nations, comment a few hours after Japan was elected a UN member, quoted by Ralph Teatsorth of the United Press in interview in New York World-Telegram and Sun, *December 21, 1956.*

INDEX OF PERSONS QUOTED

371